THE BURGESS SEASHORE BOOK
FOR CHILDREN

ALSO AVAILABLE FROM LIVING BOOK PRESS

The Burgess Animal Book for Children (in color)
The Burgess Bird Book for Children (in color)
The Burgess Flower Book for Children (in color)

To see a complete list of all our releases or if you wish to leave us any feedback please visit www.livingbookpress.com

The Burgess Seashore Book

for Children

THORNTON BURGESS

ILLUSTRATED BY
W. H. SOUTHWICK AND GEORGE SUTTON

This edition published 2022 by Living Book Press

This edition published by arrangement with Little, Brown and Company, New York, New York, USA. All rights reserved.

Original edition published in 1929 by Little, Brown and Company.

ISBN: 978-1-922634-62-7 (softcover)
        978-1-922634-61-0 (hardcover)
        978-1-922634-63-4 (black and white softcover)

All rights reserved. No part of this publication may be reproduced, stored in a retrieval system, or transmitted in any other form or means – electronic, mechanical, photocopying, recording or otherwise, without the prior permission of the copyright owner and the publisher or as provided by Australian law.

 A catalogue record for this book is available from the National Library of Australia

Contents

	Preface	1
I.	Danny Meadow Mouse Goes to the Seashore	3
II.	Getting Acquainted	8
III.	Danny Meets Tattler	13
IV.	A Meeting with Crabs	17
V.	A Crab Town and a Hermit	24
VI.	Danny Gets an Eyeful	30
VII.	Clams and More Clams	37
VIII.	Reddy Meets Barker the Seal	43
IX.	Reddy Fox Meets Big Claw	47
X.	A Lobster and a Crab that Cannot Pinch	53
XI.	Graywing Knows His Crabs	57
XII.	A Queer Host and a Queerer Guest	64
XIII.	The Queer Fellow Who Could Open Oysters	70
XIV.	When Seeming Loss Is Really Gain	76
XV.	The Innocent-Looking Drillers	82
XVI.	Collars of Sand and Mermaids' Purses	88
XVII.	Prickly Porkies of the Sea	95
XVIII.	Shells that Swim and Shells that Walk	102
XIX.	The Curious Home of a Fish	108
XX.	Pa Stickleback Does His Duty	113
XXI.	The Queer Jelly	118
XXII.	Reddy Fox Sees a Queer Garden	124
XXIII.	More Garden Folk	130
XXIV.	Graywing's Little Joke	135
XXV.	The Horse that Wasn't a Horse	140
XXVI.	Some Upside Down People	144

XXVII.	The Queer Disappearance	150
XXVIII.	The Ink Maker	155
XXIX.	Queer Climbers and their Relatives	159
XXX.	Reddy Learns Something About Snails	165
XXXI.	Reddy Learns About Some Seaweeds	173
XXXII.	Reddy Finds Himself Mistaken	180
XXXIII.	Reddy Finds Graywing in Trouble	185
XXXIV.	Some Curious Worms	192
XXXV.	Reddy Finds Some More Worms	197
XXXVI.	A Worm That Isn't a Worm	204
XXXVII.	Reddy and Jimmy Go Fishing	208
XXXVIII.	Some Feathered Beach Folk	212
XXXIX.	The Stake Driver	218
XL.	Two Long-Legged Cousins	224

Preface

The seashore has a natural history all its own. It has been my experience that few of the host who seek the seashore every summer have the slightest acquaintance with the life of the beach, the rocks and the salt marshes. I recall how, as a boy, I was forever picking up things on the shore and asking "What is this?" and "What is that?" and never finding out. The Sand Dollar I knew as such. No one ever told me that it was an Urchin. I suspect that it is much the same way with the children of to-day.

It is to meet what seems to me a real need that this volume has been prepared. It makes no pretense of being more than it really is,—an introduction to the life of the seashore. Like its predecessors in this series—the Burgess Bird Book for Children, the Burgess Animal Book for Children and the Burgess Flower Book for Children—it is intended to be at once a storybook and a handbook within its limitations.

In its preparation those things most frequently seen along the Atlantic coast have been selected. A few of the rarer species have been added. The book does not pretend to cover in any degree of fullness the life of the seashore. It covers those things most likely to catch the eye and the interest of a child and does this in a way to make identification easily possible. It is hoped that it will arouse sufficient interest to lead the reader to desire to know more and to seek that knowledge in more scientific and complete works.

To Mr. W. H. Southwick I am indebted for the photographs used in the illustrations. These photographs were made by him especially for this book. Also, I am his debtor for his painstaking care to make his drawings accurate as well as beautiful. His work and the drawings of the seashore birds by Mr. George M.

Sutton do much to give the book such value as it may possess. Especially am I indebted to Mr. S. N. F. Sanford of the Boston Society of Natural History for his verification of scientific names and other helpful assistance.

As in previous volumes, the use of scientific names has been avoided in the text, where they have no place for children. These scientific names and scientific descriptions of the various subjects treated in the book will be found in the Appendix. It is offered with the hope that between its covers many little folk and some older ones may find pleasure and the answers to many perplexing questions.

THORNTON W. BURGESS

1. Danny Meadow Mouse Goes to the Seashore

Travel will, I think you'll find,
Greatly broaden out the mind.
Danny Meadow Mouse

Danny Meadow Mouse has his share of curiosity. In fact, I doubt if there is one among all the little people of the Green Meadows and the Green Forest who is without curiosity. Just now the thing that Danny was curious about was the thing that the little people call the Man-Bird. It was, of course, an aëroplane and it had landed on the Green Meadows very near the home of Danny and Nanny Meadow Mouse. At first it had filled them both with a great fear, but when it had remained there without moving and without sound for a day and a night, Danny became more curious than timid.

He had discovered for himself that this Man-Bird was not a live creature. He had discovered that when none of those great two-legged creatures called Men were about, this great birdlike thing was powerless and wholly harmless. He was possessed of a great longing to climb up it. He wanted to go all over it. But, try as he would, he could find no way of climbing in.

After the landing of the machine, the aviator had taken a mass of cotton waste to wipe off the engine, and this he had tossed down on the ground when he was through with it. Now that cotton waste was just the nicest material in all the Great World for a Meadow Mouse bed. Danny had found it and had curled up in the middle of it, after he had given up trying to climb up into that Man-Bird. In fact, Danny was sound asleep there when the aviator returned to his machine the next day. He saw the cotton waste on the ground and picking it up tossed it into the cockpit of the aëroplane. With it, of course, went Danny.

Never was there a more frightened Mouse than Danny Meadow Mouse. It had all happened so quickly that Danny didn't have the least idea what *had* happened. Now he found himself in a strange place and his one thought was to get out of sight. He scrambled out of the cotton waste. Right in front of him was a dark place. Danny darted into it. He was in a little cupboard, in which was more of that cotton waste. Danny crept under it and his little heart went pitapat, pitapat with fright. A few minutes later it almost stopped pitapatting. There was a terrible noise. Such a noise Danny had never heard, excepting when there was a thunderstorm. But this was worse than thunder, for it didn't stop. It was such a great noise that Danny didn't even hear the slamming of the little cupboard door when the aviator climbed in.

Two minutes later Danny Meadow Mouse was up in the air. He didn't know it, but he was up in the air, being carried away in that little cupboard of the aëroplane. For a long time Danny was too frightened by that terrible noise to even wonder where he was. He just made himself as small as possible at the back of that little cupboard under the cotton waste and wondered what would happen next.

He whimpered and cried a little, for he was a very little fellow, you know, and he was a prisoner. He felt the trembling of his prison, which was the vibration from the engine, and he in turn trembled.

By and by, after what seemed to Danny a very long time, but which really was only a little more than half an hour, the terrible noise ceased as suddenly as it had begun. There was a gentle bump or two and then the great Man-Bird came to a stop. Danny heard the voice of the aviator and the voices of other people who had gathered around. Presently the aviator opened the little cupboard door and pulled out some of that cotton waste. He didn't discover Danny, but he did leave the little door open.

Danny drew a long breath of the fresh air. Then he sniffed. That air was different from any air he had ever known before. He ran his tongue along his lips and they tasted salt. Now Danny was as eager to get out as ever he had been to get in that great Man-Bird. It seemed to him that those people never would go away.

At last Danny no longer heard voices. He ventured to poke his head out. Then he went out altogether. There was no one in the great Man-Bird. Danny ran all about inside, for once more his curiosity had possession of him. Then he climbed up where he could look out on the Great World. He caught his breath. It wasn't at all the Great World he was used to. In two directions, as far as he could see, was shining sand. In front of him was water. He had never dreamed there could be so much water. It stretched away and away until it seemed to meet the sky. Back of him was what looked much like the Old Pasture at home. In the distance he could see the houses of those two-legged creatures called Men.

The sight of that water reminded Danny that he was very, very thirsty. He wanted a drink and he wanted it right away. Not far off he saw a little puddle of water. Anxiously he looked this way and that way. He saw no one to be afraid of. He jumped down from the aëroplane and ran swiftly through the coarse, stiff grass growing out of the sand. When he reached that puddle, he plunged his little nose in the water. He took one good swallow and then such a wry face as he made! My, my, my, such a wry face as Danny Meadow Mouse did make! You see, that water was salt. Danny was at the seashore. He didn't know it, but that is where he was.

"Bah!" exclaimed Danny in his squeaky little voice, and a disgusted little voice it was. Then he ran back into the grass, for he didn't dare stay out there in the open. That taste of salt water made him even thirstier than before. "Now what shall I do?" thought Danny. "I just must have food and water. I'll have to go exploring."

So Danny went exploring. Presently he came to a bathhouse, although of course he didn't know it was a bathhouse. There was fresh water there,—sweet, fresh water dripping from a faucet. A very little was all Danny needed. When he had had that little he felt like a new Meadow Mouse. He crept under the bathhouse. That seemed to be the safest place. He decided he would stay there a while. He was filled with the spirit of adventure. Curiously enough, he never once thought of home. He didn't even wonder if he would ever get back there. Now that he was out in the Great World, he wanted to see more of it.

"There must be a lot to see here," said Danny right out loud, in that funny, squeaky voice of his.

"There is," said another voice close to him. It gave him such a start that he almost squealed aloud. When he discovered who the speaker was, he was more startled than before. It was a member of the Skunk family. Yes, sir, it was a member of the Skunk family. His coat was nearly all black. Danny scurried across to the other side, for he knew that a plump Meadow Mouse is sometimes enjoyed by members of the Skunk family.

"Who are you?" squeaked Danny.

"I'm Jimmy Skunk," replied his neighbor.

"You're not either!" squeaked Danny. "I left Jimmy Skunk back at Farmer Brown's, and he has a big, white stripe down the middle of his back."

"That's all right," replied the stranger goodnaturedly; "I may not be the Jimmy Skunk you know, but I'm Jimmy just the same. Anyway, that is what they call me. Who are you and where are you from?"

"I'm Danny Meadow Mouse and I came from the Green Meadows," replied Danny. And then he told how he happened to be there.

"Are you going to stay?" asked Jimmy. "If you have never been to the seashore, there is a lot to see here."

"I—I should like to see it," replied Danny. "I know all about the Green Meadows, but I don't know anything about the seashore. I don't know what to be afraid of, or what enemies to watch out for."

"Oh," replied Jimmy, "just you stay near me. Then you won't have anything to be afraid of." He spoke just as Jimmy Skunk back on the Green Meadows always spoke. It was clear to Danny that this Jimmy was just as independent as the other Jimmy.

"I guess it runs in the family," thought Danny. Aloud he said, "Aren't there any Hawks here?"

"Oh, there's one now and then," replied Jimmy carelessly.

"Aren't there any Owls?" asked Danny.

"I suppose so, but they don't bother me," replied Jimmy.

"And what about Foxes?" demanded Danny.

"Oh, there are Foxes," replied Jimmy Skunk. "You don't suppose with such good living as can be found along the seashore, there would be no Foxes, do you? But don't worry; just keep along with me and there'll be nothing to fear."

II. Getting Acquainted

Back of the bathhouse under which Danny Meadow Mouse had found shelter were sand dunes. Back of these sand dunes was an old pasture. This in turn ended on the edge of a great marsh. Just a little way from the bathhouse this marsh came almost to the sand dune. All this Danny learned in course of time. But for the rest of that day he was satisfied to curl up in a little hollow in the sand in the darkest corner under the bathhouse.

With the coming of the first Black Shadows Danny crept out. For a moment he sat there, testing the Merry Little Breezes. It was funny, but they left the same taste on his lips that he had found in that water where he had tried to get his first drink at the seashore. Every time he ran his tongue along his lips he tasted salt. He rather liked it.

Danny scrambled up a sand dune. It was the hardest scrambling he had ever done. You see, he slid back almost as fast as he went up. When at last he did get to the top, he was all out of breath and his legs ached. There he found the queerest grass he had ever seen. It didn't grow like the grass of the Green Meadows. The blades were far apart, coarse and stiff, and when he tried eating one he didn't like it. It had a sharp edge. The blades didn't grow close enough together to hide him and he felt very uncomfortable.

As soon as he could get his breath, Danny went on. By and by he reached what he called "real land." The grass was short, but it was real grass. There were patches of bushes here and there. In fact, this place was very like the Old Pasture back home. Danny felt more comfortable.

Presently Danny found an old log partly covered with dry seaweed, where the pasture joined the marsh. The old log was hollow, but the only opening was a knothole so small that no one bigger than Danny could possibly get in. Danny went in and gave a little sigh of thankfulness. Then he carried in some bits of dry seaweed and some of the softest dry grass he could find. "Now," said he in that funny, squeaky little voice of his, "I have a new home at the seashore, and I am going to find out what it is like around here. Just one thing is needed to make me feel really at home."

Just then there was a sniffing sound at the end of the log and a familiar scent reached Danny's nose. It was the scent of a Fox. Danny chuckled down inside himself. "Now," said he, "I *do* feel at home. If only Nanny were here, it would be perfect." For a wee minute he felt a bit lonely.

As soon as it was safe to do so, Danny started out exploring. In the excitement of doing this he forgot all about Nanny. First he made a little passage for himself under the dry seaweed along the old log. Then he cut a little path down to the edge of the marsh. All along the edge of the marsh were masses of dry seaweed which had been stranded there by a high tide. Never had Danny found it so easy to keep under cover. In running from one mass of seaweed to another, he had to expose himself for only a moment.

Finally Danny ventured out to see what the marsh was like. It looked very like the Green Meadows back home, for it was covered with grass. However, when Danny tasted that grass, he found it very different from the grass he was used to. It tasted a wee bit salt. He rather liked it. There was no sweet clover. The grass was tall enough for him to feel well protected, so he started in at once to cut little paths. The ground was rather wet. Day by day and night by night Danny carried his little paths farther out into the marsh.

Danny actually begrudged time to sleep. You see, he was all the time finding new and strange things. On the sand at the edge of the marsh were curious little creatures called Beach Fleas or Sand Hoppers, and he found them in the grass too. They made him think of giant Fleas. He soon discovered that they were good to eat, so after that he did not have to depend on grass alone. Then, when he had explored a little farther, he found that there were tiny shellfish, also good to eat when small enough for his sharp teeth to crack them open.

Twice every day the water came creeping, creeping up over the marsh. Sometimes it quite covered the grass. Other times just the tops of the grasses were above it. Then after a short time all that water would disappear. It was the coming and going, or rising and falling, as it is called, of the tide. Sometimes after the tide had fallen, Danny would find that it had left behind it more of these little shellfish. Occasionally, very tiny fish would be left stranded in little pools. Then Danny turned fisherman.

When he wanted a complete change, all he had to do was to go up on the high land back of the marsh. There he found seeds and berries and sweet grasses, such as he had been used to at home. Altogether, Danny liked the seashore. He liked it very much.

Every day when the tide went out, Danny would return to the marsh. Always there was something new to see. Sometimes he would come to little pools, and looking into them he would see minnows darting in all directions. Then one day a little path that he was making suddenly opened on to a broad patch of mud. Danny sat there at the end of his little path, looking out. The mud was brown, almost black. Not a single spear of grass was growing there. It was very soft in most places and out in the middle a little water was standing.

"That is no place for me," thought Danny. "There isn't a thing to hide under. Anyway, it isn't interesting. I don't believe there is anything out there that I want, or that anybody else wants."

"Pee-eet, pee-eet, pee-eet," said a voice right over his head.

Danny looked up to see a bird that reminded him of Teeter the Sandpiper, whom he had seen along the Smiling Pool. In fact, at first he thought it was Teeter. But when he had had a good look, he saw that it was a stranger. It was, if anything, a little smaller than Teeter and it was not spotted as was Teeter. Danny remembered that Teeter's legs were yellow, while the legs of this fellow were rather greenish.

"Pee-eet!" said the stranger, who had alighted and was running about rapidly and continually picking up something from the mud.

GREATER YELLOWLEGS OR TATTLER.
Totanus melanoleucus.
SEMIPALMATED SANDPIPER OR SANDPEEP.
Ereanetes pusillus.
LEAST SANDPIPER OR MUD-PEEP.
Pisobia minutilla.

"Who are you?" demanded Danny in his squeaky little voice, when the stranger came near enough.

The little stranger stopped abruptly and stared very hard at Danny. "I am Peep the Least Sandpiper," said he.

"Then you must be cousin to Teeter the Spotted Sandpiper," said Danny.

Peep nodded. "I am," said he. "There are many of us Sandpiper cousins. Cousin Teeter seems to like the fresh water best, but give me the mudflats on the salt marshes and the sand of the shore at low tide. Excuse me, I'm very hungry and I hear some of my family coming. I must get what I can while I can."

A moment later Danny saw a whole flock, each of whom looked exactly like Peep. Their wings were long and narrow. They turned in the air together so exactly that it looked as if they must have been trained to do it. They saw Peep running about on the mudflat and immediately alighted and all began to run about. It was fun to watch them. They would make little short runs this way and little short runs that way. Then down would go their slender bills and Danny knew that something good to eat had been found. They ran along the very edge of the water and all over that mudpatch. They seemed to be having a splendid time. Such busy little people Danny had never seen. He was tempted to go out and try to get better acquainted, but just as he started to do this, away they all went, crying "Pee-eet, pee-eet," and Danny was left to stare after them.

"Well, anyway, I've made the acquaintance of some of the shore people," thought Danny. "I wish they had stayed and let me talk to them. There's such a lot I want to know, and however am I going to find out things if I cannot ask questions? Now, I wonder who that is whistling. It isn't Farmer Brown's Boy, because Farmer Brown's Boy isn't at the seashore. But it is just as loud a whistle as Farmer Brown's Boy's. Hello, I do believe it is up in the air!"

III. Danny Meets Tattler

Danny Meadow Mouse looked up in the air. Then he squatted down so that the grass would hide him. A big bird was coming his way. At least, it looked big to Danny, and Danny is always suspicious of big birds. This one was whistling. There was no doubt about it,—that whistle was coming from this bird. "Whyee!" exclaimed Danny. "It must be a giant Sandpiper! Yes, sir, that fellow must be a giant of the Sandpiper family. Anyway, he looks a lot like Peep and Teeter, only he is ever so much bigger. His bill is longer, his neck is longer and his legs are longer. I wish he would come down here where I could get a good look at him."

It was as if the stranger had heard him. He swung around just overhead, his long legs stretched out behind and his long neck and bill stretched straight out in front. As he passed over Danny his pointed wings were set and he was sailing. Then he began to beat his wings again and presently he sailed once more. Finally, with his wings set, he sailed down until he could drop his long legs and touch the mud. He ran a few steps, stopped, stretched his wings straight above his back and then carefully folded them. A moment he stood there with head up, looking and listening, a picture of watchfulness. Satisfied that there was no danger, he began to run about in the shallow water. Danny suspected that he was catching tiny fishes, and this is exactly what he was doing.

At last the stranger began to pick up things on the mud and so at last arrived very close to where Danny was hiding. His legs were yellow, his neck and breast and sides were grayish-white, heavily spotted with dark. His back was dark, spotted with white. His long straight bill was black. As he stood before Danny he teetered on those long legs of his somewhat after the manner of Teeter the Spotted Sandpiper, whom Danny had known at the Smiling Pool.

Danny moved ever so little. Instantly the stranger's bright eyes were fixed on him and the stranger's wings were lifted just a little as if for flight.

"Don't go," squeaked Danny. "Please don't go."

"Who are you?" demanded the stranger suspiciously.

"I am Danny Meadow Mouse. If you please, who are you?" replied Danny.

"I am Tattler the Yellow Legs," replied the stranger.

Danny chuckled. "Do you know," said he, "I thought you were a giant. Yes, sir, I did. I thought you were a giant Sandpiper."

"We do belong to the same family," replied Tattler. "However, my name is Yellow Legs. So don't forget it,—Tattler the Yellow Legs."

As he stopped speaking, he stretched his neck up and looked over the marsh. Then hastily he took to his wings and away he went, whistling as only he can whistle. Danny could hear that whistle when Tattler was so far away that he couldn't be seen. It was evident that everybody else heard it too. Up from the bed of a creek a short distance away flew Longlegs the Heron. From a little farther along Black Crown the Night Heron flapped his way up into the air. Peep and his friends came skimming past just over the tops of the grass. Without being told, Danny somehow knew that it was all on account of Tattler's whistle. He had a feeling that Tattler had seen danger and given warning.

This is exactly what had happened. Tattler is the watchman of the marshes. He is always on the watch, and the instant he sees anything suspicious he gives the alarm. Because his whistle can be heard so far, all the marsh folk look on him as their watchman and are on guard whenever they hear his whistle. So Tattler is true to his name. It is, of course, a nice kind of tattling, because he is doing his neighbors a good turn. It makes him, however, greatly disliked by some who miss a dinner because of his tattling.

Danny decided that as long as he didn't know what the danger was, the wisest thing he could do was to go back home. So away he went, as fast as his short legs could take him. Just as he reached the hollow log on the edge of the marsh, a familiar voice said, "Hello! So this is where you are living."

Danny gave a funny little squeak of startled surprise. Then he found his voice. "Hello!" said he. "Yes, this is where I am living. My, how you startled me, Jimmy Skunk!" It was his old friend of the bathhouse.

"What were you running so fast for?" inquired Jimmy.

"I don't know," confessed Danny. "Tattler the Yellow Legs gave an alarm and everybody seemed to take it as a danger signal, so I ran home."

Jimmy grinned. "If you run every time you hear Tattler whistle down there on the marsh, you'll spend a great deal of your time running," said he. "Tattler is a good watchman, but sometimes he whistles when there is no need of it. He is a great traveler, that fellow is."

"Is he any greater traveler than the other feathered folk who go south in the winter?" inquired Danny.

"He travels twice as far as most of them do," replied Jimmy. "Anyway, that is what I have been told. They say that few birds go as far south as he does in winter. In the spring he goes almost as far north. Perhaps it is the dangers of these long journeys that make him so watchful and suspicious. By the way, I thought you were going to let me show you things. Why not come over to the beach with me to-night? That is the place to see things. It will be moonlight to-night and we'll take a walk down the beach. As long as you are with me there will be nothing to fear. I shall be looking for you."

After Jimmy had gone Danny wished he hadn't agreed to meet him that night. Then he remembered what Jimmy had said about seeing things on the beach, and at last curiosity actually made him impatient for the coming of the Black Shadows.

When at last Danny reached the bathhouse that evening he was tired. He tried to be polite, but he couldn't help showing that he was tired. Jimmy Skunk saw this. "You'd better rest a while," said he. "The moon doesn't rise until late to-night and, what is more, the tide is not out yet. When the tide goes out we'll go down on the beach and I'll show you things."

Meanwhile, Danny had been poking around and had discovered a dry, brittle, queer-looking thing. It was shaped like a star. Yes, sir, it was shaped exactly like one of the stars which Danny had often seen twinkling high overhead. "If you please," said he, "what is this thing?"

Jimmy Skunk came over to look at it. "Oh," said he, "that's a dead Starfish! I'll show you some live ones by and by."

"A fish!" exclaimed Danny indignantly. "Do you think I'm so innocent that I do not know a fish when I see one? The idea of telling me that this is a fish! You must be joking, Jimmy Skunk. You must be just trying to have fun with me."

"Nothing of the kind," replied Jimmy. "I said what I meant and I meant what I said. I don't suppose it really is a fish, but it moves in the water when it is alive and it is called a Starfish. So there you are!"

Danny looked very hard at Jimmy Skunk. "I suppose if you say it is so, it must be so," said he, trying to be polite. "But how a thing like that can swim I don't understand at all."

"Pooh!" said Jimmy. "That's nothing. A Starfish can turn itself inside out."

This was a little too much for Danny. He just couldn't believe a word of it. Later he was to learn that it was true. But just then Jimmy Skunk changed the subject and Danny forgot all about it. They talked about this and that and rested, until at last silvery Mistress Moon came up and made the beach almost as light as by day. The tide had gone out.

"It is time for us to start," said Jimmy. "You follow me and I'll show you things you have never dreamed of."

So Jimmy led the way from under the bathhouse and Danny Meadow Mouse followed a little behind him. He didn't want to get too near Jimmy, but he didn't dare get too far away. At one and the same time, he felt both safe and unsafe, which you will admit is a queer way to feel.

IV. A Meeting with Crabs

"What are we going to look for?" Danny Meadow Mouse asked timidly, as he trotted along behind Jimmy Skunk.

"First," replied Jimmy, "we are going to look for something to eat. Almost always there is something to eat along the beach after the tide goes out. Dead fishes can be found, if nothing else."

Danny thought to himself that he didn't care about fish, but he wasn't impolite enough to say so. Jimmy led the way down on to the hard sand. All along were rolls of seaweed which had been washed up by the water when the tide was high. Jimmy began to poke about in these, looking for a dead fish. While he was doing this, Danny was doing a little exploring on his own account.

Suddenly Danny was confronted by a terrible creature. In all his life he had never seen such a thing. He thought it was a Spider, but he had never even dreamed that a Spider could be so big. It seemed to be looking at him with two curious raised popeyes. On each side were four queer legs that were jointed and looked as if they were stiff between the joints. In front the creature held up two great jointed legs ending in wicked looking pincers. That is, Danny called them legs, because he didn't know what else to call them, although they were not used as legs at all. They were used more as arms, and the pincers were used like fingers. The creature was green spotted with yellow, and it wore a shell, as Spotty the Turtle does, only it was a different kind of shell. Suddenly it moved with surprising quickness. But instead of going straight ahead, it went sideways. It ran sideways right at Danny Meadow Mouse.

Danny squealed right out with fright. If this was a Spider, it was the most awful Spider he had ever seen. He took to his heels and ran straight to where Jimmy Skunk was poking over the seaweed.

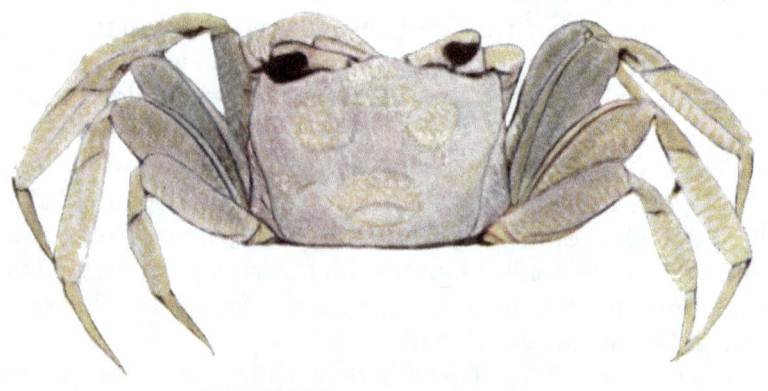

GREEN CRAB.
Carcinides Maenas.

GHOST CRAB OR SAND CRAB.
Ocypode albicans.

"What is the matter?" demanded Jimmy.

Danny couldn't find his tongue. All he could do was to point at that dreadful thing. Jimmy took two or three steps towards it and away it scuttled, going sideways surprisingly fast.

"Did you ever see such a dreadful Spider?" gasped Danny, when Jimmy returned.

Jimmy Skunk laughed right out. "Bless your heart, Danny," said he, "that wasn't a Spider. That was a Crab. That was a Green Crab. Did you see him run away from me? Probably he's hiding right now under a stone. I almost always find that fellow on the beach after the tide has gone out. Look out for those big pincers of his, Danny. He cannot bite, but he certainly can pinch. I suppose you'll laugh at me again if I tell you that he is a fish. Of course, he isn't a real fish, but he belongs to what is called the shellfish family. I have heard it said that he is one of the highest forms of crustaceans, whatever they may be."

It was only a few moments later when out of a hole almost at Danny's feet popped another Crab. It was quite different from the first one, but quite as startling to Danny. In the first place, Danny hadn't seen any hole there. In the second place, this fellow was so very near the color of the sand that, when he wasn't moving, it was difficult to see him, even when looking right at him. He was so close to Danny that he had a good look at him.

"Oh! oh!" squealed Danny suddenly. You see, that Crab had suddenly raised himself right up on the tips of his toes, so to speak; and then he had raised his eyes right up out of his head. Anyway, that is the way it looked. Those two eyes were on the ends of little stalks and when those stalks were raised, so that their owner might look all around, the effect was rather startling.

"Now, what is it?" demanded Jimmy Skunk.

"That fellow there!" replied Danny, pointing to the Crab standing on tiptoes.

Jimmy turned. At his first move away went the Crab. Danny had thought that the Green Crab had moved rapidly, but it was nothing to the way this fellow scuttled across the sand. Like the Green Crab, he traveled sideways, but he went so fast that it would have taken a good runner to catch him.

"There goes another of the Crab family," said Jimmy Skunk,

chuckling. "That one is called the Ghost Crab, and sometimes the Sand Crab. I guess he is the fastest runner of all the family, and he can dig about as well as he can run. It is too much work to chase him and bring him back for you to look at. You know I never like to hurry. Anyway, you will have plenty of chances to see him, for he and his friends are always running about on the sand. They do like the moonlight. They don't come out so much daytimes, but they certainly do like to run around at night."

"What do they eat?" asked Danny.

"Oh, any old dead fishes they can find, or any other dead matter. Then they catch and eat Beach Fleas," replied Jimmy.

"Beach Fleas!" exclaimed Danny. "What kind of Fleas are Beach Fleas?"

"Well," said Jimmy, "some folks call them Sand Hoppers. There goes one now! Catch him. You will find it good eating."

Danny caught it. It was good eating as he had already found out on the marsh. Though he didn't know it, it wasn't an insect at all. It was a crustacean, like the Crabs. It looked much like a giant Flea, only sand-colored. Danny saw another and caught that. While he was chasing this one, he ran down almost to the edge of the water. There he surprised another Crab. It was unlike either the Green Crab or the Ghost Crab. It was white or greenish-yellow, covered with spotted rings of red and purple. The two hind legs were not as much like legs as those of the other Crabs. They were really two paddles, for this Crab is a very good swimmer and uses these paddles when swimming. This was the Lady Crab, also called Sand Crab, although quite different from the Ghost Crab, which likewise bears the name of Sand Crab. This one scuttled away into the water. Danny was still staring after it when Jimmy Skunk joined him.

"What are you staring at?" asked Jimmy.

Danny pointed out the Crab. "Is that all?" exclaimed Jimmy. "You'll get used to Crabs pretty soon. I wouldn't mind a soft-shelled Crab this very minute."

"What is a soft-shelled Crab?" asked Danny.

"Just that and nothing more," replied Jimmy. "It is a Crab with a soft shell."

LADY CRAB.
Ovalipes ocellatus.

BLUE CRAB.
Callinectes sapidus.

"How can it be a shell if it is soft?" demanded Danny. "All the shells I have ever seen were hard."

Jimmy thoughtfully scratched his nose. "It does seem queer to speak of a soft shell," said he. "Perhaps it isn't a shell until it gets hard. Anyway, those Crabs have a soft covering which later becomes hard. I'll show you, if we have any kind of luck."

After a while they came to a little pool from which the water had not run out when the tide went down. There was a rock on the edge of it and seaweed attached to the rock and lying in a mass in the water. Jimmy pulled away this seaweed and suddenly scooped something out on to the sand. "Here's one!" he cried.

"Here's what?" asked Danny, hurrying up to see.

"A soft-shelled Crab," replied Jimmy. "Just touch him and you'll see that he hasn't any hard shell."

It was a small Crab and Danny at last ventured to touch it. Sure enough, it was soft. Those pinching claws were perfectly harmless. There was no pinch in them. "Do you mean to say," squeaked Danny, "that this fellow ever will have a hard shell like those others I have seen?"

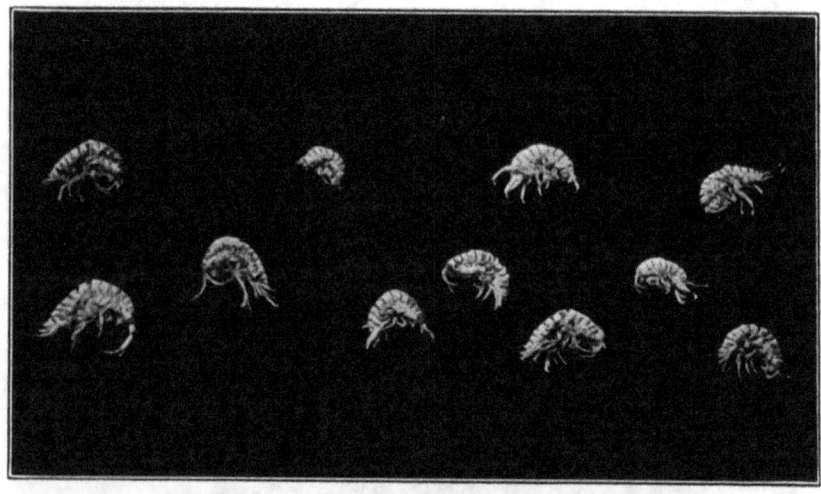

COMMON BEACH FLEAS.
Orchestia agilis.

Jimmy's eyes twinkled. "No," said he, "I don't mean anything of the kind. This fellow will never have a hard shell, but if he were not such good eating, or if he hadn't been caught, he would in time have a hard shell."

"Are you going to eat him?" demanded Danny.

"I certainly am," replied Jimmy, suiting the action to the word.

"I suppose," said Danny thoughtfully, "that it was because he was so small that he had a soft shell."

"Nothing of the kind," replied Jimmy. "Big Crabs are the same way sometimes. They have to get out of their hard shells in order to grow. So once or twice a year they shed their shells and grow new ones. It is when they are out of their shells that they are called soft-shelled Crabs. Didn't you ever see a caterpillar shed its skin when growing?"

"Yes," replied Danny, "but a skin is one thing and a shell is another. How can one of those fellows get out of his shell? Do you mean to tell me that he gets every bit out,—legs, pincers, and everything?"

"So I'm told," replied Jimmy. "When a Crab gets ready to leave his old shell, the latter cracks in places and the Crab squeezes himself out. Then he keeps hidden as much as possible until the new shell hardens. You see, when it is soft, fishes and other creatures, including Men and myself, are all the time looking for it. I've seen those two-legged creatures called Men take home big baskets filled with soft-shelled Crabs. That was a Blue Crab you saw, and it is the Blue Crab that is considered the best eating when it is soft-shelled. There is one now with a hard shell."

Danny looked. The top shell was about twice as broad as it was long. It and the claws were dark green in color. Underneath the Crab was a dingy white. The feet were blue. The rear legs were like those of the Lady Crab,—swimming paddles.

v. A Crab Town and a Hermit

WHEN THE stars began to fade and it was almost time for jolly bright Mr. Sun to begin his daily climb up in the blue, blue sky, Jimmy Skunk returned to his home underneath the bathhouse and Danny returned to his home in the old log on the edge of the marsh with a little sigh of thankfulness. Danny curled up in his snug bed to sleep. Then he dreamed of Crabs. He dreamed of big, pinching claws always reaching for him. When he awoke, the first thing he thought of was Crabs. He still couldn't get over the idea that Crabs were nothing more or less than Spiders wearing shells,—great big armored Spiders. He was sure he would never get used to them.

When Danny went exploring again it was out on the salt marsh. He felt more comfortable there in the grass, even though it was a different kind of grass from what he was used to. By and by he came to the bank of a creek, which you know is a stream of water. And there unexpectedly he came to a town. He didn't know it was a town, but that is what it really was. All about were holes,—in the bank and back from the bank a little way. Never had Danny seen so many holes at one time.

"I wonder who made these and if anybody lives in them," said Danny to himself.

As if in answer, out of a hole almost under Danny's nose popped a little Crab. Danny was so startled that he almost fell over backward. It was the funniest Crab Danny had yet seen. Instead of two big big pinching claws it had only one, and this was carried up and across in front of it in the funniest way. The other pinching claw was small.

Fiddler, for this is what he was called, being a Fiddler Crab, did not see Danny. Almost at once another Crab appeared from another hole, and this did not have the big pinching claw, the two pinching claws being small. It was Mrs. Fiddler. A minute later Crabs were popping out of the holes all around Danny. Some had the big pinching claws and some did not. And how they did scuttle about! Every now and then there would be a fight and it was fun to watch.

Danny was wondering if it could be possible that these funny little Crabs had dug all those funny little holes. He didn't have to wonder long. He saw a Crab scrape up the mud and form it into a little ball. This little ball of mud it tucked underneath three of the back feet and there carried it, using the other legs to walk with. The little mud ball was carried off four or five feet. Then the Crab came back to get another. Then Danny noticed that some of the Crabs coming out of the holes were also carrying little mud balls. He knew then that this Crab in front of him was just starting a new hole.

Now the eyes of these funny little Crabs were on the ends of funny little stalks, which were movable. Danny wanted to laugh aloud as he watched a Crab move these little stalks this way and that, while he looked all around. Each one bringing out a load of mud would do this before carrying the mud away. It was clear that they were very suspicious people.

It seemed as if everybody in that Crab town was out when something frightened them. Such a scuttling as there was then! Instead of making for his or her own hole, each Crab made for the nearest hole. The result was that sometimes a Crab would find a hole already occupied. Then the newcomer would try to pull the other one out. Sometimes he succeeded and sometimes he didn't. As soon as all was quiet, out popped all the Crabs again.

Watching them day by day, Danny learned a lot about Mr. and Mrs. Fiddler. But there was no one to tell them that there are different kinds of Fiddler Crabs. Farther up, along that same creek, there was another Crab town. The dwellers in this town were a little larger than the others. They were the largest of the Fiddler Crabs, and at the joints of their legs were red spots. If Danny could have visited this town, he would have found that many of the holes had over them little archways of mud. With this convenient arrangement the owner could sit in his doorway

FIDDLER CRAB.
Uca pugilator.

 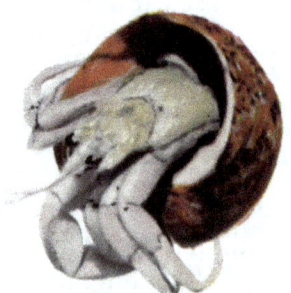

HERMIT CRABS.
Pagurus longicarpus.

and look out without being seen from overhead. These little Fiddler Crabs live on vegetable matter.

Danny thought the Fiddler Crabs the queerest of all the Crabs, until one day a door was shut in his face. Yes, sir, a door was shut right in Danny's face. He had discovered a very small Crab who seemed to be carrying on his back the shell of a snail. The little Crab was not only carrying it, but actually was running away with it.

"Now, I wonder what that Crab is doing with that shell," muttered Danny to himself. "My, he must be strong to carry that around on his back! It covers him so that I can see only his legs. I'd like to see just what he looks like without that shell on his back. I believe I'll just knock it off."

So Danny scampered after the funny little Crab with the shell on his back. Like all the rest of the Crab family, this one ran sideways. Danny was just about to knock that shell off, or at least try to, when the Crab disappeared so suddenly that it was nothing short of mysterious. One instant Danny saw those scuttling little legs beneath the shell, and the next instant that shell was lying on its side with no sign of a Crab.

"He must have a hole in the sand," thought Danny, "and has gone down in that, leaving the shell behind him."

Danny reached out and poked the shell aside. There was no hole in the sand. You should have seen Danny's face! At first he looked everywhere but at that shell. At last he looked at this and discovered that it wasn't empty. Anyway, he couldn't see into it. He looked more closely. There were two claws right across the opening. Those two claws fitted in tightly, just like a door. Even then Danny didn't understand. He sat down and stared. Perhaps it was because he sat still so long that Mr. Crab thought he had gone away. Anyway, suddenly those legs appeared once more and away raced the shell.

"Oh!" exclaimed Danny, and started after it. When he was almost up with it the legs disappeared again. Once more the shell lay apparently deserted. As before, a door made of claws closed the opening. This time Danny kept his eyes fixed on that door. After a while it was pushed out. The legs followed, and away scuttled that Crab with the shell on his back.

Danny had seen enough now to know that the shell wasn't being carried on the Crab's back the way he first thought it was. He knew now that the Crab had simply backed into the shell and made a door of his big claws. He suspected that while he was running the Crab was still partly in the shell. Danny was right. He was watching Hermit the Hermit Crab.

But Danny couldn't understand it yet. He couldn't see how a Crab with a hard shell could back into the narrow opening of a snail shell and then carry the shell around with him. "That," said Danny, "is the queerest performance I have ever seen. I certainly must get acquainted with that fellow."

But this was more easily said than done. Hermit was bashful. Every time Danny came near, Hermit ran away. Then, when Danny ran after him, Hermit retired inside his shell and closed the door in Danny's face. Finally Danny gave it up.

Had Danny had a little more patience he might have seen Hermit get a new house. The reason that Hermit carried that snail shell about with him was because he had no shell of his own. No, sir, he had no shell of his own. This funny little Crab had a soft body and, had he not been protected in some way, he would long before have been gobbled up. Old Mother Nature having failed to give him a shell, he had remedied the latter's oversight by finding a shell for himself. Actually, he was better off than some of his Crab cousins with shells of their own.

You will remember that Danny had found out how other Crabs grow by getting out of their old shells and hiding until new and better shells are formed. Hermit thinks he has improved on that plan. He doesn't have to wait hidden away for a shell to harden. He doesn't have to run any risk as the others do. He simply finds a new and bigger empty shell and takes possession. He was househunting when Danny discovered him.

After Danny finally left, Hermit peeked out cautiously. Then off he started in his usual hurry. Presently he came to a shell. He looked to see if it were empty. It seemed to be just about the right size. He examined the opening. There was another Crab in there. Hermit tried to pull him out. Yes, sir, he tried to pull that Crab right out of his house. He couldn't do it, so he gave up and went on his way.

Presently he found another shell. This one was empty. He looked all around to be sure that no one was watching him. Finally, sure that he was alone, he came out of his shell and backed into the other so quickly that had you been there you would hardly have known what he was doing. Then he started off again. He stopped. He wiggled around. He didn't like the way it fitted. He came out and backed into it again. Then he returned to his old shell, backed into that, adjusted himself, and away he went, still with his old house.

Hermit was busy for some time. He tried several shells before he found one that suited him. At last he found one that seemed to be just the right size. But this one was already occupied. Hermit undertook to pull the other Crab out. For a few minutes they had a great fight. At last Hermit managed to get hold of the other just right and out he came. Quick as a flash, Hermit was out of his old house and had backed into the new one. The other Crab, feeling helpless without any kind of a house, backed into Hermit's old shell and in his turn went looking for another.

What Danny didn't know and didn't discover, and what you may not be aware of, is that Hermit isn't a really, truly Crab at all. He is, strictly speaking, more nearly related to Big Claw the Lobster. But wherever he is found, he is called a Crab, and only a few folk seem to know that he isn't one. But, Crab or not, he certainly is an amusing little fellow.

vi. Danny Gets an Eyeful

There wasn't a minute while Danny Meadow Mouse was awake that he wasn't filled with curiosity. Most folks are curious in a strange place, so it is no wonder that being at the seashore for the first time in his life, Danny was curious over many things which, to the people who lived at the seashore, were not curious at all.

When he had nothing else to do Danny would run over to Crab town to watch the Fiddler Crabs. This was, as you know, on the bank of a creek. When the tide was very low there was little water left in the creek. Then there were big mudflats and sandbars. Often he saw Peep the Least Sandpiper and his friends running about there, and sometimes Tattler the Yellow Legs. One morning Danny ventured to run out on a mudflat a little way from the sheltering grass. Right away he noticed a number of little holes in the mud. They were nowhere near as big as the holes over in Crab town. Of course, Danny knew that some one had made those holes and he was very curious to know who. Peep the Sandpiper came running along.

"Hello, Peep!" cried Danny.

"Hello, Danny!" cried Peep, for by this time they had become well acquainted.

"Is there anything down in this hole?" Danny asked.

"I can't say, but I fancy so," replied Peep.

"Is it a Crab?" asked Danny.

"I don't think so," said Peep.

"If I wait, will it come out?" Danny demanded.

"No," replied Peep, and flew over to join some of his friends on a little sandbar.

"It must be a Worm," thought Danny. "I guess a great big

HERRING GULL OR HARBOR GULL.
Larus argentatus.
COMMON TERN OR SUMMER GULL.
Sterna hirundo.

SOFT-SHELL CLAM OR NANNINOSE.
Mya arenaria.

RAZOR CLAM.
Ensis directus.

DANNY GETS AN EYEFUL

Worm must have made this hole. Still, when the water comes in, the worm would drown. I wonder if I can dig out whoever is down there."

Danny leaned over and tried to look down that little hole. Of course, he couldn't see anything. He was still trying and wondering what could be down there, when without any warning a stream of water hit him right in the eyes. Danny got an eyeful. In fact, he got two eyes full. It was salt water too, and it made his eyes smart, to say nothing of the way it scared him. And that stream of water had come straight up from the hole Danny had been looking down. You should have seen Danny scamper for the shelter of the grass! Once there he felt safe, and sat down to watch those little holes.

It wasn't long before Tattler the Yellow Legs came walking along. He stepped near one of those little holes and Danny saw a stream of water come up. Tattler paid it no attention, no attention at all. He just went on about his business and seemed to take it as a matter of course. But Danny fairly ached with curiosity. What could have made water squirt up that way?

"Oh, Tattler," he called, "what did that?"

Tattler paused to look at Danny. "What did what?" he asked.

"What made that water squirt up out of the mud in front of you just now?" Danny asked.

"Oh," said Tattler, "a Clam did that."

"What is a Clam?" demanded Danny.

"Ha, ha, ha! Ho, ho, ho! The idea of not knowing what a Clam is!" cried Tattler. "A Clam is—why, it's a Clam. My goodness, here comes one of those two-legged creatures! You watch him and you'll see Clams, for he is coming after them, or I am greatly mistaken." With this, Tattler flew whistling away across the broad green marsh.

Danny remained safely hidden in the grass, but where he could peep out and see all that happened on the mudflat. The two-legged creature was, of course, a man. He had a pail and a queer-looking hoe. It was a hoe with teeth like a rake. He stopped right in front of Danny and began hoeing up the mud where Danny had seen all those little holes. Really, he was digging. Every other minute he stooped and picked up something and tossed it into a pail. By and by he tossed something over his shoulder and it fell close to Danny. You should have seen Danny scamper away. But after a bit curiosity drove Danny back again to see what it was that had fallen there. He found something that at once reminded him of the fresh-water mussels he had seen Jerry Muskrat opening and eating at the Smiling Pool. However, this one was white. The shell had been broken and that was why the man had thrown it away. Danny could see inside that broken shell. What he saw reminded him again of the fresh-water mussels or Clams of which Jerry Muskrat was so fond.

When at last the man went away, Danny went out to the place where he had been digging. There he found a number of small things just like the one that had been thrown up beside him. These, however, were not broken. While he was looking at them, one of them pushed out a long neck. Just then along came Tattler the Yellow Legs.

"Well," said Tattler, "I see you have found out what a Clam is."

"Are those Clams?" Danny asked rather stupidly.

"Of course they are Clams," replied Tattler. "See, there is one with the shell partly open. If you would like to get pinched good and hard, just put a paw in there."

"No, thank you," replied Danny. Even as he spoke, that Clam withdrew its long neck and closed its shell. "I suppose," said Danny, "that if Jimmy Skunk were here, he would say that a Clam is a fish."

"I don't know what Jimmy Skunk would say," replied Tattler, "but a Clam is called a fish; at least it is called a shellfish. There are several kinds of Clams. This one is called the Soft-shelled Clam and the Long Clam and in some places the Nanninose or Maninose. It is found mostly in sand and mud, in such places as this. I have seen it way up north where I go to nest, and I have seen it a good way south."

"Huh," said Danny, "I don't call that shell soft." You see, while Tattler had been talking, Danny had been trying his teeth on a bit of clam shell that he had found.

Tattler chuckled. "Well," said he, "it may not be soft, but it breaks a lot easier than the shell of some other Clams."

The Clams gave Danny something to think about. It seemed

to him that with the shell closed a Clam was just about as safe as any one could be. When he found that he couldn't get so much as a claw in one anywhere, he said aloud in his funny, squeaky little voice, "Well, nothing can happen to you. If I had a house like that, I never would worry. No, sir, I never would worry."

Probably the Clam wasn't worrying, for I doubt if Clams do any worrying. Just the same he *had* cause to worry, only he didn't know it. Had Danny been told it, he wouldn't have believed it. However, you sometimes have to believe what you see, and there came a day when Danny saw that a Clam was not as safe as he seemed to be.

Danny was fond of watching Graywing the Herring Gull as he sailed high overhead. Sometimes he would see Graywing sitting out on a sandbar. Once when he had climbed up on a sand dune and looked over towards the ocean, he saw Graywing sitting on a rock. At that distance Graywing seemed to be all shining white save his wings. They were a soft gray and gave him his name.

Danny often wondered what Graywing ate. He knew that Graywing ate fishes, because he had seen him swoop down and catch them. But he wondered if this big bird had to catch all those fishes alive. He didn't know that Graywing got a great deal of food floating in the water, thrown over from ships. And then one day he saw Graywing get a dinner in a most surprising way.

The man whom he had first seen digging Clams had returned for more. After he had gone Graywing alighted where the man had been digging and began to walk around. Presently he picked up a big Clam that had been overlooked.

"Now what under the sun will Graywing do with that?" thought Danny. "He certainly will choke to death if he tries to swallow it."

Up went Graywing with the Clam, and up and up and up. And then Danny caught sight of something dropping. It came down so fast he could hardly follow it with his eyes. It struck on a rock and Danny heard something crack. And when he looked up again, Graywing was coming down. He alighted close by the thing that had fallen and picked it up in his bill. Then Danny saw that it was the Clam that Graywing had carried aloft. Now the shell was broken all to bits and Graywing was pulling off the pieces. A moment later he swallowed the Clam and then went to look for another and did the same thing over again.

"I've learned something," muttered Danny. "I doubt now if anybody is absolutely safe. I didn't suppose any one could possibly get at one of those Clams inside such a hard shell. But Graywing the Gull has been smart enough to find a way. Live and learn; live and learn."

VII. Clams and More Clams

You ought to know Graywing the Herring Gull. He is quite worth knowing. There isn't much that Graywing doesn't know about the seashore. It's his business to know. Just take the subject of Clams. There are Clams and Clams. Graywing can tell you all about them. You see, he likes Clams to eat. The Clams that Danny Meadow Mouse saw him carry up in the air and drop on the rocks were the so-called Soft-shell or Long Clams. If you have ever been to a clambake and eaten steamed clams, you know what they are. You know, too, that Graywing knows what is good.

But there is another member of the Clam family which, though quite as delicious eating, is so difficult for Graywing to get that it isn't often he has the treat. He sees this Clam often enough, but seeing is not tasting. This is a long Clam,—quite six inches long, narrow and shaped very much like the handle of an old-fashioned razor. It doesn't look as if it were able to take care of itself. It looks not one bit smarter than any other Clam. But try to catch one, as Graywing has tried more than once.

Graywing knows just where to look for the Razor Clam, as it is called. He knows a certain sandbar where at low tide this Clam may be found with the upper end of the shell projecting from its hole. It is a tempting sight to Graywing. Yes, indeed, it is a tempting sight. Many times has he darted at one of these Clams in the hope of catching it. But at the first movement, down goes the Clam, and Graywing has nothing but an exasperating hole in the sand to look at.

Now, the surprising thing is that this Clam can go down into the sand faster than you can dig down with a spade. Yet it has no feet, no hands, no claws. To look at it, you wouldn't think it had a thing to dig with.

I have said that this Clam has no feet. This is true, but it has what is called a "foot." It isn't shaped like any foot you ever have seen. It looks like a long fleshy part pushing out from the lower end of the shell. But it is with this that the Razor Clam burrows so fast in the sand. This queer so-called "foot" stretches out into a point. This is pushed right down in the sand. Then through the other end the Clam draws in water. The water is forced right down into the foot, so that the latter swells and pushes away the sand around it. Then the point becomes a little disc that clings to the bottom, and the Clam pulls its shell right down. This process is repeated over and over, and so the Clam goes down in the sand very fast.

Does it surprise you to be told that there is one Clam that is a good swimmer? It would have surprised Danny. But Graywing has seen that swimming Clam many times. It is a little Clam, not over three-quarters of an inch long. The shell is thin and flexible. The surface is a rich brown color marked with yellow lines. This little Clam uses its foot for swimming and it can go either backward or forward for a considerable distance without touching bottom. It is called the Swimming Clam.

Then, too, Graywing is acquainted with the Sandbar Clam. This queer fellow is fond of pure salt water. He is fussy about it. Like other Clams, he burrows into the sand, but only for a short distance. His shell is covered with a sort of brown skin, which makes it look as if it were polished. Graywing says that this fellow has an unusually powerful foot and can skip along the surface with its aid, helped by flapping the two halves of the shell.

There is still another Clam that Graywing is acquainted with,—a pretty little Clam that has a name which is not pretty at all. It is called the Bloody Clam. This is because the gills and the liquid which corresponds to the blood in other animals, is red. This little Clam has a little brown shell with about thirty-two ridges radiating from the hinge. It usually is found fastened to stones.

Graywing the Gull is not the only one acquainted with members of the Clam family. Jimmy Skunk one time made their acquaintance and now he doesn't think as much of Clams as

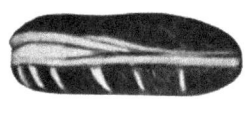

SWIMMING CLAMS.
Solemya velum.

HARD-SHELL CLAM OR QUAHAUG.
Venus mercenaria.

he used to. At the time he thought he knew all there was to know about them. It was his mistake. It is doubtful if any one knows all about anything. Jimmy found that he didn't know all about Clams.

Jimmy was poking around in the seaweed one moonlight night. He was looking for anything which appeared good to eat. Finally he found what he knew right away was a Clam. It differed from the Clams he was familiar with, but there could be no doubt that it was a Clam. It was in some seaweed in a little pool of water. Jimmy noticed right away that it wasn't long like the Soft-shelled Clams. The shell was partly open, but this Jimmy didn't notice. He wanted to look that Clam over close to, so he reached out his paw to pull the Clam towards him up on the sand.

What happened then happened so suddenly that for a minute even Jimmy himself didn't know what was the matter. You see, one toe had slipped into the opening of the shell. Instantly the Clam had closed its shell, pinching that toe of Jimmy Skunk's. And, my goodness, how it did pinch! Could you have seen him, or heard him, and not known what was the cause, you certainly would have thought that he was having a fit, or else had gone quite crazy. That is what Reddy Fox thought. He is cousin to Reddy Fox of the Green Meadows and looks just like him. He had long ago discovered that he could pick up a good living along the beach. It had become his favorite hunting ground.

Reddy Fox happened along just as Jimmy Skunk was caught by the Clam. Jimmy was snarling and growling and jumping up and rolling over as if he had quite lost his head, instead of having merely been caught by a toe. You see, he was as much frightened as he was hurt. His first thought was that he had been caught in one of those dreadful steel traps.

"Why, it's nothing but a Clam," said Reddy Fox. At this, Jimmy Skunk stopped dancing and stared long and hard at that Clam. It was more round than long. Jimmy tried his teeth on it. That shell was so hard that Jimmy was afraid he would break his teeth if he bit any harder.

"I—I didn't know what I'd caught," he said lamely.

Reddy Fox began to laugh. "You didn't catch anything," said

he. "It caught you, so far as I can see." Then he went off about his business, but as he trotted away he was still chuckling.

"Now what am I going to do?" said Jimmy Skunk to himself, as he glared down at the Clam which was holding him fast. "What am I going to do? If I were caught in a trap, I could pull and pull and pull my toe off. I wouldn't want to do that, but I *could* do it. I can't do it with this thing, however, for when I pull, it comes along with me. Perhaps if I keep quiet a little while, it will open and let me go."

Now if Jimmy had thought to put the Clam back in the water and sit beside the little pool quietly a little while, the Clam might have opened. But he didn't think to do that. Fortunately for Jimmy, it wasn't a very big Clam. It was what is called a Littleneck Clam. That is the kind that is served on the half shell in hotels and restaurants. If it had been a little bigger, it would have been called a Cherrystone Clam. And had it been fully grown, it wouldn't have been called a Clam at all, but a Quahog. It was well for Jimmy that it wasn't full grown.

Jimmy remembered how he had seen Graywing the Herring Gull carry Clams high in the air and drop them. "I wish I had wings," said Jimmy. "If I had wings, I'd fly away up and drop the thing." Then Jimmy began to laugh at himself. Yes, he did. You see, he had remembered that he couldn't drop the Clam if he wanted to. He was just as well off without wings as he would have been with them.

Then it occurred to him that perhaps by pounding it on a rock he could make the Clam let go. It was some distance to the nearest rocks. His whole foot ached by the time he got there. He didn't waste any minutes. He lifted his foot with the Clam and brought it down hard on a rock. "Ouch!" cried Jimmy. Then he looked at the Clam. Mr. Littleneck was still on the job. There was no crack in the shell. Jimmy began to realize how very hard that shell was. He tried the same thing several times, always with the same result.

Now there were little pools of water in among those rocks and at last Jimmy put that aching foot in the water, hoping that it would take the ache out. He held it there for a few minutes. When he lifted it from the water, he nearly tumbled over in surprise. The Clam had let go of that toe. There it lay down in the water.

These Clams, by the way, are not commonly found above the low-water mark. Probably some man had dropped this one where Jimmy found it. To this day Jimmy has the greatest respect for Clams.

VIII. Reddy Meets Barker the Seal

AT A certain point on the beach were many rocks. Some of these were far out in the water, so that when the tide was high they were entirely covered. When the tide was low some of them would be entirely out of water and some of them would be partly covered with water. They were big rocks. Seaweed partly covered some of them and among them lived all sorts of curious little seafolk. Both Jimmy Skunk and Reddy Fox had discovered that when the tide was out things very good to eat could sometimes be found among these rocks. So at night, when the tide was low, they were in the habit of going down there to see what they could find.

It happened one night that Reddy Fox was poking about among these rocks at the water's edge. Beyond he could see the flat tops of great rocks standing in the water, but these didn't interest him in the least. He couldn't get out on them, so why think about it? He had just found a fish that had been washed ashore,—a fish that looked like a very good fish. He opened his mouth to pick it up, when suddenly there was a sharp bark right behind him.

Reddy didn't pick up the fish. He didn't even take time to look behind him. He raced up the beach as fast as his legs could take him. Several times he heard that bark, and each time he heard it he tried to run a little faster. When he was safely back of a sand dune he stopped to listen.

At first he heard no sound. Then far away he heard that barking again. He crept up to the top of the sand dune. You should have seen how crafty he was. When he was near the edge, he flattened himself right down on the sand and crawled. He crawled until he was right behind a little bunch of coarse grass growing on the edge of the sand dune. He peeped between the blades of grass. It was bright moonlight and he could see almost as well as if it were daylight. No dog was following him. He looked over to those rocks. No dog was there.

Such a funny, funny look as came over the face of Reddy Fox. It came to him just then that no dog could have been barking behind him when he was away down on the edge of the water, for no dog could have come by way of the water. Slowly Reddy got to his feet and stared back at those rocks. His black ears were pointed forward. There it was again,—that bark. It came from out in the water. Slowly, taking a step and stopping, then taking another step and stopping, Reddy moved forward. He was ready to run at the slightest hint of danger. At last he was almost at the very edge of the water. The barking still came from out beyond.

Reddy's sharp eyes caught sight of something moving on a great rock out in the water. His first thought was that somehow a dog must have reached that rock. Then, as the moonlight fell full on it, Reddy saw that it wasn't a dog at all. Whoever it was was smooth-bodied and in the moonlight shone sleekly. The head was round. It reminded him somewhat of the head of Little Joe Otter, only it was very much bigger.

Once more he heard that bark and this time he saw the stranger life his head and open his mouth. He knew then that it was this stranger who had fooled him. A moment later the stranger flopped clumsily across the rock and slipped into the water. Reddy saw that round head moving swiftly above the surface. Then it disappeared.

"Well," said Reddy, "I should like to know who that was."

Have you guessed who it was? It was Barker the Seal, one of the seafolk.

Every night after his first glimpse of Barker, Reddy visited the place where the rocks were. For several nights he was disappointed. He saw and heard nothing of Barker.

"Probably he was just resting here that time," thought Reddy, as one night he made his way down to the rocks. "Probably I shall never see him again. I'm sorry. I should like to get acquainted with him."

Reddy stopped abruptly. On a flat rock almost within jumping distance from the shore was the stranger. Seeing him so near, Reddy somehow didn't feel so anxious to become acquainted. It was the stranger who spoke first.

"Hello!" said he. "Who are you?"

"I'm Reddy Fox. Who are you?" replied Reddy.

"I'm Barker the Seal," said the stranger, who looked very sleek and glistening in the moonlight.

Reddy put on his politest air. You know he can be very polite when he wants to be. "I am pleased to know you," said he.

"You don't know me," replied Barker rather gruffly.

Reddy corrected himself hastily. "I am pleased to make your acquaintance," said he.

"That is different. I am glad to make yours," replied Barker.

"If you please, Mr. Seal, where do you live?" Reddy asked.

Barker stared at Reddy so long and so hard that Reddy began to feel uncomfortable before Barker demanded in his gruffest voice, "Where do you suppose I live?"

"I haven't an idea. Truly I haven't," Reddy hastened to say. "This is only the second time I have seen you. I thought I knew everybody who lives on this part of the shore."

"Shore!" snorted Barker. "Shore! Do you think I live on the shore? I should say not! I live in the sea."

Then for the first time Reddy noticed that Barker had no legs. At least, they were like none Reddy had ever seen. Where his front legs should have been, according to Reddy's idea, were what looked like two paddles. Reddy could see no hind feet. When Barker moved he flopped about. No one who could only flop about like that could make much of a success living on shore. But it was equally hard for Reddy to imagine anybody but a fish living in the water all the time. "Are you a sort of fish?" he inquired.

"No," snorted Barker, and he looked more indignant than ever. "Fish, indeed! I am no more of a fish than you are, but I live in the sea just the same."

"I should like to have you come ashore and visit me, Mr. Seal," said Reddy in his most polite manner.

Barker looked at him a little suspiciously and inquired, "Where do you live?"

"Oh, not very far away," replied Reddy. "It is just over those sand dunes and back on the shore a little way."

"Thank you, Mr. Fox," replied Barker. "Thank you for your invitation. I must refuse, however. If I could swim there, I would accept in a minute. As I cannot, suppose you come and visit me instead."

Reddy grinned. "Thank you, Mr. Seal," said he. "If I could swim, I would."

Barker pretended to be very much surprised. "Do you mean to tell me," said he, "that such a smart fellow as you cannot swim?"

Again Reddy grinned. "Oh, I can swim," replied he. "I can swim just about as well as you can travel on land."

It was Barker's turn to grin. "Then you wouldn't be very comfortable in the water," said he.

That was a shrewd guess on Reddy's part that Barker wasn't at home on the land. Never once had he seen him come ashore. "What I should like to know," said Reddy, "is how you breathe under water. I watched you dive one night and you did not come up for a long time. Do you breathe through your skin like Grandfather Frog?"

"I don't know anything about Grandfather Frog," replied Barker, "but I can tell you I don't breathe through my skin. I have a perfectly good pair of lungs and I breathe just as you do. When I dive I hold my breath until I come up again."

Reddy sighed. "I don't see how you do it," said he. "I wish I could hold my breath that way. I believe you eat fishes. How do you catch them?"

Barker looked at Reddy as if he thought that a silly question, as indeed he did. "The same way you get your food," said he. "I surprise my food or run it down in the water, just as you surprise or run yours down on land."

"Where is your home?" inquired Reddy.

"Wherever I happen to be," replied Barker.

"And I believe you said you are not part fish," said Reddy.

As before, Barker fairly snorted. "Just because I am at home in the water, and eat, sleep, play and work there, I can see no reason for thinking me a fish. I am as much an animal as you are, and I wouldn't trade places with you for anything in the Great World. Give me the water every time. Watch me dive through that wave that is coming in!"

Barker slid from the rock just as a wave was going to break over him and Reddy saw no more of him that night.

IX. Reddy Fox Meets Big Claw

Because you've never seen a thing,
Don't say it cannot be.
The strangest thing you've ever seen
May common be to me.
Barker the Seal

And this is a shoe that fits the other foot just as well. The thing that is unbelievably strange to you may be very commonplace to me, and the thing that seems impossible to me may be so familiar to you that you do not give it a thought.

Of course, Reddy Fox knew a whole lot about Crabs. He was quite accustomed to seeing these funny fellows scuttling sideways when he came along. He had found out that some of the biggest ones could pinch hard enough to make him yelp. They really are very queer looking fellows, but Reddy was so accustomed to them that it never occurred to him that they were queer.

But when one day, for Reddy occasionally visited the beach in daytime, he found on the beach a dead, odd-looking creature that had been cast up by the waves, he was a surprised Fox. Never had he seen anything like this. At first he thought it was some kind of Crab. It had legs very much like the legs of a Crab. Then he discovered that the body was altogether different. It was long instead of round, and the rear part was jointed, or hinged. And then the pinching claws! Never since he had first come to the seashore had Reddy seen such great claws as these. There were two, one being a little bigger than the other.

"I don't want to be pinched by either of those claws," declared Reddy most emphatically.

The shell of this fellow was dark green which looked almost

COMMON LOBSTER.
Homarus americanus.

SPINY LOBSTER.
Panulirus argus.

black, and on the big claws were places that were red. Barker the Seal was lying on a big rock not far off and he called to Reddy to ask what he was staring at.

"I don't know what it is," replied Reddy.

"Bring it over where I can look at it," said Barker.

Reddy hesitated. He didn't like to admit that he was afraid to pick that thing up, but he was. You see, he wasn't quite sure that it wasn't alive. Finally he took hold of it by the tail and dragged it over.

Barker merely glanced at it. "Pooh!" said he. "That's nothing but a Lobster. There's nothing queer about that. It's a dead one, anyway."

"What is one of these things like when it's alive?" inquired Reddy. "It's queer I've never seen one running around on the beach."

At this Barker began to laugh.

"What are you laughing at?" demanded Reddy.

"The idea of Big Claw running around on a beach," replied Barker.

"I suppose by Big Claw you mean this Lobster," said Reddy. "Crabs run around and this thing looks something like a Crab. Anyway, it has legs like a Crab and claws like a Crab, only bigger. Why shouldn't it run around the same as Crabs?"

"Because a Lobster lives in the water and not on land; that's why," replied Barker. "If that one were alive it wouldn't be up there. And let me tell you that if you ever do find a live one, you want to keep away from those big claws."

"Huh!" replied Reddy. "You don't have to tell me that. I wonder if it's good to eat."

"Good to eat!" exclaimed Barker. "If there is anything better to eat than Big Claw the Lobster, I don't know what it is. But you want to get one when he hasn't any shell."

Reddy looked at Barker suspiciously. "Say that again," said he.

Barker did so. Reddy looked down at the Lobster at his feet. If ever anybody was thoroughly protected it was that Lobster.

"When does a Lobster have no shell?" inquired Reddy.

"When it has outgrown its old one and is waiting for a new one to harden," replied Barker.

"What becomes of its old one?" inquired Reddy.

"Oh, it is left kicking around," replied Barker carelessly.

Reddy looked at the Lobster's big claws and then over at Barker. "What about those big claws? Do you expect me to believe that any one with big hard-shelled claws like those can change his shell?" demanded Reddy.

Barker laughed. "Will you please tell me, Brother Fox, how you think a Lobster could grow without getting rid of his old shell every so often and growing a new one?"

This was too much for Reddy. The more he thought it over, the more clear it became that a Lobster inside a hard shell could grow no more than just to fill that shell out. But it was just as hard for him to see how it was possible for a Lobster to get out of his shell. "Have you ever seen a Lobster out of his shell?" he asked.

Barker smacked his lips. "I should say I have," said he. "Just talking about it makes me hungry."

"How does he do it?" cried Reddy.

"Easily enough," replied Barker. "Those joints become soft and he draws the flesh of those claws back through. Then the shell cracks in places and he draws himself out. Then he hides. You see, there are many fishes that are tickled to death to find Big Claw out of his shell, not to mention some of the rest of us. Big Claw just lies low until he gets a new shell."

"How long does it take him to get it?" inquired Reddy.

"About a week," replied Barker.

"Can he pinch then?" asked Reddy.

"Can he pinch!" exclaimed Barker. "Can he pinch! Just let a good big Lobster get hold of one of your paws in one of his claws, and then tell me what you think about pinching."

Reddy was full of questions. "Does he ever lose one of those big pinching claws?" he inquired.

"Often," replied Barker.

"What does Big Claw do then?" inquired Reddy.

"Grows another," said Barker in the most matter-of-fact way. "He grows a new claw, or he grows a new leg, if he happens to lose one. It seems to be no trouble at all. Of course, it may be inconvenient to lose a leg, but it will soon be replaced. After all, when one has ten legs I doubt if one or two can be missed much."

"Who has ten legs?" demanded Reddy.

"Why, Big Claw, of course! Isn't that whom we are talking about?" inquired Barker impatiently. "Big Claw the Lobster has ten feet, including those two big pincers."

"But those are not feet," protested Reddy.

"If they are not, what are they?" demanded Barker.

Reddy didn't know, so he kept on with his questions. "What does he use those big pinching claws for?" inquired Reddy.

"To tear his food to pieces," explained Barker.

"But I thought you said those big claws were feet," said Reddy.

"So I did," replied Barker. "You can scratch yourself with your hind feet as well as walk on them, can't you?"

"Of course!" snapped Reddy. "What has that to do with the matter?"

"Well, do you see any reason why Big Claw shouldn't use a pair of feet for something besides walking?" inquired Barker.

Reddy looked foolish. He felt that way. Now it occurred to him that all the Crabs he had seen—and it seemed to him that they must at least be second cousins to Big Claw the Lobster—always went sideways. "Does a Lobster travel sideways when he is walking?" inquired Reddy.

"Of course not! What put such an idea into your head?" exclaimed Barker. "He walks straight ahead, the same as you do."

"Can he swim?" inquired Reddy.

"Certainly," replied Barker. "He swims backward. What are you laughing at?"

"I was just wondering," explained Reddy, "if he were to be in a race which was to be walked for half the distance, and swum for half the distance, where he would be when he finished. Can he do anything else besides walk and swim?"

"He can dig," replied Barker. "He digs holes in the sand under water and backs into them. Then he is ready to grab anything that comes his way and looks good to eat."

"That reminds me," said Reddy. "What does Big Claw eat, anyway?"

"He isn't a bit fussy," replied Barker. "He likes dead fishes. Now, I'm a bit fussy. I want my fishes alive. But Big Claw will take his dead and he doesn't care how long they've been dead either. Once in a while he catches a little fish alive, or some of the other things that live in the sea. Altogether he picks up a very good living."

"How often does he change that shell of his?" demanded Reddy.

"Twice a year, I believe," replied Barker. "Mrs. Lobster changes hers only once a year."

"Are Lobsters always the same color?" inquired Reddy.

Barker shook his head. "No," said he, "usually Lobsters are dark green with red and blue markings, but sometimes they are almost all blue or almost all red. If you ever get a chance to catch one out of his shell, do try it."

Reddy grinned. "I will," said he. He knew that this was a little joke of Barker's, for already Barker had told him that the Lobster changes his shell only in the water.

X. A Lobster and a Crab that Cannot Pinch

Barker the Seal was good-natured. It was just as well that this was so, for Reddy Fox was full of questions. Reddy isn't a bit bashful. That is, he isn't a bit bashful where he is not suspicious. He meant to find out all about Lobsters, if asking questions could get him the information. "Is there only one kind of Lobster?" he inquired.

"There is only one kind around here," replied Barker, "but I'm told that there is another kind of Lobster that has no claws."

Reddy's eyes opened very wide. "Do you mean that he hasn't any legs?" cried he.

"I didn't say legs; I said claws," retorted Barker rather sharply.

"But only a few minutes ago you told me that the claws are feet, so how should I know?" retorted Reddy.

"I mean those big pinching claws," said Barker. "This Lobster I speak of is found in the warm water way down south. And I have heard that he is also found on another shore called the Pacific Coast. Instead of having eight regular feet and two big pinching claws, this fellow has ten regular feet and no pinching claws. At least, that is what I have been told. I have never seen him myself."

For a few minutes Reddy thought this over. Then he was ready with another question. "If he hasn't any big pinching claws, how does he protect himself?"

"Sharp spines," replied Barker. "He has a lot of sharp spines on his shell and so they called him Spiny. Like his cousin Big Claw, Spiny is a very good swimmer and he swims backward."

"I wonder if he has the same colors that Big Claw has," remarked Reddy.

"I am told he is quite a handsome fellow as Lobsters go," replied Barker. "Spiny is blue and yellow and brown mixed together. He likes the rocks, where he can find places to squeeze into and so be safe from enemies. Sometimes an enemy will get him by a leg and try to pull him out, but this can't be done."

"Why not?" demanded Reddy, looking very much interested. "Is Spiny so strong that he cannot be pulled out? What does he do,—hang on with all his feet? I don't see how he can hang on to a rock."

"He doesn't have to," replied Barker. "He just throws that leg off. The enemy gets the leg, but that is all."

"Say that again!" exclaimed Reddy.

"I said he just throws the leg off," replied Barker somewhat sharply.

"I suppose you mean that it gets pulled off," said Reddy.

"You have no business to suppose anything of the kind," retorted Barker. "Spiny doesn't even try to keep his leg from being pulled off. He lets go of it and so gets rid of it."

Reddy remembered a certain Lizard that could do the same thing with his tail. Then it wasn't quite so difficult to believe that Spiny the Lobster could let a leg go. "Does he ever get that leg back again?" he inquired.

"That is a silly question!" snapped Barker. "Of course he doesn't. But the next time he gets a new shell, he gets another leg in its place."

"I'd like to see Spiny," said Reddy. "I wonder if he is as good eating as Big Claw, the Lobster who lives around here."

"They say he is," replied Barker. "I know no reason why he shouldn't be. Why all the excitement?"

Reddy had begun to dig in the sand furiously. When Reddy starts to dig in earnest he certainly can make the sand fly. This sand was rather wet, for it was just above the water. So it wasn't quite as easy digging as it would have been had it been dry. Reddy did not reply at once. He was too much occupied. But after a minute or two he gave up. "I missed him," he grumbled.

"I say," repeated Barker, "why all the excitement?"

"I was trying to catch something," replied Reddy.

"Oh," said Barker, "that was it. Well, it is a good thing for me that I do not have to dig in order to catch things."

Reddy grinned. You know Barker the Seal has no feet to dig with. "That is quite true, Barker," said he. "It is equally true that if I had to catch things by swimming for them, I should soon starve to death. I should like to know what that thing was that I tried to catch just now. It certainly was some digger!"

"What was it like?" inquired Barker. "If you can tell me what it was like, perhaps I can tell you what it was."

"I didn't get a good enough look at it to describe it," confessed Reddy. "It was sort of like a big bug. Wait a minute! There's one now swimming in this little pool of water right in front of me. If it will keep still long enough perhaps I can tell you what it is like."

But it wouldn't keep still and Reddy's patience didn't hold out. That little pool of water was very shallow and Reddy made a dash to try to scoop out the queer little creature. He didn't succeed; it promptly burrowed in the sand. And once more Reddy dug in vain.

"You don't seem to have much luck," said Barker.

Reddy paid no attention. You see, he had discovered that a little farther along on the beach were a number of these queer little creatures. One of them was still, not far away. Reddy got a good look at it. It was about two-and-a-half inches long and about half as broad. The back seemed to be rounded quite high and was smooth. In fact, it was a hard yellowish-white shell. The rear part of the little creature was folded forward along the under side of the body, reaching nearly to the front. There were two eyes, each very small and on the end of a long, slender stalk. The legs were so short and small that they hardly seemed like legs at all. Growing out from the head, instead of the round, long feelers that Big Claw the Lobster has, were two little feathery feelers, something like those that Reddy had often seen on a big moth.

Reddy might have been wondering to this day what these little creatures were, had not Graywing the Gull happened along. "What are you looking at so intently," Reddy?" Graywing asked.

"I don't know," replied Reddy. "I wish I did."

Graywing hovered overhead, looking down. Of course, he

saw instantly what it was that Reddy was looking at. "That's a Sand Bug," said he. "That is Hippa the Sand Bug."

"I didn't know that there were any bugs on the seashore," said Reddy. Graywing alighted on a rock a short distance away, near enough to talk. "Hippa isn't a real bug," said he. "He is a Crab."

"He is what?" cried Reddy.

"I said that Hippa is a Crab," replied Graywing. "It must be that you are a little hard of hearing, Reddy Fox."

"No," replied Reddy, "I'm not hard of hearing, but that fellow looks so little like a Crab that I didn't think I heard aright. Are you quite sure that it is a Crab?"

"Certainly," replied Graywing. "Hippa the Sand Bug is just as much a member of the Crab family as is any other Crab. He is most nearly related to Hermit, the fellow who lives in somebody else's shell."

"But Hippa hasn't any pinching claws," persisted Reddy.

"Neither has Spiny the Spiny Lobster," interrupted Barker, who had been listening.

"That's so," exclaimed Reddy. "I had forgotten that. Well, I've learned something. I have learned there is a Lobster without pinching claws and a Crab without pinching claws."

"Huh!" exclaimed Graywing. "If you stay around the seashore long, you'll learn a lot of stranger things than these."

"Well, I'm always ready to learn," replied Reddy.

XI. Graywing Knows His Crabs

"Speaking of Crabs," said Graywing the Gull, "there are some curious fellows in that family."

"I know," replied Reddy. "A fellow can't hunt along the beach without knowing that. I've met a lot of them."

"Of course you have," said Graywing. "But I've seen some you haven't met. That is the advantage of being a traveler. Did you ever see the Box Crab?"

Reddy shook his head. "If I've seen him, I don't know him by that name," said he. "What is he like?"

"You haven't seen him, or you wouldn't ask," replied Graywing. "But then, you wouldn't see him along here, anyway. I've seen him rolled up on the sand farther south. This fellow lives on sandy and muddy bottoms and comes ashore only when the waves roll him up there."

"Is he a little Crab or a big Crab? And why do they call him a Box Crab?" demanded Reddy.

"Oh," replied Graywing, "he is of rather medium size, but thicker through than most Crabs. When he's scared he just draws his legs in and folds his big pinching claws, which are broad and flattened, so that they fit close together across the front. It is just as if he were shut up in a box then."

"That reminds me of some one," said Reddy. "Did you ever see Slowpoke the Box Tortoise? He is one of the Turtle family who can shut himself up the same way."

But Graywing was thinking about Crabs and paid no attention to what Reddy said. "Then there are the Spider Crabs. Have you ever seen any of the Spider Crabs, Reddy?"

"Huh!" exclaimed Reddy. "They all look like Spiders to me. How should I know whether I've seen the Spider Crabs or not?"

"Well," said Graywing, "if ever you have seen a Crab planting seaweed on his own back, you have seen a Spider Crab."

Reddy looked up quickly and there was suspicion in the way in which he regarded Graywing. "Say that again," said he.

Obligingly, Graywing repeated what he had said. Then he added, "There are different kinds of Spider Crabs. I suppose they get their name of Spider Crabs from their long, slim legs. They certainly are a queer lot."

"But what about this planting seaweed on their backs?" interrupted Reddy.

"It's a fact," replied Graywing. "That is the way they hide. Some of them not only have seaweed all over their backs, but sponges and even some of the other queer little living creatures of the sea. It is their way of hiding."

"But do you mean to tell me that they put them there themselves?" inquired Reddy.

"I mean just that," replied Graywing. "I have seen a Spider Crab break off pieces of seaweed, chew the ends, and then with his claws reach up and stick the bits of seaweed on his back. His back was more or less covered with hairs. And I can tell you more than that. I've seen one of those Spider Crabs take care to cover himself with only the particular kind of seaweed immediately around him."

"I didn't think that Crabs were that smart," said Reddy. "How many kinds of Spider Crabs are there?"

"I can't say exactly," replied Graywing. "Here, come over to this little pool of water."

Reddy did as he was bidden and stared down into a little pool between the rocks. "Well," said he, "I don't see anything."

"Look again," said Graywing. "Don't you see some seaweed growing down there?"

"Yes," replied Reddy, "I see that. Why, some of it is moving around!"

"Certainly," replied Graywing with a chuckle. "You are looking down on one of those Spider Crabs I have been telling you about, one that has covered himself with seaweed. That particular one is called a Toad Crab, because his body is shaped a good deal like that of a Toad. There's another one of these Spider Crabs that is also called a Toad Crab, and he looks even more like a Toad than this one. I've been told by some of my relatives whom I've

TOAD CRAB.
Hyas coarctatus.

KELP CRAB.
Pugettia producta.

MUD CRAB.
Panopeus herbstii.

ROCK CRAB.
Cancer irroratus.

met 'way down south, that there is still another Toad Crab off the northern Pacific Coast. Along that coast the most common Spider Crab is called the Kelp Crab. I am told it is almost the exact color of the kelp or seaweed around it."

"You seem to know a lot about Crabs," said Reddy.

"Why shouldn't I?" replied Graywing. "I've spent most of my life along the seashore and there isn't a great deal going on that I don't know about."

"I don't doubt that," replied Reddy. "I can understand how you can know about the things that are on the shore, but some of these Crabs you have mentioned spend all their lives in the water."

"What of it?" exclaimed Graywing. "Don't you suppose I can see 'em just the same?"

"I hadn't supposed so," replied Reddy. "I can't see anything on the bottom except when I am right over a little, shallow pool."

"You forget," replied Graywing, "that I can look straight down. Now that makes all the difference in the world. When the water is smooth, I can see the bottom and all that goes on down there, even though the water is quite deep. So I know about some of these Crabs that you wouldn't be likely to know much about on shore. Speaking of Crabs, there are some more that you really ought to know. Have you ever met the Mud Crabs?"

"Not that I know of," replied Reddy, who was beginning to feel that he didn't know much after all. "I suppose they must live in the mud and so have been given the name of Mud Crabs."

"That's it," replied Graywing. "They like muddy shores. They live under stones in muddy places, or in burrows in muddy banks or marshes. They are all rather small Crabs. Have you ever seen the Rock Crab?"

By this time Reddy was getting rather confused. He had had no idea there were so many Crabs. "I don't know," he confessed quite frankly. "Perhaps I have and didn't know it from any other Crab."

Graywing took to his wings and flew slowly along the beach just above the water. It was low tide. Suddenly he dropped down on the sand and called to Reddy to come over there. Obediently, Reddy trotted over. Just in front of Graywing was a fairly

ORCHID CRAB.
Gecarcinus lateralis.

JONAH CRAB.
Cancer borealis.

good-sized stone, half-buried in the sand. "Pull that stone over," commanded Graywing.

Wondering what it was all about, Reddy did as he was told to do. At once a Crab which had been hiding under the stone ran out and began to bury itself in the sand. The upper shell was red, speckled with small, brownish spots, while the under shell was yellow. It was a fairly good-sized Crab. Along each side of the front edge of the upper shell were nine blunt smooth-edged teeth. Reddy noticed right away that the claws were sharp and that there were no swimming paddles. He knew then that it must be a crawling Crab and not a swimming Crab.

"That," said Graywing, "is a Rock Crab."

Reddy nodded. "I've seen that kind of Crab lots of times," said he. "Especially where the shore is rocky."

"He has a close relative," explained Graywing, "called the Jonah Crab. I've seen that fellow many times on rocky shores where the waves come thundering in. It has a rougher shell than the Rock Crab, and those teeth on the edge of the shell are saw-edged. It is a little bigger Crab than the Rock Crab and is a bold fellow. There is no hiding away under the rocks the way this fellow does."

"Well, anyway," remarked Reddy, "I am glad there are no land Crabs. I don't like the looks of these fellows and I don't like to think of them as running around on land away from the shore."

"That's all you know about it," exclaimed Graywing. "Away down south there *are* land Crabs. They are not very far from the water, but they don't live in the water. They live under damp logs, or leaves, and dig burrows. You ought to see those fellows travel. And they are good fighters, too. More than that, they can climb."

Once more Reddy Fox looked at Graywing with suspicion. "What do you mean, they can climb?" he asked.

"Just that," replied Graywing. "They can climb trees. I've seen them do it."

"Well, all I've got to say," barked Reddy, "is that I'm glad that I don't live there. What is that land Crab called?"

"The Orchid Crab," replied Graywing.

XII. A Queer Host and a Queerer Guest

OFTEN REDDY Fox met Jimmy Skunk on the beach. They were excellent friends. There was plenty to eat, so of course there was no occasion to quarrel over food. Now and then they would find a dead fish washed up on shore, a fish big enough for a whole party. So it happened that they often dined together.

Just after sunrise one morning, when the tide was out, Reddy went exploring along the water's edge. A day or two before there had been a heavy storm and many things had been washed up along the beach. Presently Reddy discovered that Jimmy Skunk was down there too. Jimmy was poking at something black at the water's edge and Reddy went over to see what it was. It appeared to be nothing but a queer rock. Part of it was smooth. Attached to this and, as Reddy supposed, a part of it, were a number of queer projections. Some were small and some were nearly as big as a man's hand. They were very rough, very rough indeed.

"What are you fooling with that queer looking rock for?" asked Reddy.

Jimmy's eyes twinkled. "Just wishing that one of these fellows would open up just long enough for me to scoop him out," said he.

Reddy looked about curiously. "What fellows?" he demanded. "I don't see anything that can open up around here."

Jimmy put a black paw on one of the rough pieces of the queer looking rock. "One of these," said he.

"That's nothing but a piece of rock!" exclaimed Reddy.

Jimmy's eyes twinkled more than ever. "Guess again," said he. "This isn't a rock; it is an Oyster."

"What is an Oyster?" grunted Reddy.

"An Oyster," replied Jimmy, "is an appetizer. You eat one and it gives you an appetite."

"Huh!" exclaimed Reddy. "I don't have to eat any Oyster to give me an appetite. But how do you eat a thing like that?"

"You don't, the way it is," replied Jimmy, "any more than you eat a Clam with the shell closed. This fellow has two halves to its shell, just as a Clam has, only this fellow's shell is a lot thicker than a Clam's shell. If you are lucky enough to find one open, and can scoop the Oyster out before it can close the shell, you've got something better than a Clam. But there isn't a chance to get one when they're shut up the way these are. You see, all these Oysters became attached to this stone when they were tiny and they've grown up together in a bunch. They do that sometimes. I suppose the storm washed them up here. It's tantalizing. That's what it is, tantalizing."

"Where did you learn so much about Oysters?" demanded Reddy, as he in his turn poked over those Jimmy had found.

"What is the good of a tongue if you don't use it?" chuckled Jimmy. "I have been asking questions. Hello, here comes Graywing. If you don't believe what I've told you, ask him."

Graywing alighted close to Reddy and Jimmy. "What are you fellows looking at?" said he.

"Oysters," replied Jimmy Skunk. "Oysters that we can't eat."

Just then Reddy Fox spied a Hermit Crab scuttling along with his house on his back. Reddy never grew tired of watching these funny little Crabs. They amused him, and you know we all like to be amused. "Do you know," said Reddy to Graywing, "I think those Crabs are the smartest of all the Crab family."

"Why so?" asked Graywing, looking somewhat surprised.

"Because," replied Reddy, "they have been smart enough to find shells that will protect them better than their own shells would, if they had any. None of their relatives has been smart enough to do that."

"Is that so?" exclaimed Graywing. "Never make a statement, Neighbor Fox, until you *know* you know all there is to know about that particular thing. Come along with me."

Graywing flew along the shore to where a boat had come in with some Oysters that morning just at daybreak. Reddy followed along the shore, and behind Reddy ambled Jimmy Skunk, for Jimmy was also interested. Some Oysters had been opened on that boat. Graywing looked around among the open shells. Presently he picked up something and dropped it where Reddy could see it. "Look at this," said he. "What do you make of it?"

Reddy walked over to it. It was a very tiny Crab. It was a teeny-weeny Crab. It had no pinching claws and its legs looked too weak for it to walk on. "That," said Reddy, looking very wise, "is a baby Crab."

"Guess again," retorted Graywing. "That Crab is fully grown."

Reddy's eyes opened very wide. "I don't like to say that I don't believe you," said he, "but you can see for yourself that this Crab cannot run around. He isn't big enough yet."

"That isn't a 'he,'" retorted Graywing. "That is a 'she.' That is Mrs. Crab, and it is quite true that she cannot run around or swim around. She doesn't have to and she doesn't want to. You never saw her before, did you?"

"No," replied Reddy, "I never did."

"Well, you wouldn't see her now, had it not been that some one opened an Oyster and she fell out," said Graywing.

You should have seen the sharp ears of Reddy Fox prick up! "What do you mean by that?" he demanded.

"I mean," replied Graywing, "that this is Mrs. Oyster Crab and that she has lived nearly her whole life within an Oyster shell with an Oyster. She went in there when she was a baby and she never left there until now. That is why she hasn't any strength in her legs, nor any pinching claws. She hasn't any use for them. You think those Hermit Crabs are well protected in those shells they carry around with them, but you'll have to admit that those shells are nothing compared with Oyster shells."

"Does she live on the Oyster?" asked Jimmy Skunk, who had been listening.

"No," replied Graywing. "She lives *with*, not *on*, the Oyster. They are the best of friends."

"Imagine," chuckled Reddy, "any one having an Oyster for a friend."

"If that is Mrs. Oyster Crab, where is Mr. Crab?" inquired Jimmy Skunk.

FEATHERFOOTED SHRIMPS.
Mysis stenolepis.
OYSTER CRAB.
Pinnotheres ostreum.

EDIBLE SHRIMP.
Penaeus setiferus.

"Goodness knows," replied Graywing. "He may be almost anywhere in the water."

"Oh!" exclaimed Jimmy. "Doesn't he live with an Oyster, the way Mrs. Crab does?"

"No," replied Graywing, "he is even smaller than little Mrs. Oyster Crab, but he has a hard shell. Yes, sir, he does so. He may be little, but he is hardshelled just the same. He believes in having a good time seeing the world."

"Am I to understand that little Mrs. Oyster Crab doesn't ever have a hard shell?" inquired Jimmy Skunk.

"If that is your understanding, it is correct," replied Graywing. "She has only a skin in place of a shell, and that is what makes her such good eating."

"Good eating!" exclaimed Reddy Fox and Jimmy Skunk together. And both eyed that little Crab with new interest.

But before either could move, Graywing had picked up little Mrs. Oyster Crab and she had disappeared at one gulp. "I hope," said he, "that sometime you may find out what an Oyster Crab tastes like. You know it isn't often that one is found. They never leave the Oysters with which they are living, and it is only when an Oyster is opened that there is a chance to get one of these little dainties."

"Look at that baby Crab down there!" cried Reddy Fox. "That's the smallest Crab I ever have seen."

Graywing looked. Just disappearing under some seaweed in the water was a mite of a Crab, but he was a sure enough, regular Crab. Little as he was, Reddy could see that he had two pinching claws just like the bigger Crabs, and there was nothing weak about those tiny legs, as had been the case with Mrs. Oyster Crab. He was traveling sidewise in regular Crab fashion.

"Well, you are lucky!" exclaimed Graywing. "It isn't every one who has a chance to see little Mr. Oyster Crab. That is whom you are looking at. He has a shell, and all that, like a regular Crab, but he is such a tiny fellow that his shell isn't very hard and always there are hungry fishes looking for him. That is why he scuttled out of sight so quickly just now. However, tiny as he is, he is a regular fellow, for he would rather take his chances and see something of the great world than live as Mrs. Oyster

Crab lives—secure and safe, but with nothing more exciting happening than the opening and closing of an Oyster shell. It is said that the most important thing in life is safety. Mrs. Oyster Crab has it. She certainly has it. As for me, I prefer a little less safety and a lot more excitement."

"The same here," replied Reddy. "Isn't that a hunter with a terrible gun heading this way along the beach?"

"I believe it is. I just remember that I have a fishing date," replied Graywing.

As for Reddy Fox and Jimmy Skunk, they disappeared quickly behind the sand dunes.

XIII. THE QUEER FELLOW WHO COULD OPEN OYSTERS

ONCE MORE Reddy Fox and Jimmy Skunk had met at the water's edge at low tide.

"Have you had any appetizers lately?" inquired Reddy politely.

Jimmy's eyes twinkled. "I suppose you mean Oysters," said he. "Have you tasted one yet?"

"No," confessed Reddy, "I haven't, but I should like to. I suppose that Oysters are just about as safe as anybody can be. I don't suppose that they have any enemies that they need really to fear. Hello, I wonder what that thing is! Look, Jimmy, down there in the water!"

Jimmy looked. Just beyond where they stood, and where they could look right down into it was a pool of water. On the bottom lay two or three Oysters, their shells closed. A big Starfish was close to one of these Oysters. The Starfish was the queer thing Reddy had seen.

It was creeping along the bottom of the pool. It was a queer fellow indeed, having five divisions, so that it made a perfect star, which gave it its name of Starfish.

Now, the Starfish isn't a true fish, in spite of the fact that it is called Starfish. Both Reddy and Jimmy had seen Starfishes before, many of them. They had found them cast up on the shore dead. At least, they supposed them to be dead. It had never occurred to either to think that these queer things could ever have been alive. So when they saw this one actually crawling along the sand at the bottom of the little pool, it was almost more than they could believe.

"I wish you'd tell me how a thing without any legs, and without any fins, can move the way that thing is moving," said Reddy.

"I don't know any more than you do," replied Jimmy. "I wish we were a little closer, so that we could see. Look, he's crawling right over that Oyster."

Sure enough, the Starfish had moved over on to one of the Oysters, and had stopped moving. Just then the attention of Reddy and Jimmy was drawn to something else and for a little while they forgot about the Starfish. At last Reddy happened to remember it and looked down in the pool to see if it had moved. "Jimmy!" he cried excitedly. "Will you look at this?"

Jimmy looked. At first he didn't see anything unusual. Then he noticed that the Starfish seemed to be folded partly around that Oyster. Yes, sir, that is the way it looked.

"What do you suppose he's doing?" asked Reddy.

"I haven't the least idea," replied Jimmy. "Let's watch and see."

Having nothing better to do, Reddy and Jimmy sat down and watched. For a long time they could not see that anything was happening. Then Jimmy suddenly leaned over with his nose close to the water that he might see down in it better. Anyway, he thought he could see better that way. "As I live!" he exclaimed. "That Oyster is opening! Now what do you know about that?"

Reddy leaned forward. Sure enough, it did look as if the edges of that shell were parting. They looked at the other Oysters. None of these was opening.

"I wonder," said Reddy, "why that particular Oyster is opening. I wouldn't expect it to open with that fellow fastened to it."

"Do you know what I think?" said Jimmy.

"What do you think?" demanded Reddy.

"I think that somehow or other that fellow is making that Oyster open," replied Jimmy.

"Nonsense!" exclaimed Reddy. "I don't believe anything could open an Oyster. Certainly that thing cannot."

But there was no doubt that the Oyster was slowly but surely opening, and it looked decidedly as if that Starfish had something to do with it. "I tell you," said Jimmy Skunk, "that Oyster isn't opening because it wants to. It is being opened and that fellow clinging to it is doing it."

Jimmy was right. On the under side of that Starfish were

hundreds of little sucker-like feet. These were clinging fast to the two halves of the shell and by means of the five arms, or parts, of the Starfish, the shell was being pulled open. It didn't seem possible—no, sir, it didn't seem possible. But it *was* possible and it was being done right under the very eyes of Reddy Fox and Jimmy Skunk.

Reddy and Jimmy were so interested that they forgot all about everything else. They watched that shell open to a certain point. Then for some time they couldn't see that anything was happening. But by and by the Starfish let go of the shell and began to crawl away. Now they could look down into the partly opened shell.

Then Reddy looked at Jimmy, and Jimmy looked at Reddy, and both looked down at the half-open shell once more. There was nothing in it. No, sir, there was nothing in it. It was as empty as a shell could be. Once more Reddy looked at Jimmy, and Jimmy looked at Reddy, and such funny expressions as there were on those two faces.

"Do you suppose," said Reddy, "that the shell was empty all the time, and that was the reason why it opened so easily?"

Jimmy Skunk shook his head. "No," said he, in a most decided way, "I have seen a lot of closed Oysters and a lot of Oyster shells. Empty shells are never closed tight, the way that one was. There certainly was an Oyster in that shell. It looks to me very much as if that Oyster had been eaten right under our very noses. Look! There comes another one of those things. Let's watch him."

Sure enough, another big Starfish came creeping into view. Jimmy and Reddy watched. This one passed right over the empty Oyster shell without paying any attention to it. But when it reached the next Oyster it stopped. Reddy and Jimmy saw it fold its arms about this Oyster. Then they saw precisely the same thing happen that happened with the first Oyster and the first Starfish. Slowly, very slowly, the shell opened. When it had opened wide enough, the Starfish was very busy for a while, although it seemed to be just resting there. By and by it moved away and it left an empty shell. Then Reddy and Jimmy knew beyond a doubt that somehow those Starfishes opened

COMMON STARFISH.
Asterias forbesii.

BLOOD STARFISHES.
Henricia sanguinolenta.

the Oysters and ate them. They were surprised enough as it was, but they would have been even more astonished could they have seen just how the Starfishes ate the Oysters.

What had happened was this: When the Oyster had been opened sufficiently, Mr. Starfish simply pushed his stomach out of his mouth and turned it wrongside out over that Oyster inside the shell, and that was the end of the Oyster. That is his rather handy way of eating. He doesn't have to go to the trouble of biting, chewing and swallowing his food. He just turns his stomach inside out around the food. That is all there is to it.

Now, Oysters look as if they are perfectly safe in those thick, heavy shells. But you see they are not. The Starfishes are the worst enemies they have. Against these queer fellows they are quite helpless. Starfishes eat other mollusks, such as Clams and Mussels, but there is nothing they like quite so much as a good, fat Oyster. Small mollusks are swallowed whole and the shells afterwards pushed out through the mouth. You see, a Starfish does have a mouth. It is right in the center of the star.

One of the Starfishes moved over until he was right under the nose of Jimmy Skunk and Reddy Fox. Once he turned in such a way that they saw the underside of one of the five rays, or points. They saw that it was covered with queer little feet. These are like little tubes with a disk on the end of each, a sucking disc that clings to whatever it touches. It is by means of these that the Starfish travels along and clings to rocks and pulls open Clams and Oysters. At the end of each of the five points was a little red spot like a little eye. In a way, these little spots are like eyes, for they are sensitive to light.

The Starfish that Reddy and Jimmy were watching was what is known as the Common Starfish. Almost always it has five arms. Once in a great while there will be one with six arms, or perhaps with only four arms.

Just as Jimmy and Reddy were turning away, a little wave rolled a Starfish up on the beach just beyond them. It fell on its back, so that Reddy and Jimmy had a chance to have a good look at its under side. They discovered that those little tube-like feet were arranged along a deep groove extending down the middle of each arm. While they were looking at it the Starfish bent two arms backward beneath the body and then lifted until it had turned itself over.

"What do you know about that?" exclaimed Jimmy Skunk. "Let's turn him back and see him do it again."

But before they could do this a wave came rolling in and took the Starfish back with it.

XIV. When Seeming Loss Is Really Gain

REDDY Fox had new respect for a Starfish. He felt that any fellow who could open an Oyster was entitled to respect. But Jimmy Skunk is no respecter of persons, so when Jimmy found a Starfish that had become entangled in some seaweed rolled up on the beach by the water, Jimmy decided to see if the Starfish would be good eating. So he got hold of one arm and pulled it off. Then he decided that he didn't care for Starfish.

"If you are not going to eat him, what did you pull his arm off for?" demanded Reddy, just as if he would never be guilty of such a thing himself.

"Oh, he doesn't mind a little thing like that," said another voice, before Jimmy could make reply. They turned to find Graywing the Herring Gull who had alighted on the beach just back of them.

"Why doesn't he mind it?" demanded Reddy. "I guess you would mind it if some one pulled a wing or a leg off."

"Certainly I would mind it," replied Graywing. "It makes me shiver just to think of such a thing. But then, I couldn't grow another wing or another leg. But that fellow there can grow another arm to take the place of the one Jimmy Skunk pulled off."

"Do you mean that a Starfish can grow an arm in place of one that's torn off, the way Big Claw the Lobster can grow a new claw to take the place of one that is lost?" inquired Reddy.

Graywing nodded. "You have the idea, Reddy," said he. "That Starfish won't miss his arm, because he'll grow another in its place. What is more, I suspect that the arm Jimmy has torn off will by and by become another Starfish."

You should have seen Jimmy Skunk stare at that arm and at Graywing the Gull. "You don't really and truly expect me to believe that, do you?" he inquired.

"Whether you believe it, or don't believe it, makes no difference," retorted Graywing. "I know what I know. All my life

I have lived along the seashore and I've seen this thing happen dozens and dozens of times. I believe you fellows have been getting acquainted with Oysters."

"Not exactly getting acquainted," said Reddy Fox. "I haven't actually tasted one yet, and I won't feel really acquainted until I do. But we've been learning something about them, as you know. Ever since I found out that one of these fellows can pull open an Oyster, I have had a lot of respect for them. Opening an Oyster is more than any one else that I know of can do."

"You forget those two-legged creatures called Men," said Graywing. "They can open Oysters. They are very fond of Oysters. But they hate Starfishes. It is because they are so fond of Oysters that they hate Starfishes. I've seen Starfishes fairly cover the bottom of the ocean for a long distance. You have no idea what a lot of them there are in the sea. They would just clean out all the Oysters where they happened to be. Then they would move on and try to find more."

"Now Men want the Oysters for themselves," continued Graywing, "so they used to catch the Starfishes around where the Oysters were and then chop them up. Then they would throw the pieces overboard into the water. Wasn't that a joke?"

Jimmy scratched his nose thoughtfully. "I don't see the joke," said he.

"Oh," exclaimed Graywing. "Each one of those pieces in time became a new Starfish. So, instead of making fewer Starfishes, those Men were making more. It always made me laugh when I watched them doing it."

"Do they still do it?" asked Reddy.

"No," replied Graywing. "They finally found out what they were doing. Now they kill the Starfishes in hot water."

Reddy and Jimmy turned to look with increased interest at the Starfish which now had only four arms. The tide was coming in. Presently the Starfish and the arm Jimmy had torn from it were both in the water.

"You found one Starfish and made two," said Graywing.

"I suppose," remarked Reddy, "that all the Starfishes are pretty much alike."

"Yes and no," replied Graywing. "There are different kinds

of Gulls and different kinds of Foxes and different kinds of Skunks. Now, that fellow you have been looking at is the Common Starfish. Let me see if I can't find you another one."

Graywing walked along the edge of the water for a short distance. Then he called to them. Reddy and Jimmy went over there. In a little tide pool was another Starfish. It had five arms like the one they had already seen, but it was somewhat smaller and it was pink or reddish, though, as they found out afterwards, it was sometimes purple and sometimes yellow and sometimes orange. When it moved they noticed that two of its arms were forward. It looked as if it were dragging the other three. "This," explained Graywing, "is a Blood Starfish. I have found this kind very common up along the northern coast when I have been north in summer."

There was one thing about this little Starfish that made it very different from other Starfishes, a thing that even Graywing doesn't know. Most other Starfishes cast their eggs into the water, where those that are not eaten by fishes in time hatch into baby Starfishes and must look out for themselves. The Blood Starfish doesn't do this. The eggs are held by the mother around her mouth until they have developed into tiny Starfishes, each one ready to look out for himself.

"What is the biggest Starfish you have ever seen?" inquired Reddy.

"Oh, that," replied Graywing, "was the Giant Starfish. It lives 'way down in the Sunny South, where the water is warm. It is the largest of all the Starfishes. It has five arms, but they are short and very thick. The upper surface is covered with little blunt spines, and between these are queer ridges. It is brown, or brownish-yellow, and it lives in deep water. You were interested in what I told you about Starfishes growing new parts. Why, there are some Starfishes called Brittle Stars, that can throw off pieces of their arms, and do so when they are frightened. I've been told that they sometimes throw off all their arms. But that doesn't matter, for of course they grow new ones. These are sometimes called Sea Spiders, because they are rather spidery looking. You see, their arms are long and very narrow and they are quite sharp-pointed and curl up at the ends. They are very active fellows. There is one that you would hardly recognize as a Starfish at all. I believe I've heard it called

MUD STARFISH.
Ctenodiscus crispatus.

GIANT STARFISH.
Pentaceros reticulatus.

BASKET STARFISH.
Gorgonocephalus agassizii.

BRITTLE STARFISH.
Ophiopholis aculeata.

the Basket Star, though sometimes it is called just Basket Fish. Its arms are divided into so many branches that it looks more like a plant than a living creature. Little fishes try to hide among its branches sometimes and that is the end of the little fishes."

"How so?" asked Reddy Fox, looking surprised.

"Because those little branches immediately seize the little fishes, and the little fishes go the way that Oyster did that you watched," replied Graywing.

"It's queer I've never seen any of these Brittle Stars along the shore," said Jimmy Skunk. "My eyes are pretty good. I don't miss much."

"Oh," exclaimed Graywing, "most of the Brittle Stars are in deep water. It is only when one happens to be washed up that you are likely to see it. There's another Starfish that I am told is quite common in deep water, but the only ones I have ever seen were some that were washed ashore. This is the Mud Starfish. The feet of this Starfish have no suckers on the ends, so they cannot cling the way the common Starfish does. It likes a muddy bottom and that's where it is usually found."

Jimmy Skunk was looking thoughtful. "My goodness!" said he at length. "I should think if every time one of those Starfishes gets broken up and each part becomes another Starfish, there wouldn't be room for them in the great ocean after a while."

"Oh, they have their enemies, just like the rest of us," replied Graywing. "Sometimes great numbers of them are thrown up on the shore in a storm and are unable to get back to the water. Then they die."

"Well," said Reddy Fox, "since I have been coming to the seashore I have seen some queer things, but a Starfish opening an Oyster beats anything I've seen yet. If I hadn't seen it done, no one could have made me believe it could be done."

"You'll see a lot more queer things if you stay around here long enough," said Graywing.

"I'm going to stay," declared Reddy.

"So am I," said Jimmy Skunk.

"Good!" said Graywing. "I'll probably have a chance to show you some of the other queer things myself."

XV. THE INNOCENT-LOOKING DRILLERS

JIMMY SKUNK had said that he didn't miss much. He had spoken the truth. He had learned to use his eyes. He was observing. You know it is an excellent thing to be observing. Some folks can go along and never see anything and have perfectly good eyes. They have good eyes, but they do not know how to use them. Or, if they do know how, they do not use them.

Now in his wanderings along the beach Jimmy Skunk had frequently noticed a certain thing. This was a tiny, perfectly round hole in a Clam shell or an Oyster shell. He saw this so often that he became curious about it. He knew, of course, that some one or something had made each of those tiny round holes. He called the attention of Reddy Fox to one of these.

"I've noticed those holes myself," said Reddy. "They are always in empty shells. Let's ask Graywing about them."

So the next time that Graywing came along they asked him about those little round holes in the shells.

"Oh," said Graywing in the most matter-of-fact manner, "those holes were made by some one who wanted to get the Clams or the Oysters inside the shells. You don't find those holes in big Oyster shells, but you will find a lot of small Oyster shells with holes in them. If I look around a bit perhaps I can show you the fellow who makes those holes."

"I wish you would, Mr. Gull," said Jimmy in his politest manner. "I wish you would. I certainly would like to see that fellow."

"All right," replied Graywing. "You wait here a few moments and I will see what I can do."

Graywing flew along the beach just at the edge of the water. Back and forth, back and forth he flew, all the time looking down with those wonderful eyes of his. Little is missed by Graywing's eyes. Presently he alighted on the beach close to the water's edge and in his harsh voice called to Jimmy Skunk and Reddy Fox.

"Come over here if you want to see one of those hole-makers at work," said Graywing.

For once, Jimmy Skunk actually hurried. He did so. You see, he was brimming over with curiosity. When he and Reddy got there Graywing showed them a Clam. On the shell of the Clam was what Jimmy and Reddy both called a small Snail.

"There you are," said Graywing. "There is one of those hole-makers. I have an idea that he has drilled his hole and is living on that Clam right now."

Jimmy Skunk turned and simply stared at Graywing. You see, he thought that Graywing was having a little fun at his expense. But Graywing didn't seem to be joking. "Why," exclaimed Jimmy, "that's nothing but a Snail."

"Certainly, it's a Snail. Who said it wasn't?" retorted Graywing.

"But Snails can't make holes in anything so hard as a Clam shell or an Oyster shell," declared Reddy Fox.

"Oh, can't they?" exclaimed Graywing. "Perhaps the Snails you are acquainted with cannot, but this one can." He reached over and picked up the little Snail. Sure enough, right where the Snail had been was a little round hole in the shell of the Clam. "There you are!" exclaimed Graywing triumphantly. "What did I tell you? He had his hole drilled and I guess I have interfered with his dinner."

Reddy Fox was blinking in a most perplexed manner at that hole in the shell. "I don't see yet what it's all about," declared Reddy. "What did he make that hole for?"

"Why, to get to the Clam inside," explained Graywing.

"But he can't pull the Clam out of that little hole," declared Reddy.

"Who said anything about pulling the Clam out of that little hole?" demanded Graywing. "He simply eats the Clam right through the hole. He eats the Clam with the same thing he drills the hole with."

"And what is that?" asked Jimmy Skunk.

"His tongue, of course," replied Graywing. "He drills the hole with his tongue. Please notice what a nice, neat job he made of it.

And when he gets the hole drilled, he uses his proboscis to suck in the Clam gradually. He treats a small Oyster the same way."

"But I don't see how he can make a hole with his tongue," protested Jimmy Skunk.

Graywing chuckled. "That used to bother me too," said he, "but I have found out that that queer little tongue of his is covered with tiny, very sharp, horny teeth, and it is with these little teeth that he cuts away the shell until he has a hole made. They call him a Drill,—the Oyster Drill. You see, next to the Starfish, this is the Oyster's worst enemy."

Reddy Fox and Jimmy Skunk looked at that little Snail with new interest and something very like respect. He wasn't much to look at. The shell was less than an inch long, a dull, brownish-gray and covered with ridges. It was hard to believe that such an unimpressive little fellow could possibly be feared by anybody.

"Tongues are funny things," said Jimmy Skunk. "There's that handy, hind-side-before tongue of Old Mr. Toad's. I used to think *that* one of the most wonderful tongues in all the Great World, but now that I've seen the work this little fellow's tongue can do, I'll have to admit that it is quite as wonderful as Old Mr. Toad's tongue."

"Oh," said Graywing, "if you stay around here long enough you'll find plenty of wonderful things. Do you see that big fellow over there?" He nodded towards what looked to Jimmy like a giant Snail. It had a coiled or twisted shell on the plan of a Snail's shell. It was rather pear-shaped with a long tapering snout. It was by far the largest of the shellfish of this kind.

Jimmy Skunk admitted that he saw the big fellow.

"That," said Graywing, "is a Whelk,—a Giant Whelk. That fellow likes Oysters and Clams, just as the Starfishes and that little Drill do."

"I suppose," spoke up Reddy Fox, "that you'll be telling us that that fellow has a wonderful tongue too."

Graywing chuckled. "Go to the head of the class, Reddy," said he. "That is exactly what the Whelk has. It has a ribbon-like tongue and the surface of it is covered with a great number of very tiny teeth. He can use that tongue just as well as the little Oyster Drill can use his. If you use your eyes around here,

OYSTER DRILL.
Urosalpinx cinerea.

PERIWINKLES.
Litorina littorea.

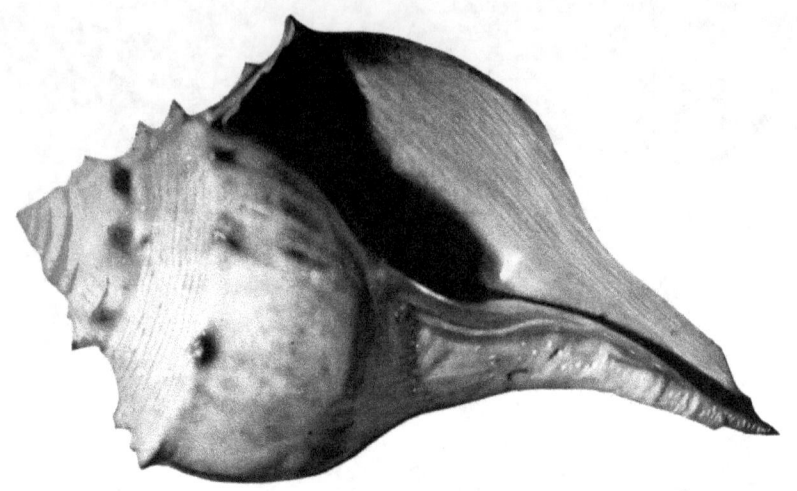

KNOBBED WHELK.
Busycon carica.

CHANNELED WHELK.
Busycon canaliculatum.

you'll soon find that a lot of the most innocent-looking things on the beach, just as is the case on the Green Meadows and in the Green Forest, are living on other things. Oysters and Clams may look to be safe when they have their shells tightly closed, but they are not. They are about the most helpless things I know of. That Whelk, by the way, is called a Channeled Whelk. Do you see that path plowed in the sand there?"

"Of course I see it," said Jimmy Skunk.

"A Whelk did that," said Graywing. "If we follow it we'll probably find him."

Sure enough, that little path plowed in the sand led around a rock and there was a Whelk. But this one was a little different from the one they had been looking at. Reddy Fox noticed it right away and mentioned the matter.

"Oh," explained Graywing, "this is a different kind. You noticed that other fellow had a sort of hairy-looking skin on the shell, while this one hasn't. Then, too, this one has a lot of little knobs. It is called the Knobbed Whelk. What have you found now, Jimmy?"

"You tell," said Jimmy. "It is a new one to me." Lying on the sand in front of Jimmy was what looked like a lot of little yellowish discs strung on a cord. They were smaller at one end, bigger in the middle, and became smaller towards the other end.

"Oh," said Graywing, "those are the eggs of a Whelk. Each one of those little discs has about two dozen eggs in it."

Reddy and Jimmy looked at the curious string of discs with a lot of curiosity. It was very hard to believe that those queer little discs contained the eggs of anything. But they had learned that to refuse to believe often is to expose one's ignorance. And, after all, it was no more wonderful that these little discs on a string should contain eggs, than that a little Snail should drill a hole in a shell with his tongue.

XVI. Collars of Sand and Mermaids' Purses

Jimmy Skunk was wandering along the beach, pulling over this, poking his nose into that. Never had Peter Rabbit had any more curiosity than Jimmy Skunk possessed right then. Well, perhaps it wasn't to be wondered at. There were so many curious things on the beach that Jimmy was constantly finding something new and unexpected and queer.

Farther along the beach Reddy Fox was pulling over this and poking his nose into that. Reddy was quite as full of curiosity as Jimmy Skunk. That beach was a wonderful place. Every time the tide went out—and that was twice a day—strange things were left washed up on the beach. It was then that Jimmy Skunk and Reddy Fox went looking for what they might find.

Jimmy Skunk glanced over towards Reddy and discovered that Reddy was looking very intently at something on the sand. "I wonder what he's found," thought Jimmy. "He certainly has found something. I wonder if it is anything new—anything that I haven't found. I'll go over and see."

So Jimmy shuffled along over to where Reddy Fox was still standing staring down at something at his feet. "Reddy," said Jimmy, "you look puzzled. What have you found now?"

"I wish you would tell me," replied Reddy. "There it is. It seems to be made of sand, but I've never seen anything like it before. Just look at that thing! How can sand hold together in a shape like that?"

Jimmy looked down at the thing Reddy was staring at. It looked a whole lot like a collar. The shape was like one of those big, white collars that little boys used to wear. But this collar was made of sand. It looked to be, anyway. Very gently and cautiously Jimmy Skunk reached out his black paw and touched it. It felt like sand. Jimmy turned it over and it still retained its shape. It didn't crumble and go all to pieces, as you would expect a thing made of sand to do. This was as puzzling as was the shape of the thing. How could anything as thin as this collar be made of sand and not break when turned over? Jimmy looked at it very closely. It certainly was made of sand. He could see the grains. Yes, sir, he could see the grains of sand.

Just then Graywing the Gull came sailing over. He saw Jimmy and Reddy and he saw that they were very much interested in something. You know nothing escapes those sharp eyes of Graywing's. He swung in a circle and then alighted on the beach near his two friends.

"What are you two fellows looking at?" he inquired.

"You tell us," retorted Reddy.

Graywing merely glanced at that collar of sand. "Oh, that?" said he. "That is nothing but a lot of eggs."

"Eggs!" exclaimed Jimmy scornfully. "Eggs! Say, what is the matter with your eyes, Graywing? Can't you see that this thing is made of sand? Eggs!"

Now Graywing would have been quite excusable if he had taken offense at the manner in which Jimmy Skunk had spoken. But he didn't take offense. He chuckled. "I see the sand all right," said he. "But you'll find that there's a lot more than sand there."

Reddy and Jimmy bent over the sand collar and looked at it more closely. But, though they looked and looked, they couldn't see any eggs. "Where are the eggs?" demanded Jimmy.

"Covered with the sand," replied Graywing. "Do you see that big, round Snail over there?"

Reddy and Jimmy looked. Sure enough, right close by was a great, big Snail, one of the round kind. It was bluish-white and it was moving very, very slowly away from that collar of sand.

"Certainly we see that Snail," said Reddy. "What of it?"

"Nothing much," replied Graywing. "Only she made that thing that has puzzled you so much, and it is her eggs that are in it. You see, those eggs are very tiny and there is a great number of them. When they are first deposited by Mrs. Snail, they are covered with a sticky material. In this the eggs are arranged in regular rows. The sand sticks to the outside and the whole thing hardens. And so it looks as if it were made of sand. If nothing happens to that thing, a lot of baby Snails will one of these days come out of that. So now you know what a sand collar is."

"Of course, Graywing, if you say it is so, it must be so," replied Jimmy politely. Then he sighed. "But it is hard to believe," he added.

Reddy Fox was watching Mrs. Snail. He shook his head slowly. "I've seen eggs and eggs," said he. "I've seen all sorts of things in which eggs are placed. But this is the queerest egg case I have yet seen. By the way, what do they call that Snail?"

"Oh, the Sand Collar Snail," replied Graywing carelessly. "By the way, she has one of those tongues with teeth and she likes to bore into Clams and other shellfish. She makes a nice, neat, round hole through the shell, and through this sucks out the Clam."

Meanwhile, Jimmy Skunk had turned his back on the sand collar and its maker and was exploring a little farther down the beach. Presently he came to a curious creature that had been cast up by the waves. It was dead. Jimmy supposed it must be some kind of fish, but it was unlike any fish he had ever seen. It was big and flat and thin. In shape it was rather circular, with a fairly long, spiny tail. Its mouth was on the under side. Jimmy isn't over particular about what he eats, but somehow this thing didn't look appetizing. He turned up his nose at it. When Graywing came walking over to see what he was looking at, Jimmy asked what it was.

"It's a fish," replied Graywing.

"Thank you," said Jimmy. "It is nice to learn that what one already knows is so. What kind of a fish?"

"It is a Skate," replied Graywing, "a Common Skate."

"A what?" exclaimed Reddy Fox, who had come up just in time to overhear what was said.

"A Skate, a Common Skate," repeated Graywing.

"All right, I suppose it is, if you say so," replied Reddy. "But whatever it is, it is a mighty funny-looking fish, if you ask me."

"Do you call this a funny-looking fish?" asked Graywing

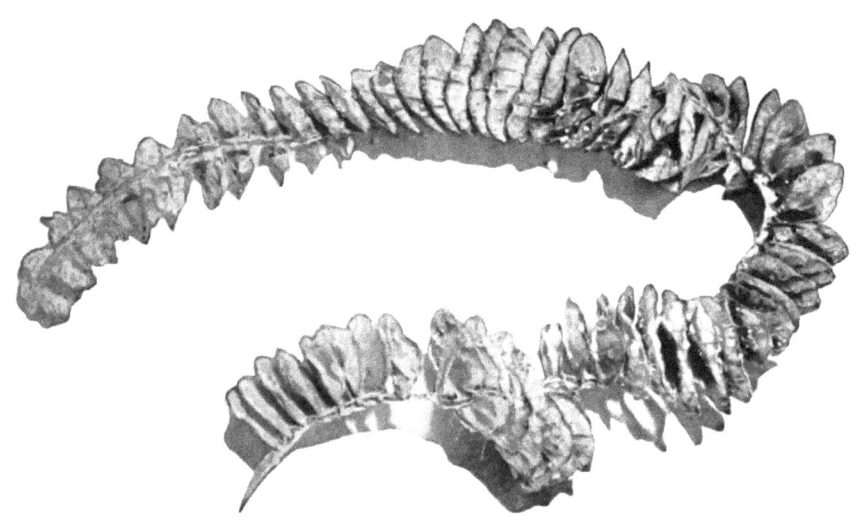

EGGS OF CHANNELED WHELK.

EGG-CASE OF COMMON SKATE.

SAND COLLAR SNAILS.
Polinices heros.

SAND COLLAR.
Egg Case of Lunatia Heros.

presently. "You wouldn't if you had seen some of the really funny-looking fishes that I have seen. You'll have to admit that this does look in some ways like a fish. But there are fishes that do not look like fishes at all. By the way, when you have been poking around in the seaweed on the beach, haven't you found any Skate eggs?"

Reddy shook his head and Jimmy Skunk shook his. "Not that we know of," replied Reddy, speaking for both. "But since being told that those sand collars are really egg cases, I begin to think that I don't know anything about eggs. Are the eggs of the Skate rolled up in sand too?"

"No," said Graywing. "You must have found some of the empty shells around in the seaweed. If you haven't, you haven't used your eyes."

"I've used my eyes all right," retorted Reddy, beginning to be a little provoked. "I've used my eyes all right and I certainly haven't seen any eggs, or any empty eggshells. Now what are you laughing at?"

Graywing was chuckling. There was no doubt about it. Reddy had a suspicion that he was being laughed at and he didn't like it. "You've got one paw on an eggshell right now," said Graywing, and chuckled more than ever.

Reddy looked down and Jimmy Skunk moved over where he could look too. Reddy's forefeet were resting on a roll of seaweed which had been washed up by the waves. Under one paw was a curious-looking black thing. It was about two and one-half inches long by two inches wide. At each of the four corners was a long, black, stringlike thing which was hollow. The whole thing was leathery looking, shiny, and unlike anything Reddy had ever seen. He had taken it for granted that it was part of the seaweed.

"Do you mean this thing?" he inquired, lifting his foot.

Graywing nodded. "Yes," said he, "that is the shell of a Skate's egg."

"What are these long strings on the corner for?" inquired Reddy, who for the life of him could see nothing egglike about the thing.

"Oh," replied Graywing, "that egg was laid in the water and

those strings wound around the seaweed and clung to it. If that seaweed had not been washed up by the waves, that egg case wouldn't have come up on the shore. It simply came along with the seaweed."

"Huh!" said Reddy. "If you ask me, I'll say that a Skate is a queer fish and its egg is just as queer. Anyway, I'm glad to know what these things are. I find I'm learning a lot from you, Graywing, and I'm much obliged to you."

"The same here," spoke up Jimmy Skunk.

"Pray don't mention it," replied Graywing. "I find I am learning some things myself."

"What?" inquired Reddy curiously.

"How little some folks know," answered Graywing, and off he flew.

There was one thing that Graywing did not tell Reddy Fox and Jimmy Skunk. There is another name for the Skate's egg. It is sometimes called a Mermaid's Purse.

XVII. Prickly Porkies of the Sea

> The Prickly Porky of the sea
> Says: "When you find me, let me be."

HE DOESN'T say it in words. Goodness, no! But he does say it just as the Prickly Porky of the land says it, and just as a chestnut bur says it. It is said without words. You have merely to look at Prickly Porky of the sea to know that it is best to leave him alone.

Who is the Prickly Porky of the Sea? Ask Jimmy Skunk. Jimmy found out by being careless. He was poking around under some rocks to see what he could find there. "Ouch!" he cried, and jumped back, holding up one little black paw. He had pricked that little black paw on something sharp. Very cautiously he looked to see what it was. There, just under that rock, was something that looked very much like a big green chestnut bur. It was covered all over with little, sharp-pointed spines. They pointed in all directions. It was all very curious. Jimmy didn't have the least idea what he was looking at. He didn't know whether it was a plant or some kind of sea animal. Certainly it didn't look as if it could move about.

"What are you staring at?" inquired Reddy Fox, coming up behind him.

"You tell," replied Jimmy, pointing to the queer thing under the rock.

"Let's get it out where we can see it better," said Reddy.

Jimmy turned his head aside to hide a grin. "That's a good idea," said he. "You pull it out."

So Reddy reached in a black paw to pull the thing out. "Ouch!" cried Reddy, and the queer thing remained right where it was.

"What's the trouble?" inquired Graywing the Gull, coming along just at that moment.

"There isn't any trouble," replied Reddy crossly. "We are just wondering what this thing is here."

"Well, pull it out and let's look at it," said Graywing.

"Pull it out yourself," retorted Reddy.

"Oh, if that's the way you feel about it, I will," replied Graywing, and reaching under the rock with his stout bill, he pulled the queer-looking thing out. It looked more than ever like a big chestnut bur.

Jimmy Skunk remembered to be polite. "If you please, Neighbor Gull," said he, "we should like to know what this thing is. Is it alive? We have never seen anything like it before, excepting 'way back on land where the chestnut trees used to grow. There every fall when the nuts dropped they were in coverings that looked a whole lot like this thing."

Graywing's eyes twinkled. "This," said he, "is the Prickly Porky of the sea. It is a Sea Urchin, a Green Sea Urchin, and it is very much alive. It is sometimes called a Sea Egg, but there's no real sense in such a name as that. You'll find that underneath all those spines is a shell, and the owner of that shell lives inside. He doesn't want to be meddled with, so Old Mother Nature has given him all of those spines. Do you see that thing over yonder?"

Reddy and Jimmy looked. There was a curious pincushion-shaped shell, but without any spines on it and covered with tiny knobs. When Jimmy turned it over, he discovered a good-sized opening in the bottom. The shell was empty.

"That," said Graywing, "is the shell of a Sea Urchin."

"Oh," said Jimmy. "Thank you very much, Neighbor Gull."

"Don't mention it," replied Graywing.

"Did you ever see Prickly Porky the Porcupine?" asked Reddy Fox.

"Yes," replied Graywing the Gull, "I've seen Prickly Porky often. Why do you ask?"

"This fellow reminds me of him," said Reddy.

"There is another member of the family that would remind you of Prickly Porky still more," said Graywing, with a chuckle.

"I'd like to see one," said Reddy. "Is there one around here?"

GREEN SEA URCHIN.
Strongylocentrotus dröbachiensis.

SAND DOLLAR OR CAKE URCHIN.
Echinarachnius parma.

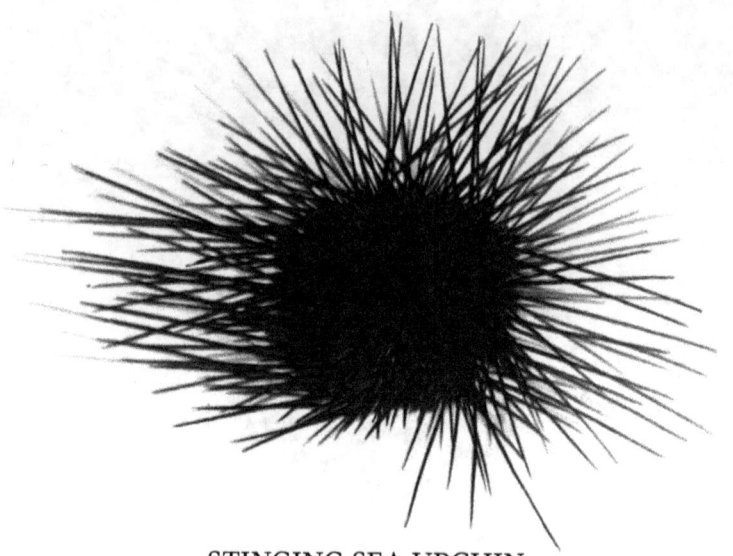

STINGING SEA URCHIN.
Diadema setosum.

PURPLE SEA URCHIN.
Arbacia punctulata.

"No," answered Graywing, "but 'way down South I've often seen this fellow. He is bigger than this one here and he is covered with spines fully as long as those little spears of Prickly Porky's. He is a bad fellow to meddle with, just as Prickly Porky is. Those spears of his are the sharpest things, and they are just as brittle as they are sharp. If one sticks into you, it breaks off in the skin, and then that place stings and is sore. They call this the Stinging Urchin. There's still another one that we ought to find along here somewhere." Graywing mounted into the air and swept back and forth over the beach, looking down. Presently he dropped down and alighted on the sand beside a little gravelly pool. He called to Reddy Fox and Jimmy Skunk and they hurried over there.

"Here is the Purple Sea Urchin," explained Graywing.

Looking in the little pool they discovered another prickly fellow. This one was quite a bit smaller than the Green Urchin, but he was just as prickly. He was almost perfectly round and his spines stuck out in every direction. This one was a deep violet color.

"You've seen the Green Sea Urchin and now you are looking at the Purple Sea Urchin," said Graywing. "But these Urchins are not always this color. Some are almost black and some are yellowish."

"Do they use those little spears for anything but to protect themselves?" asked Jimmy Skunk.

"I wish you hadn't asked me that," said Graywing.

"Why?" demanded Jimmy Skunk, looking at Graywing suspiciously.

"Because if I answer the question, you probably won't believe me," replied Graywing.

"Yes, we will!" cried Reddy and Jimmy together.

Graywing looked from one to the other. "Well," said he, "that Urchin walks by means of his spines."

"I don't—" began Reddy Fox, and then hastily changed the subject.

But Graywing had heard. "I told you you wouldn't believe it," said he. "Just look down at that fellow in the pool now."

Reddy and Jimmy looked. The Urchin was moving across

the bottom of the pool and he certainly was walking on his spines. It was like walking on stilts, with a whole lot of stilts instead of just two.

Reddy Fox had begun poking around in the seaweed not far away. Presently he found something that puzzled him. It was lying flat on the sand close by that seaweed. It was round and flat and thin. The upper side was rounded ever so little and on this upper side was a pretty pattern in the shape of a star. What it was, Reddy didn't have the least idea. He didn't like to expose his ignorance, so at first he was inclined to leave the thing and try to forget it. But of course this was no way to do, and Reddy knew it. So he looked around for Graywing and called to him. Graywing came over at once. Reddy showed him what he had found. "Have you any idea at all what that queer-looking thing is?" said he.

"I don't see anything queer about it," retorted Graywing. "It is nothing but the skeleton of a Sea Urchin."

For a moment, Reddy was sure that his ears had played a trick on him. "The skeleton of a what?" he cried.

Graywing's eyes twinkled. "No," said he, "not the skeleton of a What, but the skeleton of a Sea Urchin. Just follow me and I'll show you a live one."

Graywing again flew slowly along up and down. In a moment or two he alighted on a rock at the edge of another little pool. "Here is one," said he. Reddy and Jimmy hurried over and looked down in the water. The thing they saw didn't look any more like a Sea Urchin than had the skeleton Reddy had found. In fact, this looked a good deal like that skeleton, only they could see it was alive. It was covered with spines, but those spines were so tiny and fine that they were almost like hair. The thing was moving along, for it had sucker-like, tiny feet.

Reddy looked at the thing and then he looked at Graywing, and there was a question in his looks. Graywing nodded. "It is a Sea Urchin," said he, "a really, truly Sea Urchin. Folks call it a Sand Dollar. Some folks call it a Cake Urchin. Either name is all right, but it is just as much an Urchin as either of those you have seen."

Now, not even Graywing, wise as he is in the ways of the

seashore, knows everything about it. For instance, he didn't know that ink—a kind that cannot be erased—may be made by pounding a Sand Dollar to powder in water. So now you know something that neither Graywing nor Reddy Fox nor Jimmy Skunk has yet learned.

XVIII. Shells that Swim and Shells that Walk

"Live and learn," Reddy Fox would say. "Live and learn. I can believe almost anything since I've learned that a Lobster can get out of that hard shell of his; and that a Starfish can pull open an Oyster and then eat him. There certainly is a lot to see along the seashore. Now I wonder why I never find any of these fancy Clam shells with the owners inside."

Reddy was looking down at a shell which was almost round, excepting at the place where it should have been hinged to another shell just like it. At that point there were two little wings of shell. This shell was scalloped in the prettiest way. A lot of other shells just like it were scattered around, but, look as hard as he might, Reddy couldn't find one with the owner inside. At last he thought of Graywing and looked to see if Graywing were about anywhere. Graywing wasn't. He was off fishing. Then Reddy noticed Barker the Seal sitting on his favorite rock very close to the shore.

"I'll ask Barker about these," thought Reddy. Picking up the shell that had puzzled him so, he trotted over as near to Barker as he could get.

"Hello, Neighbor Fox, what have you there?" inquired Barker.

"It's a shell," said Reddy. "I have found ever so many just like it, but never have I found the owner of one of them."

"Where have you looked?" inquired Barker.

"Everywhere," replied Reddy.

"Excepting in the water," said Barker with a chuckle.

Reddy took no notice of this. "This looks to me like the shell of some kind of a Clam, and Clams usually are in the mud or sand. I have dug them up lots of times," said Reddy.

"You won't dig one of these fellows up," replied Barker. "Well, well, well, what do you know about that!"

Barker was staring out over the water. Just beyond the rock on which he lay the water was clear and smooth and the bottom beneath was sandy. It was over this stretch of smooth water that Barker was staring. Reddy stared too. "Did you see that?" cried Barker.

"Did I see what?" demanded Reddy, who hadn't seen anything at all excepting the water.

"Just watch right out there," replied Barker.

Reddy looked where Barker was looking. At first he saw nothing unusual. Then he saw a little break in the smooth surface of the water, and then another and another. At last he thought he caught a glimpse of something in the water, coming quickly to the top and disappearing as quickly. From where he was he couldn't see down into the water. He should have been higher up in order to see properly. "What is it?" he demanded.

"It is a party of the very folks you have been talking about. They are having a great time swimming out there," replied Barker.

"Say, what are you talking about?" retorted Reddy. "I haven't been talking about any folks."

Barker chuckled. "Well, you've been talking about their houses, anyway," said he. "Those folks out there in the water are the owners of shells just like the one you have there. They are called Scallops. For shellfishes, they swim pretty fast and easily."

You should have seen the look on Reddy's face. Yes, sir, you should have seen the look on Reddy's face. "What are you trying to tell me?" cried Reddy. "How can anything that lives in a couple of shells like this one swim? A common Clam can't swim. And if it can't swim, I don't believe one of these Scallops can."

It was a good thing that Barker was good-natured. He didn't take offense at all. "If you were up on this rock with me," said he, "where you could look down and see those Scallops, you would have to believe your eyes. They swim easily enough. They simply open and shut those shells like a pair of wings. Clams stay where they are; Scallops move about. You don't find them burying themselves in the mud. Not much! One day there will be a lot of them here and the next day not one will be found.

They have moved on. Sometimes they will stay for quite a while in one place. They seem to like to play in the water, just as you see them doing now. I wish you might see one close to. They have the prettiest blue eyes."

You should have seen the look that Reddy Fox gave Barker the Seal. He was sure now that Barker was "stuffing him," as the saying is. Barker saw the look and once more he chuckled. "You don't believe that, do you, Neighbor Fox?" said he.

"No," said Reddy quite frankly, "I don't."

"It is true just the same," replied Barker. "There is a part of a Scallop called the mantle, and along the edges of this are rows of bright blue eyes. It's a fact, even if it is hard for you to believe it."

"I'll have to take your word for it," said Reddy. "I have reached the point where I can believe almost anything. So, as long as you say it is so, I'll believe it."

Graywing the Gull had come in from his fishing and had alighted close by. Now he took part in the conversation. "There is a member of the Scallop family," said he, "that lives a little farther south. It isn't quite so large as the Scallop who lives around here. I've watched that fellow many a time escaping from an enemy. He dives into the mud and then he churns the mud all up by opening and shutting his shells, so that the water becomes so muddy that he cannot be seen and thus escapes."

Reddy Fox happened to look along the shore and saw Jimmy Skunk. At once Reddy said good-by to Barker and hurried down to tell Jimmy what he had learned about Scallops. He found Jimmy looking at a queer thing that he himself had been puzzled by very often. He had found it in all sizes from little things to some a foot or more long. They all looked alike. That is, all the live ones looked alike and all the dead ones looked alike. The live ones were black, while the dead ones were about the color of sand. Each was the shape of a horseshoe, with a regular spike for a tail. Each seemed to be chiefly shell,—a high, rounded shell. On the rounded top were some sharp points like little spikes.

But the thing that puzzled both Reddy and Jimmy was that when they turned one of these things over on its back, there seemed to be nothing inside that shell but legs. Yes, sir, that is the way it seemed. It seemed that it was simply a shell walking around on seven pairs of legs. The legs were something like the legs of a Crab.

It was a big fellow that Jimmy Skunk had found this time. It must have been two feet from the front edge of the shell to the tip of the tail. It was partly buried in the sand. Graywing the Gull had followed Reddy and was now flying just overhead. Reddy looked up. "Graywing," said Reddy, "I've just got to know something."

Graywing made a quick turn and sailed over to where he could look down directly on Reddy and what Reddy was looking at. He seemed to actually remain still in the air right over Reddy. "Well," said he, "what is it?"

"That's what I want to know," barked Reddy.

"What is it?"

"That? Why, that's nothing but a Horseshoe Crab, sometimes called the King Crab, though why I haven't the slightest idea," replied Graywing, and alighted on the beach close by.

"Crab!" exclaimed Reddy. "That thing a Crab? Why, there is nothing to it but a shell and legs! Where is its body?"

"Where it ought to be,—inside the shell," retorted Graywing rather impatiently. "You didn't suppose that legs could be walking around without a body, did you? Use your eyes, Reddy, use your eyes."

"I have used my eyes," snapped Reddy. "I've turned dozens of these fellows over. If there is a body, it must be a mighty small one. Anyway, I haven't ever been able to see it."

"Well, it's there just the same, whether you have been able to see it or not," replied Graywing. "As it is so hard for you to believe things, I presume it is a waste of breath for me to tell you that these Crabs dig holes in the sand, in which to lay their eggs."

"No," said Reddy, "it isn't a waste of breath. I have reached a point now where I could almost believe that a fish could build a nest."

Graywing chuckled. "All right, Reddy," said he. "I'm glad to hear you say it."

"Why?" Reddy demanded, looking at Graywing suspiciously.

"Because," replied Graywing, his eyes twinkling, "there *is* a fish that builds a nest. And, by the way, this fellow here isn't

COMMON SCALLOP.
Pecten irradians.

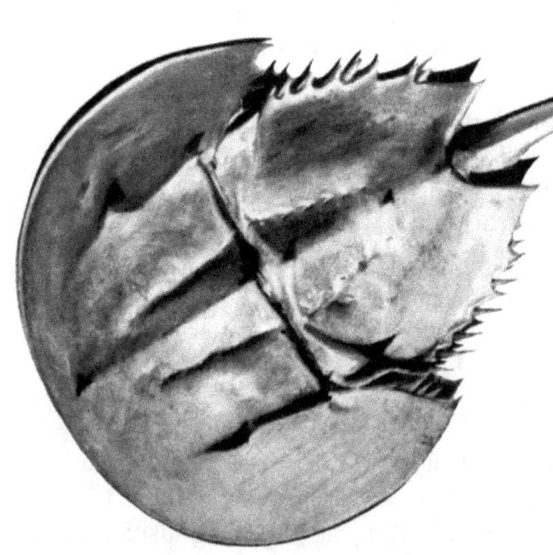

HORSESHOE CRAB OR KING CRAB.
Limulus polyphemus.

really a Crab. It is supposed to belong to a very old family,—a family older than the Crab family. It sounds queer, but it is supposed to be related to Spiders and Scorpions, rather than to Crabs. Anyway, it isn't a Crab, even if it is called so."

"All right," said Reddy, "I'll believe it." As a matter of fact, Reddy hadn't half heard what Graywing had said. You see, he was thinking of that fish that builds a nest.

XIX. The Curious Home of a Fish

YOU KNOW that it doesn't do to believe everything you hear, or even everything you see. But neither does it do to refuse to believe. Keep always an open mind, ready to believe facts when they are proved to be facts.

Reddy Fox prided himself on having an open mind. He prided himself that he was ready to believe anything, provided he could be certain that he had the real facts in regard to it. When Graywing the Gull had stated that there was a fish who builds a nest, you should have seen the look on Reddy's face. He suspected Graywing of trying to fool him. Yes, sir, he suspected Graywing.

"Did I understand you to say that there is a fish who builds a nest?" he inquired.

Graywing nodded. "There is nothing the matter with your hearing, Neighbor Fox," said he. "That is what I said."

"Did you mean it?" persisted Reddy.

Graywing tossed his head, as if a bit provoked. "I am not in the habit of saying things that I do not mean," said he very sharply.

"Just what kind of a nest does this fish build?" asked Reddy.

"Why, a nest, a regular nest," returned Graywing.

"I suppose," said Reddy, "that you'll be telling me next that this fish sits on the eggs and hatches them out, after the manner of a bird."

My goodness, how Graywing's eyes did snap then! "See here, Reddy Fox," said he, "it is quite clear to me that you do not believe what I have told you, and I am not accustomed to having people doubt my word. There *is* a fish that builds a nest. If you are going to doubt what I say, don't come to me for any more information about the things along the seashore."

Reddy saw that Graywing meant just what he said. "I beg your pardon, Graywing. I do indeed," Reddy hastened to say. "I believe every word of what you've told me. Some folks like to joke and at first I thought you might be joking. It was my mistake. I'm sorry. You see, the idea of a fish building a nest was so new to me that I couldn't believe you were in earnest. I certainly should like to see one of those fish nests. There is nothing I can think of that I should like to see more. If you should find one of these nests, Neighbor Gull, would you be willing to show it to me?"

"Certainly," replied Graywing, getting over his indignation. "I'll show you the first one I find."

"Is—is—is it likely to be on the ground, or in bushes, or where?" inquired Reddy with a little hesitancy.

Graywing laughed right out. "I see," said he, "that you are still thinking of birds, not of a fish. How do you suppose that a fish could build in a bush? A fish might make a nest on the sand under water, but not out of water. Remember, we are talking of fishes."

Reddy grinned. "I know," said he, "but it is the very fact that we are talking of fishes that makes it so hard to believe that one can make a real nest. What kind of a fish did you say makes this nest?"

"I didn't say," replied Graywing. "Excuse me now, for I have an engagement." Graywing spread his wings and rose from the sand.

"Don't forget that you are to show me one of those fish nests when you have found one," barked Reddy.

"I don't believe that you really believe it yet," cried Graywing.

Reddy grinned. "I'm trying to," he replied.

It was hardly more than an hour after Graywing left when Reddy saw him returning. He circled over Reddy. "Are your eyes good?" he called.

Reddy grinned up at Graywing. "My eyes are always good," said he. "What have you on your mind now, Neighbor Gull?"

"That nest I promised to show you," replied Graywing. "Follow me and I'll show you the nest of a fish, just as I said I would."

"I'm always ready to be shown," replied Reddy, and trotted along the beach, keeping his eyes on Graywing, who flew ahead of him. Presently Graywing turned inland and flew over the sand dunes toward the marsh. Reddy scrambled up over the

THREE-SPINED STICKLEBACK AND NEST.
Gasterosteus aculeatus.

sand dunes, and saw Graywing alighting beside a tide pool in the marsh beyond. It was a pool from which the water never ran out. Somewhat gingerly Reddy picked his way through the wet marsh grasses over to where Graywing was waiting for him. He didn't like getting his feet wet that morning.

"How are your eyes now?" demanded Graywing as Reddy came up.

"Just as good as they were when you asked me the same question a little while ago," replied Reddy.

"All right," said Graywing. "Look down in the water where those grass stems are coming up. If your eyes are really good, you will see fastened to those stems a little round ball."

Reddy leaned over and looked down in the water. "I see it," said he.

"Well," replied Graywing, "that is the nest of a fish."

There is an old saying that seeing is believing, but as a matter of fact there is nothing that can be fooled more easily than eyes. So, even though you see a thing, or think you see a thing, it sometimes is wise to be a little slow in believing. Reddy Fox felt just this way as he looked at what Graywing said was the nest of a fish. He was sure that he saw what he *thought* he saw, but it was so hard to believe that a fish could really build a nest, that now it was just as hard to believe that his eyes might not be fooling him. Attached to the grass was a little round soft-looking mass about the size of a big glass marble. It seemed to be made of tiny bits of plant growth fastened together in some way that Reddy didn't understand. There was a round doorway. It did look like a little nest, but it was hard for Reddy to believe that it was the nest of a fish. Yes, sir, that was something hard to believe.

"I'll agree that this looks like a nest," said Reddy, "but you haven't proved to me yet that it is the nest of a fish."

"Be patient," retorted Graywing. "You have been out in the Great World long enough to know that in order to see things one must be patient. If you haven't any important engagement I suggest that you stay here a little while and watch. I think you will see something that will surprise you and will convince you that this is the nest of a fish. Huh! You won't have to have patience. Here comes the owner of that nest now. It is Mr. Stickleback."

Sure enough, Reddy could see a fish coming towards that nest. It was a very small fish, hardly three inches long. Reddy would have called it a minnow. It looked to him like a minnow. Then he saw that there was a second fish. "I suppose," said he, "that one of those is Mrs. Stickleback."

Graywing bobbed his head. "Of course," said he. "Those are Mr. and Mrs. Stickleback. The one going into the nest now is Mrs. Stickleback."

"Why," demanded Reddy, "did you say that Mr. Stickleback is the owner of that nest? Isn't it just as much Mrs. Stickleback's as it is Mr. Stickleback's?"

"No," declared Graywing, "it is all his. He built it, every bit of it. Mrs. Stickleback didn't have anything to do about it, and, what is more, she won't have anything to do about it after she has laid her eggs there. That is Mr. Stickleback's nest and he is very proud of it. Sometime if you hear some one giving all the credit for the bringing up of a family to the mother of the family, just you tell him about Pa Stickleback."

"Why is he called Stickleback?" inquired Reddy.

"Look at him," retorted Graywing. "Look at his back. How would you like to bite down hard on that back of his?"

Reddy looked more closely than he had before. In the middle of the back were two spines that were sharp-pointed and looked as if they might hurt. Just in front of the back fin was a third, shorter and smaller. "Oh," said Reddy, "I guess I know now why he is called Stickleback. Did I understand you to say that he really built that nest all himself? What makes it stick together?"

"Certainly he built it all himself," replied Graywing. "He has some kind of sticky stuff with which he binds together that green stuff. I've seen a good many nests of Sticklebacks. Sometimes a nest has one doorway and sometimes it has two. I think this one has two."

Graywing walked around where he could look across the back of the nest. "Yes," said he, "this one has two doorways. If you want to see a good father and learn something about fathering, you come over here every day for a few days and watch Pa Stickleback. You will find it worth while."

XX. Pa Stickleback Does His Duty

There had been a time when, if any one had told Reddy Fox that he would spend hours watching a little fish less than three inches long, Reddy would have laughed. But here he was, doing just that thing. Whenever he had nothing else to do he trotted over to that little pool on the marsh where he could watch down in the water Pa Stickleback and his nest.

You will remember that on his first visit there he had seen Pa Stickleback bring Mrs. Stickleback there. She isn't called "Ma Stickleback" for she doesn't deserve the name. Reddy saw her go into the nest which Pa Stickleback had built. After a while she came out and swam away. That is the last he saw of her. But Pa Stickleback didn't swim away. Goodness, no! He posted himself right outside one entrance to that nest and the way he guarded it was beautiful to see. If another fish came anywhere near, even though that fish might be twice as big as Pa Stickleback, those spines on the latter's back stood right straight up and he darted at the stranger so fiercely that usually the stranger was only too glad to hurry away.

Pa Stickleback was quite handsome. He was so! You see, he had put on his very prettiest colors when he went courting Mrs. Stickleback. He was very trim and very alert and he had very big eyes. He was on the watch every instant. You see, Mrs. Stickleback had left some precious eggs in that nest and he didn't intend to allow anything to happen to them if he could help it.

Once Reddy saw another Stickleback approach. It looked to him like Mrs. Stickleback. In fact, he was quite sure that it was Mrs. Stickleback. But Pa Stickleback rushed at her as fiercely as he had at any of the other swimming folk who had approached. You see, he knew Mrs. Stickleback through and through, wherein he was more fortunate than some menfolk. If Pa Stickleback could talk to you he would tell you that he wouldn't trust Mrs. Stickleback one single little minute. He would tell you that she would like nothing better than a chance to eat those precious eggs. And that is a fact. So after Mrs. Stickleback had laid the eggs in that nest Pa Stickleback was through with her. He didn't want her hanging around and he didn't allow her to hang around.

I have told you that there were two doorways to that little nest. Reddy saw that Pa Stickleback kept guard at one entrance and with his fins he kept a little current of water moving right through that little nest, in one doorway and out the other. That was to keep the water clean and pure. If an egg got washed out, he would hasten to push it back in. Pa Stickleback was on the job every second. The wonder was that he got enough to eat. But he did. At the same time he managed to keep those eggs from all harm.

Reddy never went over there, no matter what the hour of the day, that Pa Stickleback wasn't right on the job, looking as if he had a chip on his shoulder all the time. You know that is just a way of saying that he looked as if he were ready to fight instantly. He was. Yes, sir, he was. And proud! Why, Pa Stickleback was as proud of that nestful of eggs as anybody could be. He might be anxious for fear some harm would come to them; and worried for fear they wouldn't hatch; and tired of all the time staying on guard; but he certainly was proud! You merely had to look at him to know that.

Pa Stickleback is one of the best fathers I know. If any father should be honored, it should be Pa Stickleback. Yes, sir, it should be Pa Stickleback. He may be only a little fish with spines on his back, but he certainly knows his duty to his family and does it.

Many a time Reddy Fox stole up very softly to see if he could find Pa Stickleback off guard, but he never did. Always Pa Stickleback was right there, not only ready for any trouble that might come along, but apparently looking for trouble to come along. It was eight or nine days after Reddy saw Mrs. Stickleback go into the nest to leave her eggs, that he discovered Pa Stickleback apparently breaking up the nest. Reddy rubbed his eyes. Pa Stickleback had taken such great care of that nest and those precious eggs, that when Reddy looked down in the water and saw what was going on, he couldn't believe it. But he found it was so. Pa Stickleback actually was breaking down the walls of his little nest. He was destroying his home.

Reddy thought something must have happened. Yes, sir, he thought that something must have happened. Something *had* happened! Instead of a lot of eggs in that nest, there were a lot of little Sticklebacks. From each of those eggs had come forth a little Stickleback. Anyway, Reddy supposed they were little Sticklebacks. They didn't look any more like Pa Stickleback than most babies look like their fathers, which is not at all. But they were tiny fish and Pa Stickleback was making a great fuss over them. So Reddy knew that they must be little Sticklebacks.

My, my, my, how Pa Stickleback did fuss about! He tried to keep those big eyes of his on all of them at the same time, and that was some task. Yes, sir, that was some task. To be sure, right at first those baby Sticklebacks were somewhat helpless. Newly born babies usually are somewhat helpless. These were no exception. So far as Reddy could see, they did nothing but cling to the grasses and plant stems in the water. Pa Stickleback fussed about them and kept swimming around and around. If so much as a shadow fell across the water, he would rush at it in a fury until he discovered his mistake.

Baby Sticklebacks change just as all other babies change. It wasn't long before they began to get independent. Then Pa Stickleback's troubles doubled. It was difficult enough to guard from danger so big a family of children when all were keeping still, but that was nothing to guarding that big family when none was keeping still.

But Pa Stickleback did it. To this day Reddy Fox doesn't know how Pa Stickleback did it, but he did do it. That was his job and he did it. He didn't have time for anything else, but nothing else mattered. He didn't allow any other finny inhabitant of that little pool to come anywhere near those little Sticklebacks. He even drove away their own mother. But then, that was just as well. They didn't know she was their mother, and she didn't know they were her children. Not that it made any difference. It would have been just the same if she had known that they were hers. You see, she was quite satisfied to let Pa Stickleback be both father and mother.

He certainly was qualified for the job. He stayed right with those young Sticklebacks until they were big enough to take care of themselves. Then, I suppose, he gave them his blessing and sent them out into the Great World, which was, of course, that little pool on the marsh. Anyway, they scattered and left Pa Stickleback all alone.

"There's gratitude for you," said Reddy Fox, who happened to be looking on at the time.

"*What* is gratitude?" asked Graywing the Gull, who happened along just then.

"Why, all those little Sticklebacks have left Pa Stickleback flat, without so much as saying good-by, so far as I could see," explained Reddy.

"He doesn't seem to mind it," said Graywing, looking down into the pool.

Graywing was right. Pa Stickleback didn't seem to mind it at all. The very first thing he did was to go get a good, square meal. Being father, mother and nurse to a big family of children is hungry work.

"Did I tell you the truth?" asked Graywing.

Reddy pretended not to understand. "The truth about what?" he asked innocently.

"The fish that builds a nest," said Graywing.

"You certainly did," replied Reddy. "I am prepared to believe anything now. I thought I knew something of the Great World before I came down to the seashore, but I am right here to confess that I knew very little. I don't know what I should have done without you, Graywing. I owe you a lot."

"That's all right," replied Graywing. "I am always glad to teach folk who really want to learn. My, there's a good Clam! I feel just like a Clam."

He flew over and picked up the Clam. Then he circled high up in the air. In a moment Reddy saw the Clam dropping. Graywing shot down after it and caught it in midair. Then he flew up with it again and once more dropped it. This time it hit a big rock and cracked. Graywing followed it down and picked the

Clam out from the broken shell. "Did you see me miss my aim the first time?" said he.

"Was that it?" exclaimed Reddy. "I wondered why you caught that Clam before it had a chance to reach the ground."

"It would have missed the rock," answered Graywing.

XXI. The Queer Jelly

THERE HAD been a storm. All the little folk who live along the seashore, and the big folk too, know that after a storm many strange things are likely to be found on the beach. So as soon as this storm was over Reddy Fox and Jimmy Skunk started along the beach to see what had been washed up by the waves. Many a good meal had they found there after a storm. But this storm hadn't brought much in the way of food. It didn't matter, because neither Reddy nor Jimmy was very hungry. They were more curious than hungry. It was fun to poke about and see what could be found.

Presently, as Reddy was trotting along, he came to something that looked for all the world as if some one had dropped a saucerful of soft lemon jelly on the sand. Reddy sniffed at it, but for once his nose didn't tell him anything.

"This is queer," said Reddy, talking to himself. "Now, what under the sun can this stuff be? I have never seen anything like it before. There is some more over there."

Reddy walked over to examine this second find. It was just like the other, except that there was a little more of it.

"What are you looking at?" inquired Jimmy Skunk, coming up behind Reddy.

"I don't know," replied Reddy. "I don't know what it is. What do you think it is?"

Jimmy walked all around it, eyeing it suspiciously. Then rather carefully he put out a little black paw and touched it. It felt just as it looked. It felt just as jelly would feel if you should put your finger in it. Of course Reddy and Jimmy didn't know anything about jelly. If they had known anything about Jelly, they would, I am quite sure, have suspected right away that some one had been along that way and spilled some jelly. Then, after they had traveled along the beach a little farther, they would have wondered where under the sun so much jelly could have come from. You see, for a long distance the beach was literally covered with these little masses of jelly.

Reddy was the first to discover that they were more than clear jelly. He found one that was lying on the sand perfectly flat, and as he looked down on it, he could see something like a cross, just as on the Sand Dollar he had seen a star. Could it be that these masses of jelly were not at all what they looked to be? He went down to the water's edge to see if there were any in the water. At first he didn't see any. Then he saw one just being washed up by a little wave. He hurried over to it. It looked just like the other little jelly masses. It didn't move, but lay perfectly still just where the wave had left it.

Reddy sat down and scratched his head thoughtfully. Could it be possible that that thing was alive, or ever had been alive? Jimmy Skunk joined him. Jimmy was as puzzled as Reddy was. They talked it over. They looked around for some one to ask questions of, but no one was in sight. At last they decided that it was a waste of time just to sit staring at things they couldn't understand, so they trotted off to see what else they could find. But all the time in the back of his head Reddy was thinking about those jelly masses. They perplexed him and they vexed him.

"I certainly have got to find out what they are," said he.

"How are you going to do it?" asked Jimmy Skunk.

Reddy looked far down the beach. His eyes brightened. Away down there he could see Graywing the Gull fishing. Most of the time he was circling over the water, but now and then he would alight on a big rock on the shore. "We'll go down there and ask Graywing," said Reddy. "He seems to know all about everything on the beach, so probably he can tell us about those queer things and where they come from. Come on, Jimmy."

Graywing saw Reddy and Jimmy coming and remained on the big rock until they reached him. "Hello, Neighbors," said he. "What have you on your minds now? Don't tell me that you have nothing on your minds, for I know better."

SPECKLED JELLYFISH.
Dactylometra quinquecirro.
HYDROMEDUSA.
Orchistoma Tentaculata.
THIMBLE JELLYFISH.
Melicertum campanula.

Reddy looked up at Graywing and grinned. "You must be a mind reader, Neighbor Gull," said he. "There *is* something on my mind. Perhaps I shouldn't say it is on my mind, for really it is on the beach up there. But it certainly is bothering me."

"Well, what is it?" inquired Graywing.

Reddy grinned again more broadly than ever. "That's what I want to know," said he. "What is it? I don't know how to describe it to you, so when you get through catching your breakfast, why not go back up the beach with us? I am sure you will know what it is, for you know everything."

"Tut, tut, tut, Neighbor Fox, you flatter me!" said Graywing. Nevertheless, he looked pleased.

"Not at all, not at all," replied Reddy. "When I am with you I feel as if I know nothing at all."

Graywing looked more pleased than ever. "We'll go up there right away and see what those things are," said Graywing. "You and Jimmy trot along up the beach and I'll join you by the time you get there."

"Thank you, Neighbor Gull," replied Reddy. "You will find the beach just covered with those queer things. I suppose they came out of the water, but I don't know. My, this sun is hot, isn't it?"

Graywing nodded. Then he flew out over the water in search of something more to eat. Reddy watched him a few minutes, then turned and trotted up the beach after Jimmy Skunk, who was already on the way. Presently they reached the place where they had been so puzzled by those queer jelly masses. Both stopped abruptly and blinked. Then they looked at each other with such a funny expression on their faces. Not one of those little masses of jelly could be seen.

At first they thought they couldn't be in the right place. But they were. There were Reddy's footprints in the sand and there were the footprints of Jimmy Skunk. But all those little masses of jelly had disappeared. Reddy looked at Jimmy and Jimmy looked at Reddy, and neither knew what to say.

"Well, where are those things you fellows wanted to know about?" inquired Graywing, alighting on the beach.

"I—I don't know," confessed Reddy.

"Did you say that there were many of them?" inquired Graywing.

"The beach was covered with them," spoke up Jimmy Skunk.

Now, Graywing suspected what Reddy and Jimmy had seen and his eyes twinkled. "Can you not remember just the spot where you left one of those things?" he inquired.

Reddy looked about. "Yes," said he, "I left one on the sand over there by that stone, and there are my footprints where I stood looking at it."

"There seems to be a wet spot there," said Graywing. "In fact, there seem to be many wet spots all about here. Perhaps the things you saw have melted in the sun."

Reddy went over to the stone and examined the wet place. It was exactly where one of those little masses of jelly had been lying. "You must be right, Neighbor Gull," said he. "I don't know what those queer things could have been, but they certainly have melted. I am sorry I got you up here for nothing."

"Don't mention it," replied Graywing. "It was no trouble at all. By the way, Reddy, have you ever seen one of these things?"

Graywing was looking down into a pool of water between the rocks.

Reddy jumped up on to another rock from which he could look down into that pool. At once he became so excited that he nearly fell into the pool. "There's one now!" he cried. "There's one of those things down in the water. The beach was just covered with them."

Graywing chuckled. "I thought as much," said he. "That, Reddy, is what is called a Jellyfish. Of course, it cannot live out of water, but see how pretty it is in the water."

It *was* pretty. It was a round disc shaped something like an umbrella and looked as if it were made of jelly, but the edges of it were moving and to his surprise Reddy discovered that it was swimming. From the edge hung a sort of fringe.

"Do you call that thing a fish?" cried Reddy.

"As I told you before, it is called a Jellyfish, though of course it isn't a real fish," explained Graywing. "However, it is alive and swims, as you can see."

"But what became of all those that were on the beach?" asked Reddy.

Once more Graywing chuckled. "They melted," said he. "You

see, a Jellyfish is made up mostly of water and so, when it is out on the beach in the hot sun, it disappears."

The Jellyfish in the pool was within reach. Reddy wondered if he could scoop it up on the rocks to see if it would melt. He thrust a black paw in among the little threads of the fringe, intending to slip it under the Jellyfish and scoop it out.

"Wow!" cried Reddy, and tumbled backwards off the rock. He had been stung! Yes, sir, he had been stung! The threads of that Jellyfish had stung him. How Graywing did laugh! But it was some time before Reddy could see the joke.

XXII. Reddy Fox Sees a Queer Garden

"What did it?" demanded Reddy Fox. "What did it?"

"What did what?" asked Graywing between chuckles.

"What stung me when I put my paw down there in the water?" demanded Reddy.

"That Jellyfish," replied Graywing, beginning to chuckle again. "You put your paw in amongst those threads and it was some of those that stung you."

"But how could they?" demanded Reddy.

"I don't know how they do it, but they do it," replied Graywing. "It is by means of those that the Jellyfish catches his food."

"Can one of those things eat?" cried Reddy, looking quite as astonished as he felt.

"Of course it can eat," replied Graywing. "How would it grow if it didn't eat? That is a small kind of Jellyfish down there in that pool. You ought to see some of the big ones I've seen way out at sea. Yes, sir, you ought to see one of those. Why, I've seen one with a mass of those threadlike things which are called tentacles streaming out behind for a hundred feet. Big ones like that can even catch small fish by stinging them."

Reddy had clambered back upon the rock and was looking down at that Jellyfish with renewed interest. It really was a beautiful thing. The body part, or disc, was in shape very much like an umbrella, with delicate wavy edges. Around these edges was the fringe of little threads which had stung him. The little creature was somewhat milky in color. It is called the Milky Disc and at certain seasons of the year appears in great numbers. Then there are the Speckled Jellyfish, the Thimble Jellyfish, and other kinds of Jellyfishes which are found along the shore, especially after storms. Graywing told Reddy about some of these that he had seen, for of course flying over the water as Graywing does, he sees much of the life in the sea.

"Some are very small," explained Graywing. "Some are pink and some are blue. But you ought to see the water at night when a lot of Jellyfishes are swimming about. They throw off light. They make the water look as if it were on fire." What Graywing meant was that they are phosphorescent.

"Do Jellyfishes come from eggs?" inquired Reddy.

"They do and they don't," replied Graywing. "Of course, you know how it is with a moth or a butterfly, or any other insect. The baby that comes out of the egg is not at all like its parents."

"Of course," said Reddy. "I know all about that. A caterpillar is nothing but a young butterfly or moth, though no one would ever guess it just from looking at it."

Graywing nodded. "It is the same way with Jellyfishes and some other things in the sea," said he. "Have you got anything in particular to do?"

"No," replied Reddy. "Why?"

"I should like to show you a little garden in the water and the things growing in it," replied Graywing. "It is quite a little distance from here, but if you would like to go, I'll lead the way."

"I'll go," said Reddy.

So Graywing flew up along the shore and Reddy trotted along a little behind and, of course, below him. At last Graywing stopped where the shore was very rocky. Rocks big and little were tumbled all about. Some of them made regular little caves, in each of which was a pool of water. Graywing finally stopped on a rock above one of these little sheltered pools. Reddy scrambled over the wet rocks to get there.

"Now," said Graywing. "I want you to look down in that pool and tell me if it isn't a regular little garden under water."

Reddy looked, and when his eyes had become accustomed to the somewhat dim light, they opened very wide with surprise. "Why," he exclaimed, "it *is* a garden! There are flowers growing down there!"

Graywing chuckled his familiar throaty little chuckle. "They do look like flowers," said he; "and a lot of those other things look like plants."

SEA ANEMONES.
Metridium dianthus.

"Well, aren't they?" asked Reddy.

"There are some plants,—some seaweeds," explained Graywing, "but most of those things that look like plants are not plants at all. And those blossom-like things are not flowers."

Reddy looked up in amazement. "What are they?" he asked.

"Animals," replied Graywing.

Reddy leaned over to look closer. Immediately under him was what looked very much like a flower, the petals waving in the water. It seemed to be growing on a stout-bodied little plant and was very prettily colored. "If that isn't a plant growing down there, then I never saw one!" declared Reddy. "I mean that one right there, with the flower on top of it."

Graywing's eyes twinkled. "Oh," said he, "that is what you mean. Reach in and touch it."

Reddy looked at Graywing suspiciously. He hadn't forgotten how Graywing had laughed at him for getting stung by a Jellyfish. "No, thank you," said he. "I learned my lesson."

"That was different," said Graywing. "You don't expect a flower to sting you, do you?"

"No," replied Reddy, "but I didn't expect a Jellyfish to sting me either. That flower may be all right to look at, but I guess I won't touch it."

Just then a Crab came along and touched that flower. In an instant the flower had disappeared, and there was nothing there but an unattractive, shapeless mass. Graywing caught the expression on Reddy's face. "Now what do you think of your flower?" said he.

"I don't think it is a flower at all," replied Reddy. "But it certainly did look like one. It had me fooled."

"As I told you before, it isn't a flower," said Graywing, "although it looks so much like one that it is called a Sea Anemone. It really is an animal, just the same as a Jellyfish is an animal. See, it is beginning to open up again now."

Reddy watched. Sure enough, in just a moment or two there was that flower again down in the water. What had at first looked like petals, he could now see were really tentacles. The stem, or body, was yellowish-brown, though sometimes it is pink, or salmon or orange or dark brown, or even mottled with different colors. The tentacles, or flower parts, were of varying colors. This was the Common Anemone, known as the Brown Sea Anemone. Like the Jellyfish, the Anemone has stinging threads with which it drives off its enemies.

"There's another one over there, of a different kind," said Graywing.

Reddy looked and, sure enough, in a shadowy corner of the little pool where it was quite dark, was another Anemone. The body was slender and of a delicate brown. The fairly long tentacles were white. "Do you know the name of that one?" asked Reddy.

"I believe," replied Graywing, "it is called the White-Armed Anemone."

"Oh," cried Reddy, "I suppose that over on the other side is another Anemone."

"That is a good guess," replied Graywing. "That is the Crimson Anemone."

"Well, it certainly is a handsome one," said Reddy. And, indeed, it was. It was of moderate size, but its color was a rich red. "Well," said Reddy, "those may be animals, but they look to me as if they were growing right there."

"They are," replied Graywing.

"Do you mean to say," exclaimed Reddy, "that they cannot swim around?"

"They don't exactly swim around," replied Graywing, "but they can let go and move if they have to. Some of them when they are young swim around."

"But if they don't swim around, what do they live on?" inquired Reddy.

"Oh, a lot of tiny little things that are in the water, that come within their reach. Some of them even suck little shellfishes out of their shells. You know I told you that they have little stinging tentacles and they catch their prey with these," replied Graywing.

Suddenly Reddy became much excited. "There's one moving down there now!" he exclaimed. "And it's moving fast!"

Graywing looked where Reddy was pointing. Then he began to chuckle. "Don't you see what's making him move?" he asked. "That Anemone has a partner. It is on the back of a Crab."

Now Reddy could see the Crab's legs. "What is that fellow doing on a Crab's back?" he demanded. "And how did he get there?"

"He's living there," replied Graywing, "and the Crab put him there. I told you they are partners. That is one of the Spider Crabs. He found out that if he had a Sea Anemone on his back, his enemies would not be so likely to see him. Then, too, if they should get too inquisitive, they would be stung by the Anemone."

"But I don't see any advantage to the Anemone," said Reddy.

"Why, he gets a free ride," replied Graywing. "He doesn't have to depend on having the water bring him his food. He has a constant change and more chance to get food as the Crab goes about. It really is a very fine partnership."

XXIII. More Garden Folk

Reddy Fox was still looking with interest down into the tide pool, which was so like a little garden. Presently he noticed what looked like a very delicate, prettily branched plant. It looked much like a dainty seaweed. On each branch were what looked like little flowers, or buds of flowers. It didn't occur to Reddy that these could be anything but plants. He would not have given them a second look had not Graywing called his attention to them.

"I suppose," said Graywing, "you have noticed those little plants growing on that stone down there?"

"Yes, they are very pretty," replied Reddy.

Graywing chuckled in the way that Reddy had come to recognize as preceding some astonishing statement. "Those are not plants," said Graywing. "Those are no more plants than the Sea Anemones are. Those little flowerlike things are not flowers at all, but a lot of little mouths. It really is a sort of animal. You remember what I told you about Jellyfish eggs hatching into something not at all like Jellyfishes?"

"I remember," said he.

"Well," replied Graywing, "each one of those plantlike creatures came from the egg of a Jellyfish."

Reddy looked very hard at Graywing to see if he were telling the truth. He suspected that Graywing might be having fun at his expense. Graywing paid no attention to him, but went on talking. "Those little things that look like buds down there have baby Jellyfishes in them. By and by they will open and the little Jellyfishes will be set free and swim about until they are fully grown. Even when they are fully grown they are very little fellows, but they are Jellyfishes just the same. In time they will have eggs and the eggs will turn into those funny little Sea Plumes, as they are called, and they in turn will set free more little Jellyfishes. It is like the caterpillar, the cocoon and the butterfly, only different."

"See those little Jellyfishes swimming around down there," said Reddy. "The ones with four long threads trailing behind them." Of course, Reddy meant tentacles.

"I see them," replied Graywing. "Do you see that moss growing down on that rock?"

Reddy nodded. "Of course I see it," said he, "and of course it isn't moss."

This time Graywing's eyes fairly twinkled. "You are learning, Reddy," said he. "No, that isn't moss down there. It is simply a lot of little Jellyfish mothers, or Jellyfish children, I don't know which. Those Jellyfishes you see swimming around there came from those little mosslike creatures down there. By and by there will be some eggs from those Jellyfishes and the little baby that hatches from each egg, after swimming around a little, will settle down and become fast to a rock and then grow into what looks like a little mosslike plant, which in turn will by and by set free a lot of Jellyfishes. So how can a fellow know which is mother and which is child?"

Reddy shook his head. "It's too much for me," he confessed. "If anybody but you had told me these things, I wouldn't believe them."

Now all that Graywing had told Reddy was true. These little plantlike creatures are called Hydroids, but are really members of the animal world and not of the plant world. There are many kinds of Hydroids, but all of them are plantlike in appearance. Not all of them are the children or the parents of Jellyfishes, whichever you please. But many of them are. More than one person has gathered and pressed some of these Hydroids, believing them to be seaweed.

"Oh," exclaimed Reddy, "see that cucumber down there!"

"What is a cucumber?" demanded Graywing.

"Why—why," said Reddy, hesitating a little, "it's a sort of vegetable that grows in gardens."

"Does it grow in the water?" inquired Graywing.

"No, of course not!" said Reddy.

"Well, then, how can there be one down in there?" demanded Graywing.

Reddy rubbed his black nose with one of his black paws and stared down into the water. "Well, anyhow, it looks like a cucumber,"

COMMON SEA CUCUMBER.
Cucumaria frondosa.
BRITTLE SEA CUCUMBER.
Synapta inhaerens.

HYDROID.
Bougainvillea ramosa.

said he, pointing to a curious thing that did, indeed, remind one of a cucumber. But it wasn't one, as Reddy soon found out. Even while Reddy was looking at it, it changed its shape two or three times. It became long and slender, almost wormlike. Then it became rather short and big around. At one end was the mouth, although Reddy didn't know it was the mouth. Around this were branching tentacles with which it caught its food. These added to its plantlike appearance. If Reddy had felt of it he would have found that it was soft and leathery. It had the power to move about, as Reddy soon discovered. When he said that it looked like a cucumber he was nearer to its name than he realized, for it is called the Sea Cucumber.

There is another known as the Brittle Sea Cucumber. This one is a curious creature because it can break itself up into pieces of its own free will. That is why it is called the Brittle Sea Cucumber. Another curious thing about it is that it lives in a tube made of fine sand. It makes this tube itself.

There are two other members of this queer family,—the Red Sea Cucumber and the Crimson Sea Cucumber. The Sea Cucumbers are related to the Starfishes and the Sea Urchins.

Reddy was still making discoveries in that curious little water garden.

"See," he exclaimed suddenly; "there is a Spider down there!"

"I don't see any Spider," replied Graywing, looking sharply down into the water.

"Well," said Reddy, "I don't suppose it is a Spider, but it looks like one."

"Where?" demanded Graywing.

"Crawling over that piece of seaweed down there," replied Reddy. "He looks to be all legs. Don't you see him down there—that gray fellow crawling along?"

"Oh, I see it now," replied Graywing. "They do call that a Spider, although of course it isn't a Spider at all. It looks just as if the legs were just joined together, doesn't it?"

"It certainly does," replied Reddy.

Graywing began to chuckle. "I've heard some funny things about that fellow," said he. "How would you like to carry your stomach in your legs?"

"Do what?" cried Reddy.

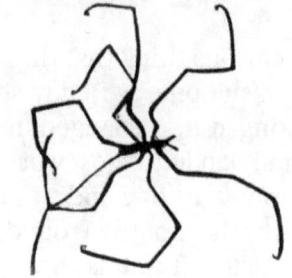

COMMON SEA SPIDER.
Anoplodactylus lentus.

"Carry your stomach in your legs," replied Graywing, still chuckling. "That is what they say that fellow does. I suppose it's because he hasn't anywhere else to carry it. I am told that Mr. Sea Spider has an extra pair of legs."

"What for?" demanded Reddy.

"He has to carry the eggs," replied Graywing.

"What's that?" exclaimed Reddy.

"I said he had to carry the eggs," replied Graywing. "You see, Mrs. Sea Spider believes in making Mr. Sea Spider do his share. She thinks she has done her share when she has laid the eggs. Mr. Sea Spider gets busy then, gathers the eggs into little balls, and fastens them to his extra pair of legs. He carries them about with him until they hatch. See, Reddy, there's another one over there! And here is one almost right under us!"

Reddy looked down. Sure enough, there was one of those curious little sea people. Suddenly his eyes opened very wide. "Look!" he cried. "He's carrying a lot of babies!"

It was so. There was a swarm of babies hanging around over their father. Reddy remembered that he had seen a true Spider with a mass of babies swarming over her, so it made this little sea creature seem even more like a Spider.

"Well," said Graywing, "I'm getting hungry. So, if you'll excuse me, Reddy, I think I'll go to look for something to eat."

"It's a good suggestion," replied Reddy. "I think I'll do the same thing."

So together they left the little water garden wherein Reddy had discovered that nothing was what it seemed to be.

XXIV. Graywing's Little Joke

Reddy Fox had seen Jellyfishes that were not jelly and sea flowers that were not flowers and moss that was not moss. Do you wonder that he was getting to be a little suspicious of new things? No one likes to be thought ignorant. Two or three times Graywing the Gull had laughed at Reddy, so now Reddy was a little slow about asking questions.

Graywing, whose sharp eyes missed very little, and who has great knowledge of things of the sea and of the seashore, had really enjoyed telling Reddy about things. He was like most other people in this respect, for most people enjoy airing their knowledge. Indeed, this is a failing with some people. They are so fond of airing their knowledge that they become tiresome. Graywing, however, wasn't as bad as all this.

After a bit Graywing noticed that Reddy was not asking as many questions as he had in the past and he wondered if Reddy were losing interest in the things of the seashore. So Graywing kept a watchful eye for things which he thought might interest Reddy. So it was that one day, happening to look down into a quiet little pool, he saw something that made his own eyes open a trifle wider.

"Well, well," exclaimed Graywing, "I wonder how this little fellow happened to get here! Reddy Fox must see him. Yes, sir, Reddy Fox must see him." At once Graywing went looking for Reddy. From high up in the sky he could look long distances in every direction. Presently he discovered Reddy taking a sun bath in a little hollow between the sand dunes. Reddy did not see him. You see, Reddy was half asleep. Graywing sailed down until he was just over Reddy and very close to him. Then he screamed. Reddy bounced to his feet as if he were on springs. He fairly glared as he looked up at Graywing. He was cross. Yes, sir, he was cross. To be startled in such a way often makes people cross.

"Well," he snarled, "what is all this rumpus about?"

"I was looking for you," said Graywing. "I have found something I think you would like to see. I'm sorry I startled you so, Neighbor Fox, but I must say that I admire the way in which you can jump. Yes, sir, I do so! I believe you used to live inland."

"I do now, some of the time," replied Reddy rather ungraciously. "What of it?"

"Then you must know what a Horse is," said Graywing.

"Of course I know what a Horse is," retorted Reddy. "Goodness knows, I've seen enough horses."

"But all the Horses you've ever seen were on land, weren't they?" Graywing asked.

Reddy grinned. "No," said he, "I once saw a Horse that wasn't on land."

Graywing looked at Reddy suspiciously. "If he wasn't on land, where was he?" he demanded.

"In the water," chuckled Reddy. "He was swimming across a river."

"Oh!" exclaimed Graywing. "Well, he was a land Horse just the same, even if he was in the water. Just a little while ago I saw a Horse in the water, but this one was a Sea Horse."

At that, Reddy pricked up his ears. "Was he swimming?" he asked.

"No," replied Graywing, "he was down under water, but he wasn't swimming."

Reddy looked disappointed. "Then he must have been drowned," said he.

"You are wrong," replied Graywing. "He was alive. He was very much alive."

"He couldn't have been alive and have been under water," declared Reddy in a most decided way. "No Horse can live under water any more than I can."

Graywing chuckled. He seemed to be enjoying something which Reddy didn't understand. "This Horse was alive and he was under water," insisted Graywing. "He was under water when I first saw him and I left him under water. In fact, he couldn't live out of water. What do you say, Reddy, to going with me to see that Sea Horse?"

SEA HORSE.
Hippocampus hudsonius

Reddy looked interested. He *was* interested, but he did not want to appear too anxious. "All my life," said he, "I have known Horses. I wouldn't go around a sand dune to look at a Horse, unless it were dead. Then I might if I were hungry."

"You have never seen a Horse like this one," explained Graywing. "As I told you before, it lives in the sea and never comes out."

At this Reddy fairly snorted. "Don't try to stuff me, Graywing," said he. "I wasn't born yesterday. I know a Horse can swim, for, as I told you, I have seen one swim. Any horse could swim a little while in the sea, but no Horse could live there."

"This one can and does," replied Graywing. "I told you that this is a Sea Horse."

"Sea Horse or land Horse, a Horse is a Horse, and you needn't tell me that there is any Horse that can live in water all the time!" retorted Reddy.

"All right, have it your own way," said Graywing. "I know where there is a Sea Horse and that Sea Horse is in the water and very much alive. If you don't want to see him, he isn't going to feel bad and neither am I. I am going over to pay him a call before he swims away and if you care to go along, I shall be very glad to have you. He is, by the way, the only Horse I know of without legs."

Once more those sharp ears of Reddy's were cocked up. On his face was a look of utter unbelief. Now he was sure that Graywing was fooling him. "Say, Mr. Gull," said he rather sharply, "just what are you talking about? There never was, there isn't now, and there never will be in all the Great World a Horse without legs. I am beginning to think that you don't know what a Horse is. A Horse without legs! Why, a Horse has four legs and knows how to use them! Without them, he would be wholly helpless."

"This one isn't," retorted Graywing. "I have an idea that if he should suddenly find himself with legs, he wouldn't know what to do with them."

"I suppose that pretty soon you will be saying that he hasn't any tail," sneered Reddy.

"Oh, no, I wouldn't say that," replied Graywing goodnaturedly. "No, indeed, I wouldn't say that! This Horse has a tail and a very useful tail."

"I suppose he uses it to switch off flies under water," said Reddy in a rather disagreeable manner.

Graywing remained good-natured. The truth is, he was enjoying Reddy's unbelief. "No," said he, "there are no flies on this Horse. Being under water, he isn't bothered with flies. He uses his tail to hang on to things with."

Reddy could stand no more. "Come on!" he barked. "Come on! Show me that Horse! I want to see a Horse that has no legs and uses his tail to hang on to things with, and lives in the sea. Yes, sir, I want to see that Horse! I am always ready to be shown things. But I can tell you one thing right now, Graywing."

"What is that?" demanded Graywing.

"If you don't make good and show me that Horse, I'll never believe anything you tell me hereafter," asserted Reddy.

"All right," replied Graywing, "that's fair enough. I am going to show you a Horse without legs and with a tail that he anchors himself with. You follow me."

Graywing spread his wings and headed over towards the beach, and then along the beach towards some quiet little tide pools. Reddy followed and he was grinning.

"That fellow doesn't know what a Horse is," he kept saying over and over to himself.

When he reached the beach, Reddy discovered Jimmy Skunk. "Hello, Reddy!" exclaimed Jimmy. "Where are you bound?"

Reddy grinned more broadly than ever. "I'm on my way to see a Horse without legs, with a tail which he uses to hang on to things with, and who lives in the sea and never comes out," replied Reddy.

"If you don't mind, I'll go with you," said Jimmy Skunk. "I should like to see a Horse like that myself. Where did you say this Horse is?"

"I didn't say," replied Reddy. "Graywing is going to show it to me. Come along, if you want to. I'll tell you what it is, Jimmy. I don't believe Graywing knows what a Horse is."

Jimmy shook his head doubtfully. "I don't believe he does either," said he. "But we've seen some queer things on the seashore. Let's go!"

XXV. The Horse that Wasn't a Horse

Reddy Fox trotted along the beach with Jimmy Skunk ambling along behind him and Graywing the Gull flying some little distance ahead of him. They were on the way to see the Sea Horse, of which Graywing had told Reddy. Of course Reddy kept his eyes on Graywing. When the latter stopped at a small tide pool, in which the water was not deep enough even to cover the body of a Horse, had one been lying there, all Reddy's suspicions returned. He was sure now that Graywing was playing a joke of some kind.

"Where is that Horse?" demanded Reddy, as he came up to the little pool.

You should have seen Graywing's eyes twinkle. "Right down there in the water," said he.

Reddy didn't even look. He knew there wasn't any Horse in any such little pool as that and he intended to tell Graywing just what he thought of him. But Graywing didn't give him a chance.

"I'm glad you've brought Jimmy Skunk along, Neighbor Fox," said Graywing. "I am going to show you something which you never would have found for yourself. And if you had found it, you wouldn't have known what it was. I told you that I would show you a Sea Horse and that is just what I am going to do. However, let me say that a Sea Horse and a land Horse are not at all alike."

"They certainly are not, if your Sea Horse has no legs!" interrupted Reddy.

Graywing paid no attention to the interruption. "I know just what you are thinking," said he. "You are thinking that a Horse of any kind must be a great big animal. That is where you are wrong. A Sea Horse is a very tiny fellow, but he is a Sea Horse just the same. Anyway, that is what he is called. And when you have looked at him, I think you will understand why. Just as a favor to me, you two fellows come over here and look down in this little pool."

Now, what could Reddy and Jimmy do? Graywing spoke so pleasantly and was so polite, and seemed so very much in earnest, that they couldn't well refuse to do as he asked. So, rather ungraciously on Reddy's part, they walked over to the edge of the pool where they could look down into it.

"Look down on that piece of seaweed growing over in that corner," said Graywing. "See what is hanging on to that seaweed by its tail."

Reddy and Jimmy looked. Both blinked, and both rubbed their eyes and looked again. Slowly, a good-natured grin crept over Reddy's face. He was looking at a curious little creature which was upright in the water, with the end of its tail curled around the stem of a seaweed.

This curious little creature was only three or four inches long. On its back was a fin. That fin led Reddy to suspect that this queer little fellow was a real fish. But it didn't look like a fish. It certainly did not! It had a head shaped like—well, when Reddy looked at it, he turned to Graywing and said at once, "I know why they call that a Sea Horse and I don't wonder they do. That head is the shape of the head of a real Horse. There is no doubt about that. I suppose it is a fish."

Graywing nodded. "Yes," said he, "that is a sure enough fish, but he is always called a Sea Horse. Watch him now!"

The funny little Sea Horse had let go of the seaweed with his tail and was swimming across the little pool. He was still upright in the water. In swimming he didn't appear to use his tail at all, but only that back fin.

"We don't see Sea Horses up here very often, but farther south I have seen a great many. Now aren't you glad you came over here?" said Graywing.

"I certainly am," replied Reddy. "I wouldn't have missed this for anything. I hope you'll pardon me for being so unbelieving, Graywing. I ought to have known that your Sea Horse couldn't possibly be a real Horse; I mean the kind of Horse I'm used to. Oh, my goodness, what's happening? What under the sun is happening?"

You would have laughed could you have seen the eyes of Reddy Fox. They looked as if they were trying to pop right out of his head. Jimmy Skunk looked much the same. Both were staring down into the water. Standing on a rock, where he could also look in, was Graywing. He did not seem at all excited.

"Can you see them, Graywing? Can you see them?" cried Reddy, growing more and more excited every minute.

"Of course I can," chuckled Graywing. "I've seen that sort of thing before."

Now the cause of Reddy's excitement was nothing more nor less than a funny little surprise party. As Reddy was watching that little Sea Horse swim across the pool, there had suddenly appeared from a big pocket of the swimmer dozens of tiny little things, which Reddy knew without being told must be baby Sea Horses. They must be, because they had come out of that curious pocket that the Sea Horse carried. Reddy thought they never would stop coming out. Some appeared to go back in, but of this Reddy wasn't sure. You see, there were so many of them that it was hard work to keep watch of all at once. They didn't look much like the Sea Horse and Reddy said so.

"What of it?" demanded Graywing. "Haven't you learned by this time that it is seldom that newly born babies look like their parents? They will in a few days, however."

"Was she carrying them all the time?" asked Reddy, nodding towards the little Sea Horse.

"No," chuckled Graywing. "No, *she* wasn't, but *he* was."

"What do you mean by 'he' was?" demanded Reddy.

"Do you remember what you learned about Pa Stickleback?" inquired Graywing. "Do you remember how Pa Stickleback took all the care of the family?"

Reddy nodded. "Yes," said he. "Do you know, I am sorry for that fellow. Whenever I think of Pa Stickleback, I feel sorry for him. But what has that got to do with Mrs. Sea Horse?"

"Didn't I just tell you that that isn't Mrs. Sea Horse, but Mr. Sea Horse?" said Graywing rather sharply. "You haven't seen Mrs. Sea Horse at all. I doubt if she is anywhere around. That is Mr. Sea Horse down there. You say you are sorry for Pa Stickleback, but Pa Sea Horse goes Pa Stickleback one better. He does so! Pa Stickleback merely takes care of the eggs in the nest, but Pa Sea Horse carries them around with him. I suppose you noticed that pocket that all those baby Sea Horses just came out of."

Reddy nodded. "Of course," said he. "I can see it now. What about it?"

"That is more than a pocket," said Graywing.

"How so?" asked Reddy.

"Well," continued Graywing, "when Ma Sea Horse lays the eggs, she is through with her home cares. She doesn't worry about her family-to-be any more than Ma Stickleback does about hers. She just leaves it to father. Pa Sea Horse gathers those eggs into that pocket and then carries them around with him until they hatch. Pa takes all the care of the children. That pocket is a nursery."

"Huh!" grunted Reddy. "I'm glad I'm not a fish."

Graywing chuckled. "Don't get the idea that it is that way with all fishes," said he. "You mustn't judge all fishes by Sticklebacks and Sea Horses. By the way, did you notice what made those babies come out?"

"I did," spoke up Jimmy Skunk. "He squeezed them out against a rock."

Graywing nodded. "That's it," said he. "He carries them around in that pocket nursery until he thinks it is time for them to come out. Then he just presses against a rock and forces them out."

"Reddy said that he thought some of them went back in again. Do they ever do that?" inquired Jimmy Skunk.

"I'm not quite sure about that," replied Graywing. "Some folks say they do. Anyway, Pa Sea Horse looks after them until they are big enough to take care of themselves."

"I wouldn't have missed this for anything," declared Reddy Fox. "Graywing, I am ever so glad that you led us over here. That is the queerest fish I ever saw. I could watch him all day. But just now I'm getting hungry."

"So am I," said Jimmy Skunk. "There ought to be a fish somewhere along here big enough to furnish us both with a good meal."

"There is," said Graywing. "I can see it, just a little farther down the shore. Eat hearty and be happy. See you later."

XXVI. Some Upside Down People

THERE is a little saying that Reddy Fox learned long ago and should have remembered, but didn't. This is it:

> "Who fails to always watch his toes
> Will soon or later bump his nose."

Nothing in the world is more true than this. A bumped nose is very likely to follow stubbed toes. The moral is, watch your step. Who watches his step will seldom fall. Usually Reddy Fox is watchful. Just like every one else, he is careless once in a while. And, like every one else, he usually has to pay for his carelessness. But Reddy is so smart that it isn't often such a thing happens, and when it does he is much upset.

Reddy had been at the seashore so long now that without realizing it he had become a wee bit careless. He wasn't watching his step as he should have been. So it happened that one day, when he jumped from one rock to another, he didn't notice that the one he was jumping from was wet and therefore slippery. The result was that his hind feet slipped. He didn't land on the other rock as he intended to. His hind feet didn't land on it at all. He tried to hang on with his forefeet, but they kept slipping. He kicked and scrambled with his hind feet, but this rock was wet too, and, despite all he could do, he kept slipping back.

Now, the side of that rock, which would be under water at high tide, was covered with white shell-like things crowded very close together. The edges were very sharp. They were not at all pleasant to slide over, as Reddy was finding out. Once he almost caught himself and then how he did try to scramble up! It was of no use. He began slipping again and this time there

ROCK BARNACLE.
Balanus balanoides.

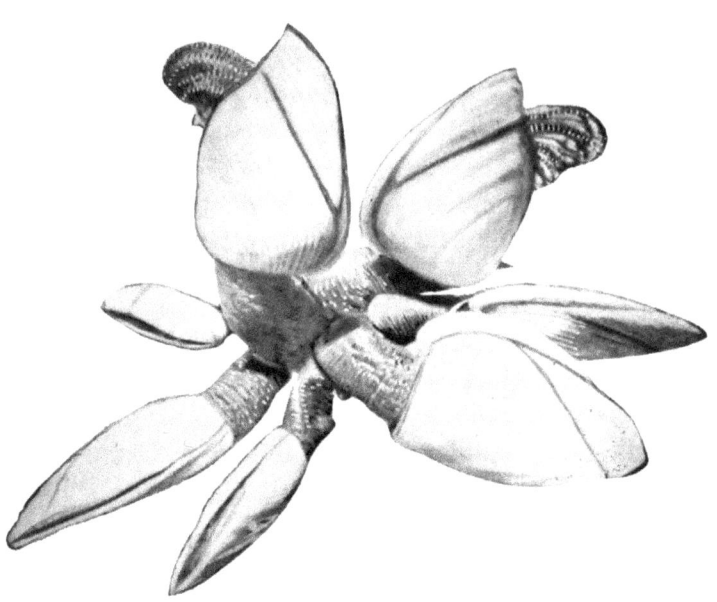

STALKED BARNACLE OR GOOSE BARNACLE.
Lepas anatifera.

was no stopping. Down he went, and in slipping he brought his nose against those sharp little shells. They took some skin off. Yes, sir, they took some skin off the end of Reddy's black nose! "Wow!" he yelped, as he landed at the bottom with a thump.

Then Reddy did the most foolish thing. His skinned nose was sore. He felt sure it would feel better if only he could get it into water. He rushed to the nearest little tide pool and plunged his nose in. "Wow!" he cried once more, and began dancing about. Of course, that water was salt, and salt water simply made that skinned nose smart all the more.

While he was still dancing about, Graywing the Gull came along. He alighted on the very rock from which Reddy had tumbled. "For goodness' sake, what is the matter with you, Neighbor Fox?" he demanded.

"Nothing," mumbled Reddy and stopped dancing.

It was then that Graywing saw Reddy's skinned nose. "Oho!" said he. "So you bumped and skinned your nose! That is too bad. It happens that I have never bumped my nose, but I guess it must hurt."

"Well, I guess that your guess is a very good guess," returned Reddy. "These are the roughest rocks I have ever seen anywhere. I don't understand what makes them smooth on top and rough down below."

For just an instant Graywing looked a little puzzled. Then he understood. "Oh," said he, "I guess you mean the Barnacles growing there."

"The what?" inquired Reddy.

"The Barnacles," replied Graywing. "Those are what you skinned your nose on. Don't you see them growing all over the lower part of that rock?"

"Growing!" exclaimed Reddy, and there was a puzzled note in his voice. "I don't see anything growing on that rock. That rock is simply white down below and dreadfully rough. What are Barnacles, anyway? I never heard of them before."

"You may not have heard of them, but you certainly have seen them enough times," replied Graywing. "As I said before, they are what you skinned your nose on."

Reddy moved over a little nearer to that rock and, for the

first time, he really began to use his eyes. He had seen those things which covered the lower part of that rock, and which covered many other rocks all about, many times. However, he had always supposed that they were part of the rocks. Never once had it entered his head that they were anything else. So when Graywing called them Barnacles, and said that they were growing on the rocks, Reddy really didn't understand.

"I don't see anything growing on this rock," said he.

Graywing started to chuckle, then thought better of it, for he knew that Reddy didn't like to be laughed at. "Of course," said he, "you don't see them actually growing, but those white things that you skinned your nose on just now are growing. They are alive and growing. And, as I told you before, they are called Barnacles."

For the time being Reddy actually forgot his sore nose. He looked more closely at those Barnacles. They were crowded together, but he saw right away that they were of different sizes and that they were of shell. He could see the sharp edges that had skinned his nose. Graywing saw the puzzled look on Reddy's face.

"I suppose," said Graywing, "that even now it hasn't entered your head that there is a living creature inside each of those queer little shells."

"No," said Reddy, "it hasn't. Is there?"

"Come over here," replied Graywing, flying to the edge of a little pool.

Reddy hurried after him. "Now," said Graywing, "just look at some of those Barnacles on that rock under water. Watch them closely and see what happens. Perhaps you may learn something."

Obediently Reddy leaned over and watched the Barnacles down under the water. Presently he discovered that the tops of some of those Barnacles were open. Then from one of them appeared what looked like feathery little legs. They were thrust out from it and began to move about in the water.

"My goodness!" exclaimed Reddy. "My goodness! Do you see that?" He looked up at Graywing.

This time Graywing really did chuckle. He was getting a lot of chuckles at Reddy's expense these days. "Now you've learned something, haven't you?" said he.

"I certainly have!" replied Reddy. "What are those funny legs waving about in the water for?"

"That fellow is kicking his food into his mouth," replied Graywing. "It is the only way he has of getting something to eat. That Barnacle lives on things too small for us to see, and those waving legs are making little currents of water which carry the food into his mouth."

"Do you mean to tell me that the thing inside that shell has a mouth?" Reddy demanded.

"Of course. Why not?" replied Graywing. "Why shouldn't it have a mouth as well as those feathery legs? I call Barnacles upside-down people."

"Why?" asked Reddy.

"Just look at them," said Graywing. "They are all standing on their heads, aren't they? They are fastened to that rock by their heads."

Reddy took a few minutes to think this over. Then he wanted to know how those Barnacles got fastened to the rock in the first place.

"Easily enough," replied Graywing. "They just attached themselves. You see, when a Barnacle first hatches from an egg he is a very tiny fellow and he doesn't look anything like a Barnacle. He swims around then. By and by he decides to settle down in life, so he butts his head against a rock, or a ship's bottom, or some other solid substance in the water, and sticks there. Then he starts in to build a house around himself. That is the shell, of course. Once he is located he is content to stay right there, and all the time he is standing on his head. When the water covers him he opens up his shell and feeds. You will notice that those Barnacles out of water are tightly closed. But as soon as the tide comes in and covers them, they will open up and begin to feed, collecting their food with their feet."

"I suppose," said Reddy, "there is more than one kind of Barnacle."

"Oh, yes," replied Graywing, "there are several kinds. But they are all pretty much alike in the way they live. There is one kind called the Goose Barnacle and also the Stalked Barnacle. This doesn't have the shell growing right down close to the thing it is fastened to. It has a little fleshy neck, or stalk. I don't suppose you know what a Whale is."

"No," said Reddy, "I don't know what a Whale is. What is it?"

"It is the largest animal in the world and it lives in the ocean," replied Graywing. "It is so big that you wouldn't believe me if I should tell you how big it is. There is a Barnacle called the Whale Barnacle, that lives fastened to the skin of a Whale. It is a big fellow."

Reddy suddenly looked up at Graywing and grinned. "It is worth a skinned nose," said he.

Graywing didn't understand at first. "What is worth a skinned nose?" he asked in a wondering tone of voice.

"What I've learned about these queer fellows who live upside-down," replied Reddy.

XXVII. The Queer Disappearance

"Hello, Jimmy. Have you found anything?" Jimmy Skunk jumped ever so little. "Goodness, Reddy Fox, you startled me that time," said he. "I didn't hear you at all until you spoke. No, I haven't found anything new or interesting, or even to eat."

"I don't suppose you've been looking in the water," said Reddy.

"No," replied Jimmy, "I've just been looking things over on the beach."

Now, by this time, Reddy Fox had learned that there were quite as many interesting things to see in the water as could possibly be found outside the water. You remember how he had seen Pa Stickleback in his home, and Pa Sea Horse and his family, and that queer fellow, the Barnacle, who stands on his head and kicks the food into his mouth. All of these had been in the water. So it was that Reddy had learned never to pass a tide pool without approaching it softly and looking into it.

For a moment or two Reddy looked up and down the beach. Then he noticed a good-sized pool which the outgoing tide had left. "I'm going over there to see what there is in it," said he. And, suiting action to the word, he trotted over towards the pool. Jimmy Skunk ambled after him in his usual leisurely way. When he reached the pool Reddy was staring intently into the water and on his face was a funny look.

"What is it?" asked Jimmy.

"You tell me," replied Reddy.

Jimmy stared down into the pool. "I don't see anything unusual," said he.

"Use your eyes!" retorted Reddy impatiently. "There it is, right down there."

Jimmy winked and blinked and stared. "I don't see a thing but sand," said he.

"You come around here and stand beside me," said Reddy.

"Now look right down there on the sand. Don't you see that queer long thing that is broad and pointed at one end and has a whole bunch of feelers at the other end?"

Jimmy winked and blinked some more. Then he saw it. It was very much the color of the sand and that was why he had not seen it at first. "There it is!" he cried. "What do you suppose it is?"

"That's what I want to know," replied Reddy.

"Do you suppose it is alive?" said Jimmy.

"I haven't the least idea," replied Reddy, "but I'm going to find out."

"How?" demanded Jimmy.

"I'm going to roll this little stone in there and see what happens," replied Reddy.

"That's a good idea!" exclaimed Jimmy.

So Reddy rolled the stone until, with a splash, it fell into the pool almost on the queer thing at the bottom. Right then a very strange thing happened. Yes, sir, a very strange thing happened! All the water in that little pool turned black! It was for all the world as if some one had emptied a bottle of ink in there. Reddy and Jimmy couldn't see the bottom at all. Of course that strange thing had disappeared. It had disappeared because the water had turned black and they could no longer see through it.

Often they had seen a fish on a muddy bottom stir up a cloud of mud. But this wasn't mud. The bottom of this pool was pure sand. There wasn't a particle of mud in it. Reddy turned to stare at Jimmy, and Jimmy stared back at Reddy.

"What do you know about that?" said Jimmy slowly.

"I don't know anything about it. Why don't you ask sensible questions?" retorted Reddy somewhat sharply. It made him a little bit cross to be so wholly puzzled. He couldn't even see the stone he had rolled in. He couldn't see anything at all in the water. Yet he hadn't the slightest idea where all that blackness had come from.

"Well, what is it this time?" cried a familiar voice, and Graywing the Gull alighted beside them.

"It is that black water," replied Reddy. "I rolled a stone into that little pool and the water turned all black. Never before have

BLUNT-TAILED SQUID OR SEA ARROW.
Loligo pealii.

SAND EEL OR LAUNCE.
Ammodytes americanus.

I seen such black water and I don't understand it. Why should that water turn black just because I rolled a stone into it?"

"You fellows follow me along down the shore," said Graywing, chuckling softly. "There's something down there I want you to see." With this he took to his wings and flew down along the shore.

Reddy and Jimmy took their time in following. When they caught up with Graywing he was waiting beside a long shallow inlet of water. The bottom was sandy.

"Do you see that fellow over there?" inquired Graywing.

Reddy and Jimmy looked. They saw it at once. It was another of those queer things they had seen in the little pool before the water turned black. It was just like the other.

"We've seen one of those before," said Reddy.

"I know you have," replied Graywing.

Reddy looked up quickly. "How do you know?" he demanded. He remembered that Graywing had not been around when they discovered that queer thing back there in the pool.

Graywing didn't answer the question. Instead, he told them to keep their eyes on that queer thing. So Reddy and Jimmy sat down to watch. After a while the thing began to move. Meanwhile, Reddy had discovered that it had two big eyes. They were round and staring and gave him a creepy feeling. They were worse than the staring eyes of the Crabs. Of course, they had no lids. At one end there was a mouth. It was in the form of a regular beak and looked as if it might bite most uncomfortably. From around this beak stretched out ten long feelers, or arms, two of them being longer than the others.

As Reddy and Jimmy watched, this queer creature changed color. It was moving very slowly. Suddenly it began to go fast. Those long arms trailed out behind it and it dawned on Reddy that this curious creature was going tail-first.

"Look!" he cried excitedly. "Look! That thing is swimming backward!"

"Why not?" inquired Graywing. "If a Lobster can swim backward—and that is the way a Lobster swims—why shouldn't other creatures swim backward?"

Reddy shook his head. "I don't know of any reason," he confessed, "but it certainly looks queer."

"Personally," continued Graywing, "I don't think much of that way of swimming. I want to see where I'm going. That fellow can go forward if he wants to, but it seems to be easier for him to go backward and so he does. Perhaps those long arms in front are in the way when he goes forward. I have seen ever and ever so many of those things dead on the beach, because the silly things ran ashore, not knowing where they were going. Once ashore, they didn't know how to get back into the water, and so they died."

Meanwhile, Jimmy Skunk had been intently watching the swimmer in the pool. "I don't see how he swims," said Jimmy.

"I don't wonder you don't," replied Graywing. "He doesn't swim like regular fish. You notice that he hasn't fins and he hasn't a swimming tail."

"Then how does he swim?" demanded Reddy.

"He swims," replied Graywing, "by taking water in and driving it out again through his mouth with such force that it shoots him backward through the water. Old Mother Nature has provided him with a curious arrangement called a siphon, just for that purpose. It seems to work all right."

Jimmy Skunk nodded. "There is no doubt about that," said he. "But that is the funniest way of swimming that I ever have heard of. What does he eat?"

"Be patient," replied Graywing. "That fellow looks to me as if he is hungry. If we watch him, we may have a chance to see him catch a dinner."

"Did you ever see one catch a dinner?" Jimmy Skunk asked.

"Often," replied Graywing. "It is quite worth seeing."

"Then we'll be patient and wait," said Reddy.

XXVIII. The Ink Maker

Reddy Fox has a little saying which is all his own. This is the way it turns:

> "It always seems to me that wishing
> Is always more than half of fishing."

I suspect that Reddy is right about that. There is a lot of truth in it. However, Reddy isn't much of a fisherman. There are some fishermen, however, who do very little wishing. Billy Mink is one. Little Joe Otter is another. Barker the Seal is a third. When they want fishes they just go get them. They waste no time wishing.

Reddy and Jimmy and Graywing were watching a fisherman who does very little wishing. It was that queer creature that had so puzzled Reddy and Jimmy, and who was now swimming backward. Presently he stopped and lay quietly on the sand. He was so nearly the color of the sand that, had they not seen him stop right there, it is quite likely they would not have seen him at all. In a moment Graywing's sharp eyes discovered a little school of small fishes swimming that way. You know Graywing has a wonderful eye for fishes.

"Watch now and see what will happen," said he.

The little fishes came darting along through the water and presently they were directly over that queer thing on the sand. Then one of those long arms shot up and touched one of those little fishes. Struggle as it would, that little fish could not get away. Another arm came up and fastened to it, and another. Then they drew it down to that beaklike mouth and a piece was bitten out of the back of the neck.

Jimmy Skunk was fairly popeyed. "Why couldn't that fish get away?" he demanded. "What made it stick to that arm that first touched it?"

"Suckers," replied Graywing. "Little suckers. Those arms, or feelers, or feet, or whatever you want to call them, are covered with little suckers on the under side. Once they touch anything, they suck right hold of it. That little fish didn't have a chance in the world."

"I guess it is a good thing that thing isn't any bigger," said Jimmy Skunk.

"Oh, as for that," replied Graywing, "there are some so big that if ever one wrapped one of its arms around you, you wouldn't have a chance in the world. But none of those big ones live around here, I'm happy to say. Why, if one of those big fellows should get hold of you, it could pull you into the water just as easily as that fellow there caught the fish."

Reddy stared down into the water and slowly shook his head. "I don't like the looks of him," said he. "I don't like those wriggly arms. I don't like the way he stares. I don't like the way he swims backward instead of forward, like an honest person. I don't like anything about him."

At that, Graywing laughed right out. "What difference does it all make to you, Reddy?" he cried.

"It doesn't make any difference, but I don't like it, just the same," replied Reddy. "And I don't like the looks of him, because he doesn't look as if he had any bones or any shell."

"Well, he has," replied Graywing. "He has a sort of shell, but it is inside instead of outside."

"If it is inside, it must be bone and not shell," declared Reddy.

"There is no must about it," retorted Graywing. "It isn't bone. It is a sort of shell. He doesn't look it, but that fellow belongs to the mollusk family. You know the Clams and the Scallops and the Oysters are all mollusks. So in a way that fellow down there is related to them. A family connection, so to speak."

"Huh! That's hard to believe. He doesn't look it," exclaimed Reddy, gazing down into the water.

In their interest in this queer fisherman, Reddy and Jimmy had quite forgotten the pool that had suddenly turned black when

THE INK MAKER

Reddy had rolled a stone into it. Now they were reminded of it. Unnoticed by either of them, Graywing had picked up a Clam. He flew up until he was exactly over that queer fellow in the water. Then he let the Clam drop. The water splashed up in Reddy's face and he was so startled that he turned tail and raced away.

"Ha, ha, ha!" laughed Graywing.

Reddy stopped short and looked back. He didn't yet know what had happened, but he was sure that in some way Graywing had played a joke on them. Reddy is just like you,—he doesn't like to have jokes played on him. He all but lost his temper. He opened his mouth to say something sharp and unpleasant, but before he could do so, he happened to glance at the water. His mouth closed with a snap. He didn't say a word. He forgot that he had been going to say something sharp and unpleasant. That water had turned black all around the place where Reddy had seen that queer fisherman.

Reddy looked up at Graywing and then down at the water. Slowly, for he was very suspicious, he crept back to the very edge of the water. It appeared exactly like the water that had so puzzled him in the little pool into which he had rolled a stone a short time before.

Now, if Reddy had been as smart as he usually is, or if he had done a little real thinking, he would have suspected that the blackness of the water had something to do with that queer fellow he and Jimmy had been watching. There had been one in that pool that had turned black, and there was one here, hidden somewhere underneath this blackness. But Reddy didn't think of this. He couldn't think of anything but the mystery of that black cloud in the water.

"Where does that come from?" he demanded, looking up at Graywing.

"Where does what come from?" inquired Graywing, pretending that he didn't understand.

"That black water," explained Reddy.

"Oh, that comes from the Ink Maker. Didn't you know that? I thought every one knew the Ink Maker," said Graywing.

"The Ink Maker! Who under the sun is the Ink Maker?" Reddy asked. His face showed how very much puzzled he was.

"You ought to know him by this time," said Graywing.

"Why ought I to know him?" demanded Reddy rather sharply.

"Because you've been looking at him long enough to know him," retorted Graywing.

"Then I suppose I've seen him, too," spoke up Jimmy Skunk.

"You certainly have," said Graywing. "Both of you have been looking at him."

Reddy and Jimmy began to look about in the most puzzled manner. They looked this way, they looked that way. Finally Reddy said, "I don't see any Ink Maker."

"Neither do I," said Jimmy Skunk.

"Of course you don't," retorted Graywing. "How could you now? He is hiding under his own ink."

It was then that Reddy suspected the truth. "Do—do—do you mean to say that queer fellow who swims backward made the water turn black?" he inquired.

"I'm glad you've waked up," chuckled Graywing. "He is the Ink Maker. He is what is called a Squid."

"But what does he make that ink for?" Jimmy Skunk inquired.

"I know," spoke up Reddy. "It's to hide himself in."

"Right!" cried Graywing. "You are beginning to wake up, Neighbor Fox. When his enemies are around, and he has plenty of them, he can disappear right under their very noses. There is another name for this fellow. Some people call him a Sea Arrow. I suppose that is because of the arrowhead shape of that broad fin at the end of his body. There are two kinds of Squids along the coast—one is the Blunt-tailed Squid, and the other is the Short-tailed Squid. Then there is the Giant Squid, of which I have already told you, but this is very rarely seen. These Squids, such as the one you have been watching, constantly change color to match their surroundings when they are swimming. They are really quite interesting."

"Just the same, I don't like the looks of them," declared Reddy. And this was Jimmy's opinion also.

XXIX. Queer Climbers and their Relatives

Both Reddy Fox and Jimmy Skunk were becoming more observing. That means that they were learning really to use their eyes. They were learning really to see things, not merely look at them. You know it is quite possible to look at things and not see them. Indeed, most of us are very apt to do that very thing. Since Graywing the Gull had shown Reddy and Jimmy so many interesting things, they had begun to pay more attention to the familiar things around them. They had discovered that the most familiar things may sometimes prove to be the most interesting things.

On the beach was a kind of shellfish to which neither Reddy nor Jimmy had paid any attention. Both thought of these shellfishes as a kind of Clam. They reminded them somewhat of the fresh-water Clams that Jerry Muskrat is so fond of. But one day Reddy stopped to look at one of these and it struck him that these particular little shell people did not live like any other Clams of his acquaintance. They did not live in the mud or in the sand. It was then that his interest became aroused, and you know that when interest is aroused, curiosity is also awakened. He called Jimmy Skunk's attention to a lot of these shell people clinging to a rock.

"I've seen those before," said Jimmy. "You can hardly go anywhere along the shore without seeing them. There are their empty shells all over the beach."

"Yes," replied Reddy, "but what are they?"

"Why, they are—" began Jimmy and then stopped. A look as if he felt rather foolish passed over his face. "Why, I've always supposed they were Clams of some kind," said he lamely.

"I've always supposed the same thing," declared Reddy. "In

fact, until this minute, I've never thought anything about them. But, come to look at them, they are not like any of the Clams I know. See how thin those empty shells are. And, instead of being white, they're bluish inside. Then, too, they are not shaped just like Clam shells. Instead of being joined together halfway around, as a Clam is, they are joined together at one end."

"That's so," said Jimmy. "I hadn't thought of that. Now you speak of it, they don't look much like Clams. Just look at the outside of this shell. It seems to be covered with a sort of brownish skin and here are some that are bluish and some almost black. Here comes Graywing. We'll ask him about them."

Graywing circled overhead for a few moments, just to tease Reddy and Jimmy, for he knew by the looks of them that they were fairly aching to ask questions. At last he dropped down on a rock close by.

Hardly waiting for him to fold his wings, Reddy Fox cried, "What are these things?"

"Mussels," replied Graywing rather scornfully. "I didn't suppose there was any one along the seashore who didn't know Mussels when he saw them. The first thing I know, you'll be asking me what stones are."

"Well, you needn't be so cross about it," replied Reddy. "I thought they were some kind of Clam. But if you say they are Mussels, why, of course they are Mussels. Anyway, they are not particularly interesting."

That was very clever of Reddy. It aroused Graywing just as Reddy had hoped it would.

"Is that so?" exclaimed Graywing. "Is that so? Well, I might have expected such a remark from you. I don't suppose there is anything interesting about them to folks who don't use their eyes. I should hardly expect you to find anything interesting in a Mussel, Reddy Fox. No, sir, I should hardly expect you to find anything interesting in just a common, everyday Mussel. Look at those clinging fast to the side of that rock. It hasn't entered your head to wonder how they stick there, has it? You never saw a Clam clinging to a rock like that. Come, own up now, you never did, did you?"

Reddy slowly shook his head. "No," he confessed, "I never did.

BEARDED MUSSEL OR HORSE MUSSEL.
Modiolus modiolus.

WING MUSSEL OR RAZOR-SHELL.
Pinna muricata.

COMMON EDIBLE MUSSEL.
Mytilus edulis.

RIBBED MUSSEL.
Modiolus demissus plicatulus.

Now that you call my attention to it, it is queer how those fellows can cling to that rock. Do they grow to it the way a Barnacle does?"

Reddy went over and took hold of one of the Mussels. It was securely fastened. He looked up at Graywing and hesitated. You see, he just couldn't bear to admit that, after all, there was something interesting about that Mussel. At last he grinned sheepishly. "I'll take it all back, Graywing," said he. "How under the sun can a thing like that Mussel hang on to a smooth hard surface like this rock?"

"Look at it closely," said Graywing. "Here's a chance to prove just how good your eyes are. If you look closely enough, you'll see a little yellow thread."

Reddy looked. Jimmy Skunk came up and looked. Sure enough, they could see little yellow threads. It was very much as if that Mussel was growing from that rock by means of little yellow roots.

"I don't understand it even yet," said Reddy. "Of course, that Mussel isn't growing out of that rock, even if it does look so."

"Right you are, Reddy," replied Graywing. "Those little yellow threads come from the Mussel himself. He makes a sticky substance and then, when it comes in contact with the air it hardens and sticks to whatever it is on. When a ship wants to stay still in one place, an anchor with a rope attached is thrown overboard. That holds the ship there. Those yellow threads are just like anchor ropes. They are called byssus threads by people who want to use big words. Would it surprise you any if I should tell you that that Mussel can climb that rock?"

"No," replied Reddy, "it wouldn't surprise me any. I've reached a point where nothing would surprise me much. If you should tell me that that simple-looking Mussel can fly, I would believe it."

You should have heard Graywing chuckle. "It can't do that, Reddy," said he. "It can't fly. But it can climb that rock. What is more, I believe it is climbing right now. That is, I mean I believe it is a little farther up on that rock to-day than it was yesterday, and it probably will be a little farther up to-morrow than it is to-day. Climbing is slow business for those shell-folk, but they can and do do it."

"How do they do it?" inquired Jimmy Skunk, who had been listening. "I can understand how they can cling to the rock by means of those little threads, but for the life of me I don't see how they can move about."

"By means of those same little threads," explained Graywing. "He throws out some of those little threads in the direction he wants to go and then pulls himself up to it. Of course, he doesn't move very fast. It takes him a long time to get anywhere, but he does get there just the same."

"Are these things good eating?" inquired Reddy.

"Certainly," replied Graywing. "There is one kind that Men are very fond of eating. In fact, I believe it is that one you are looking at."

"Then there is more than one kind of Mussel," spoke up Jimmy Skunk.

"Of course," replied Graywing. "Look at that big piece of seaweed lying over there on the beach. Go see what is fastened to the roots of it."

Reddy ran over there. "Why, it's a Mussel!" he cried. "It's the biggest Mussel I ever saw."

Graywing nodded. "That fellow lived out in deep water," said he. "That seaweed was attached to it and a storm brought them both in. Perhaps you've noticed that down on the mud flats the Mussels grow in great numbers, almost as close together as the Barnacles grow on rocks. If you look carefully, you will soon be able to find several kinds of Mussels. Some of them are rather pretty and some of them are not. There's a shell over there that is fluted, or ribbed."

Graywing took to his wings and flew down the shore a short distance. Then he called to Reddy and Jimmy. They hurried over. Among the rocks, where the water just covered it, was a good-sized Mussel. It was half buried in the sand between the stones. It was of good size and was a brown color. All around the edges of the shell the outer skin was in little rags, making a sort of yellow beard.

"This," said Graywing, "is the Bearded Mussel, or Horse Mussel. The most interesting one to me is 'way down South. It is called the Razor Shell. It is fanshaped and lives in shallow water. It is ribbed and the edges of the shell are very sharp. People don't go in wading barefooted where the Razor Shells are. Now I've gossiped enough for one day. See you later, Reddy. See you later, Jimmy."

With this, Graywing left them to go fishing.

XXX. Reddy Learns Something About Snails

Reddy Fox was gradually growing more observing. Ever since he had been at the beach he had, of course, seen very many empty shells, which he called Snail shells. Some were quite small and some were of good size. Some were smooth and some were twisted. But to Reddy they were just Snail shells and nothing more. In some places he found great numbers of these shells occupied by their rightful owners. He never gave them more than a glance. He wasn't interested in Snails.

But now that he had begun really to use his eyes, he noticed things which had escaped his attention before. Thus one morning, when the tide was out and had left bare a number of big rocks, most of which were covered with Barnacles, Reddy noticed that there were many little Snails on those rocks also. Furthermore, these Snails were on the Barnacles. He didn't think much of this until he discovered that many of those Barnacles were merely empty shells. Then he began to watch those Snails. He saw one move off a Barnacle and on to another. The one that Snail had moved from was nothing but an empty shell.

Reddy remembered the Oyster Drill, which is really a little Snail, and at once became suspicious. "I wonder," said he, speaking aloud, "if that Snail ate the Barnacle that used to be in that empty shell."

"Certainly," said a voice right over his head, and looking up he discovered his friend Graywing the Gull. "I am glad to see you are so observing. Barnacles furnish those Snails with a favorite dinner. They are very fond of them. Those are what are called Rock Snails."

Reddy was looking at them intently. "There seems to be more than one kind here," said he. "Some are brown, some are white, some are gray, and some are yellow. Look at that one there. It has a smooth shell, while the one next to it is covered with ridges."

"They are all the same kind, just the same," replied Graywing. "They are all Rock Snails. There ought to be some Periwinkles around here."

"What is a Periwinkle?" demanded Reddy.

"Just another kind of a Snail," explained Graywing. "I see some now." As he spoke he flew over to another rock near by.

Reddy followed and discovered that that rock was literally covered with small Snails that seemed to have a thick, heavy, dark-brown shall. The edge of the shell, which is called a lip, was black. "Huh!" exclaimed Reddy. "I shouldn't think the Barnacles would stand much show in these parts."

"Oh," replied Graywing, "I believe the Periwinkles eat vegetable matter. They do not bother with Barnacles. While we are talking about Snails, here is another kind on this piece of seaweed. You will notice that the color is pretty nearly the color of the seaweed. It is called the Seaweed Snail."

"By the way," said Reddy, "when I've been over on the marshes I've seen a lot of little Snails on the mud flats. I wonder if they are the same kind as these."

Graywing shook his head. "Certainly not," said he. "Those are the Mud-Flat Snails. If you had looked at them closely, you wouldn't have had to ask if they are the same kind as this Seaweed Snail. The Mud-Flat Snail is black. He is a driller too."

"Meaning, of course, that he drills holes in shells of other kinds of shellfishes and eats them, I suppose," said Reddy.

"Right again, Reddy," said Graywing. "Let's go over to that sand flat over there. I think I can show you still another. This one is called the Sand-Flat Snail."

They went over to the sand flat and, sure enough, there was a Snail about the size of the others, but somewhat different in appearance. The spiral shell was covered with grooves going around the shell and also lengthwise of the shell. Reddy discovered one that apparently was boring through the shell of another. He looked up at Graywing and grinned. "This is a nice kind of relative, isn't it?" said he.

Graywing left Reddy and slowly flew along the shore, look-

SAND-FLAT SNAILS.
Alectrion trivittata.

MUD-FLAT SNAILS.
Alectrion obsoleta.

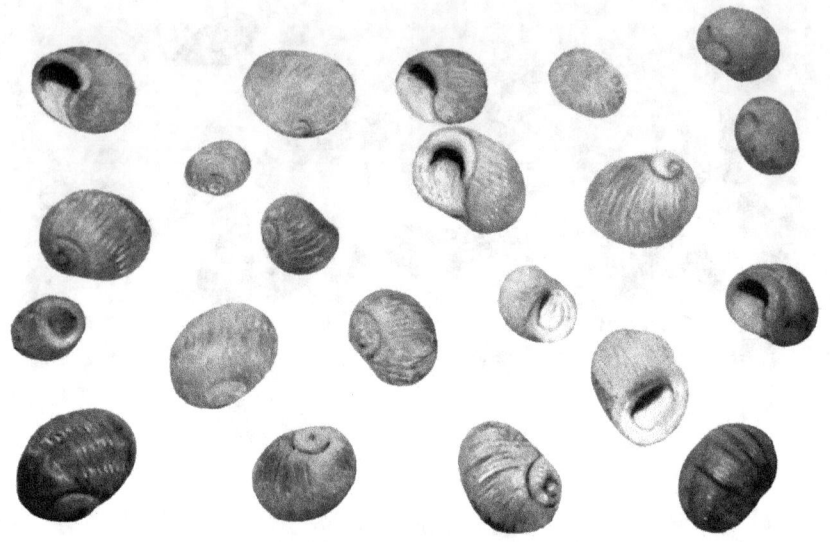

SEAWEED SNAILS.
Litorina obtusata palliata.

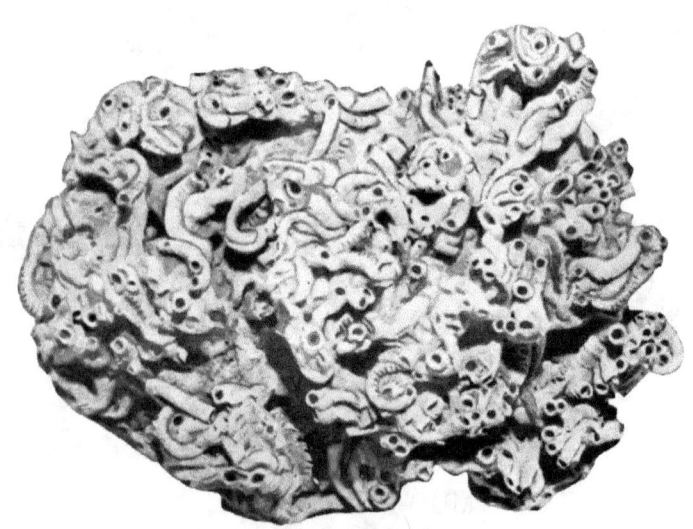

SHELL WORM.
Serpula dianthus.

ing down. Presently he dropped down on the beach and called to Reddy. Reddy hurried over. "What have you found now?" he cried.

"Just an empty shell," replied Graywing. "Just an empty shell. I thought you might like to see it."

What Reddy saw was a big shell fully three inches long. It was yellow-brown in color and grooved all the way around, so that there were ten ridges. These give it its common name of the Ten-Ribbed Snail. Inside, this shell was pure white.

"It's a wonder I found this," remarked Graywing.

"Why?" asked Reddy.

"Because," explained Graywing, "these shells are favorites with the Hermit Crabs. I am surprised that a Hermit Crab in search of a new house hasn't found this one and moved in. What have you found now, Reddy?"

"A worm shell," replied Reddy.

"A what?" cried Graywing.

"The shell of some kind of a Worm," said Reddy.

Graywing looked puzzled. "You've got another guess, Reddy," said he. "There is no Worm that has a shell to be cast up on the beach."

"There is too," contradicted Reddy. "If a Worm didn't live in this shell, I'd like to know what did."

By this time Graywing had joined Reddy and discovered what Reddy was looking at. It was a very curious shell. One end looked like the spiral end of the shell of a Snail, but the rest of it was twisted this way and that and looked for all the world as if nothing but a Worm could possibly have lived in it.

Reddy looked up at Graywing. "Don't tell me that a Worm didn't make this shell," said he.

"I don't wonder you think so," replied Graywing, "but it wasn't a Worm. That is the shell of a relative of the Snails."

"There certainly are some curious things on the shore," said Reddy, as he started along to see what more he could find. He didn't have far to go. No, sir, he didn't have far to go. The new shell he found was wholly different from anything he had yet seen. It wasn't a very big shell. It was a little less than an inch in length, but it was more spiral than any shell he had yet seen.

It was pure white and had nine ribs going lengthwise of the shell. Near by lay another one which he knew must be related, though it was slightly different. The eight spirals were crossed by almost twice as many ribs. The color wasn't pure white, but somewhat brownish.

"What kind of shells do you call these?" Reddy asked.

"I don't know," replied Graywing shaking his head. "No, sir, I don't know. I've seen them many times. They are often washed up on the shore. I think they're one of the prettiest shells I know of."

If Graywing had been a scientist he would have called the first of these shells *Epitonium angulatum* and the other *Epitonium lineatum*. The worm-like shell Reddy had found is named *Vermicularia spirata*.

Reddy stood looking down at that twisted shell. "I suppose," said he, "that those twists in the shell are made as the owner grows."

Graywing nodded. "That is the way of it," said he. "Each one of those twists shows a certain time of growth."

"Well, all I can say is that I should think that any one living in a house like that would feel all twisted up inside," declared Reddy.

"There are some very beautiful shells on the seashore," said Graywing, "and I don't begin to know all of them. Some of them that I have seen down in the South are wonderful. But there are so many of them—I mean, there are so many kinds—that I have given up trying to learn the names of all of them."

"And I used to think that a Snail was just a Snail," said Reddy, shaking his head. "Yes, sir, I used to think that a Snail was just a Snail. I hadn't the least idea that he had a lot of relatives. Well, live and learn, live and learn. This seashore certainly is a wonderful place."

"It is the finest place in all the Great World," declared Graywing. And he really meant it.

TEN-RIBBED SNAIL.
Chrysodomus decemcostatus.

ROCK SNAILS.
Thais lapillus.

Epitonium lineatum.

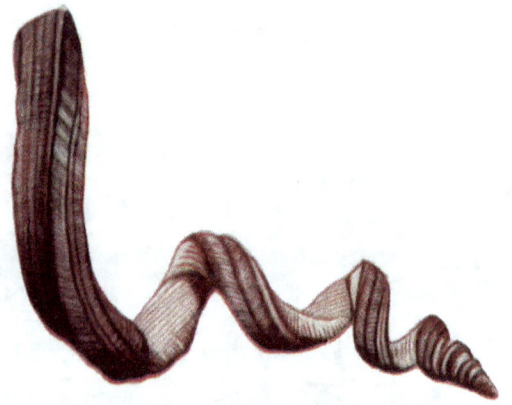

Vermicularia spirata.

XXXI. Reddy Learns About Some Seaweeds

Now that Reddy Fox was beginning to use his eyes as they were meant to be used, and really to see things, he became curious concerning many matters which, ever since he had come to the seashore, he had passed over as of no interest at all. Always along the beach were patches of seaweed. Usually just above high-water mark the seaweed lay in rolled masses, black and uninteresting-looking, where it had been dried out by the sun. After a hard storm great masses would be rolled up on the beach. Reddy always investigated these, because he was almost sure to find curious and interesting things tangled in the seaweed. But to the seaweed itself he gave no heed.

That the seaweed itself might be worth knowing something about never occurred to Reddy until one day from behind the sand dunes he watched a man going along the beach and every few minutes stopping to pick up something which he put in a basket. Naturally, Reddy's curiosity was aroused right away.

"I wonder what he is getting," muttered Reddy. "It can't be fishes, for I have already been along the beach and there were no fishes. It can't be Clams. I don't see what it can be."

The man continued along the beach, every now and then stooping to pick up something. Reddy kept his eyes on him, growing more curious every minute. Finally he saw the man drop something from his basket. Reddy kept his eyes on this, and when at last the man had disappeared, Reddy slipped out from behind the sand dunes and ran over to examine the thing that had fallen from the basket.

"It is nothing but a piece of seaweed," muttered Reddy in

disappointment, and was about to turn away when it occurred to him that it was a very curious thing that that man should be picking up seaweed. He turned back to look more closely at that little piece. It was different from the masses of seaweed about it. It was almost white with a pinkish tinge and had a flattened stem; this forked and broadened out in a leaflike way, the outer edges being irregular. It was rather pretty. But still it was seaweed and what that man could have been picking it up for was more than Reddy could imagine.

"What good is it?" said Reddy aloud, as he poked it over.

"No good to you or to me," said Graywing the Gull, as he alighted near by. "But these humans seem to have a use for it. They are forever coming along here and picking it up to carry away. What they do it for, I don't know, but it is always just that one kind. So it must be good for something."

It *was* good for something. Both Reddy and Graywing would have been much surprised had they known just why those bits of seaweed were so carefully picked up. You see, it was a very special kind of seaweed called Irish Moss, which is used along the seashore for making blanc-mange, and very delicious blanc-mange it makes.

Reddy began to poke around in a mass of wet seaweed to see if he could find another bit that the man had overlooked. "What *is* this stuff, anyway?" said Reddy. "And where does it come from?"

"It grows on the bottom of the ocean," replied Graywing, answering the last question first. "Did it ever occur to you that all sorts of plants grow in the ocean, just as plants grow on land?"

This was a new idea to Reddy and he looked up with interest. "No," said he, "it never did occur to me. In fact, I never thought anything about it. Now you speak of it, I have seen plenty of plants growing in fresh water and I suppose there is no reason why they shouldn't grow in salt water."

"No reason in the world," replied Graywing. "Just look at the mass of seaweed that is hanging to that rock over there in the water."

It was a big rock and the outgoing tide had left exposed much of it that at high tide would be under water. Hanging from the

DULSE.
Rhodymenia palmata.

IRISH MOSS.
Chondrus crispus.

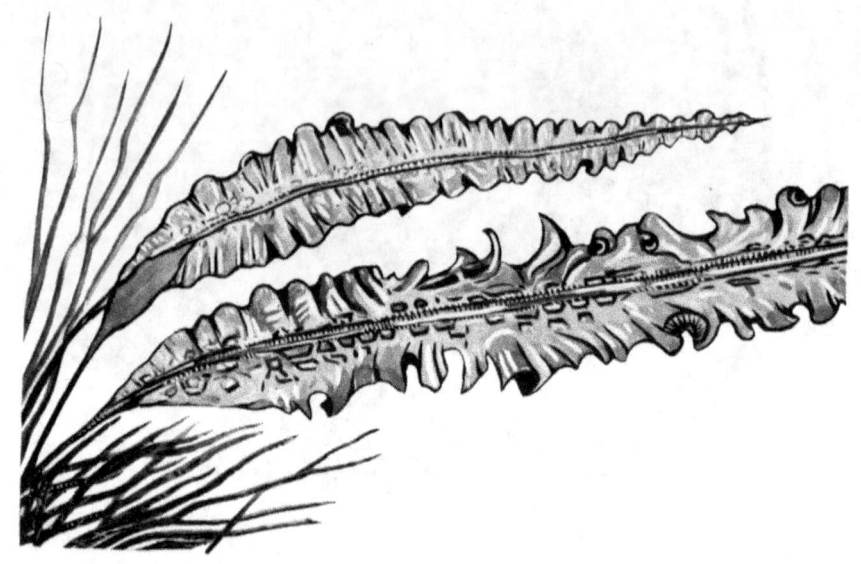

A COMMON SEAWEED.
Laminaria saccharina.

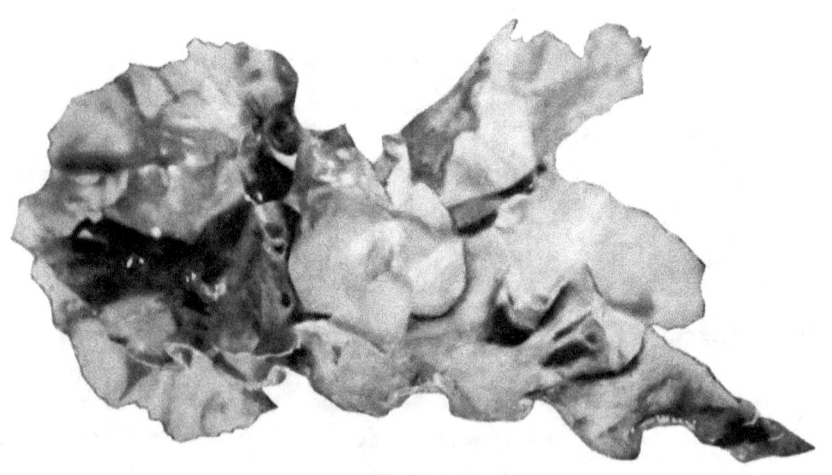

SEAWEED.
Ulva latissima.

lower side was a great mass of plants, those above water hanging straight down and those below the water line floating out and swaying back and forth with the movement of the water.

"It is just like that everywhere along the coast," explained Graywing. "A lot of those plants are attached to the rock and others grow in deep water from the bottom. That growing out there on that rock is one of the most common kinds of seaweed along the northern coast, wherever it is rocky. Here is a lot of it washed up. See all those little swellings on it?"

Reddy nodded. "I've often wondered what those were," said he. "Are they a sort of fruit?"

"No," replied Graywing, "they are what make the seaweed float. They are full of air. There are two kinds of rockweed right here in front of us. See, this one is rather broad, with those little air sacs in pairs right along the main stem. And this one here is more slender and the little air sacs seem to be a part of the main stem and its branches."

There was one thing about the first of the rockweeds that Graywing had pointed out that Graywing couldn't know, but which is rather interesting. Iodine, which mother uses to put on a cut or a bad bruise, is made from this rockweed.

"All these plants are tough, leathery things, aren't they?" remarked Reddy. "Just look at this one."

Out of the mass before him Reddy had dragged a long, leathery string. It might have been ten feet long, though sometimes this particular kind gets to be forty feet long. It didn't look like a plant at all, for it had no branches. But it *was* a plant, one of the seaweeds, and, as Reddy said, it was leathery. Graywing glanced at it. "You ought to see that growing, Reddy," said he. "When I have been flying over the water I have looked down and seen that kind growing like grass. It looked for all the world like a field of grass growing under water. You said a minute ago that it is all leathery. How about this?"

Graywing picked up in his bill what looked like a bunch of fine, dull-green plumes. It didn't look leathery at all. Instead of being leathery in appearance, it was feathery.

Meanwhile, Reddy had been poking around and now pulled out what looked very much like a broad ribbon. It had a stem several inches long, while the greenish-brown ribbon itself was several feet long. It was what is called a Sea Tangle. He was beginning to find some pleasure in seeing how many kinds of these queer sea plants he could find. Most of them were green or black, but presently he pounced on one that was somewhat the color of his own coat. That is to say, it was red. He called Graywing's attention to the color.

"Oh," said Graywing, "that's nothing. There are many red seaweeds and some of them are very pretty. It really is too bad, Reddy, that you cannot fly; then you could look down in the water and see how many beautiful things there are that cannot be seen from the land. These seaweeds washed up on the beach are not particularly pretty, but growing in the water some of them are quite lovely, especially when many are growing together. By the way, here is a red seaweed that Men use for food. Anyway, I have seen them chewing it, so I suppose they must use it for food."

Graywing had picked up a small plant, which was of a dark purplish-red. It was fan-shaped, but cut into several irregular parts. Graywing was right in saying that he had seen men chewing it. It was Dulse, and it is collected, dried and sold to people who like it. Reddy came over and tasted of it. He turned up his nose. "I don't think much of it," said he. "I would have to be pretty hungry to eat that."

"Every one to his taste," chuckled Graywing. "I don't think much of it, myself. But then, there are many things those humans eat that I don't think much of. Speaking of eating, I'm getting hungry. I think I'll go fishing, if you'll excuse me."

Reddy himself was getting hungry. He suddenly lost interest in seaweeds. His nose had brought him the odor of a fish up ahead. He promptly followed the guidance of his nose and in a few moments came to a fish that had been washed up. It was just the right size to carry nicely. Reddy picked it up and trotted away over to the sand dunes. In among these dunes he could enjoy his meal in comfort, whereas on the open beach he was always a bit nervous.

SEAWEED.
Chorda filum.

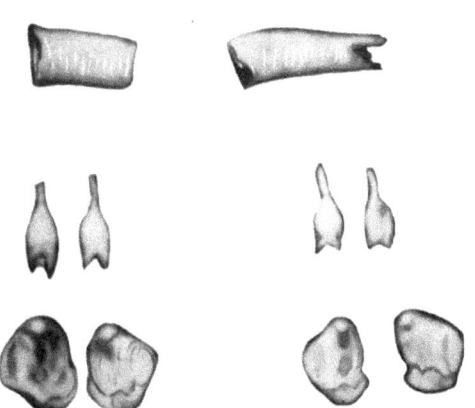

SHIPWORM OR TEREDO.
Teredo navalis.

XXXII. Reddy Finds Himself Mistaken

Reddy Fox was on the beach and, as usual, he was looking for something. He would trot from place to place, stopping to pull over the seaweed, or look into a little pool, or perhaps try to dig out a Crab that had burrowed in the sand. Jimmy Skunk was also on the beach looking for things, but he didn't trot from place to place. He ambled along in the laziest manner. You know, Jimmy seldom hurries. He believes in taking his time. He always insists that nothing is gained by hurrying.

Presently Jimmy came to a little pool of water. It was a very small pool. It had been left by the outgoing tide. Jimmy looked into it to see if there was anything of interest in it. There was. A curious little creature was swimming about. Jimmy glanced at it carelessly and his first thought was that it was a Minnow, which you know is a little fish. Then, to his great surprise, he discovered that it had legs, and no Minnow has legs.

Reddy Fox saw Jimmy looking down in the pool and hurried over to join him.

"What have you found this time, Jimmy?" asked Reddy.

"You tell me," replied Jimmy. "I don't know, but perhaps you do. Somehow, it has a sort of familiar look."

Reddy looked down in the pool and at the first glimpse he too thought it was a Minnow. Then he saw the legs and knew it couldn't be a Minnow. "I wish," said he, "that that fellow would stay still long enough for us to have a good look at him."

As if he had heard and understood—which of course he hadn't—the little swimmer stopped. He was perfectly still now on the bottom. He was just about the color of the sand. At once Reddy saw that there were two long feelers growing out from his head, like the feelers of a Lobster. There were no big pinching claws, but there were legs much like the legs of a Lobster and the body and tail were like those of a Lobster. It was about two inches long.

"Pooh!" exclaimed Reddy. "Don't you know what that is? That is one of Big Claw's children. That is a young Lobster. I should think that any one would know that just to look at him."

Jimmy shook his head. "I think you are wrong," said he.

"I think I am right," insisted Reddy. "If that isn't a young Lobster, then there isn't such a thing."

"Where is a young Lobster?" inquired a voice right over their heads. And they looked up to discover Graywing the Gull hovering just over them. "Where is a young Lobster?" he repeated.

"He's right down there on the sand in the middle of this little pool," said Reddy.

"I don't see any young Lobster," declared Graywing.

"Don't talk to me about not using one's eyes!" exclaimed Reddy. "He is right down there on the sand. Probably you don't see him because he is so much the color of the sand. Jimmy and I can see him."

Graywing shook his head. "No," said he, "you can't see any young Lobster down in that pool."

"We can too! Can't we, Jimmy?" Reddy exclaimed angrily.

"We can see something that looks as if it might be a young Lobster," replied Jimmy, "but all along I've had an idea that it isn't. Probably Neighbor Graywing can tell us what it is."

"You have forgotten that he doesn't see it," said Reddy.

"I didn't say that I didn't see anything down there," said Graywing. "I can see what you see down there, but it isn't a young Lobster. That is where you have made a mistake, Reddy. Big Claw the Lobster wouldn't own one of those fellows as one of his children. You see, that fellow is fully grown."

"What?" exclaimed Reddy, showing the surprise he felt.

"That fellow is fully grown," repeated Graywing, "and, of course, there never was a fully grown Lobster as small as that. You are looking at something else altogether."

Reddy had had his head turned away from the little pool while Graywing was speaking. Now he once more looked into the pool. "He's gone!" he exclaimed. "He isn't there! Did you catch him while I wasn't looking?" Reddy's eyes were full of suspicion as he looked at Graywing.

"How could I," retorted Graywing, "without you seeing me? You were looking right at me all the time."

"But he isn't there," protested Reddy. "There isn't a thing for him to hide under, and I tell you he isn't there!"

"Oh, yes, he is!" spoke up Jimmy Skunk. "I can see him. Do you see that little pebble down there? Look just to the right of it. You'll see that fellow's eyes and feelers. The rest of him is in the sand. I saw him go in."

"Good for you, Jimmy!" exclaimed Graywing. "He is pretty apt to do that thing if he is at all frightened. I'll tell you something more about him. Now, he is just about the color of that sand. If he should swim out where the bottom is mud instead of sand, he would become dark-colored. He has a way of becoming very much like his surroundings in color. I am told that some of them turn green when they are surrounded by green seaweed, and red when they are surrounded by red seaweed."

"You haven't told us who he is," protested Reddy.

"Oh, haven't I?" exclaimed Graywing. "Excuse me. He is what is called a Shrimp,—the Common Shrimp. The family is represented all up and down the coast. This fellow is very good eating, but there is a member of the family 'way down south that is even better eating."

"Why is it better eating?" asked Reddy.

"Because it is bigger," explained Graywing. "This fellow is only a bite, but the one down south is a whole mouthful. He grows to be three times as long as this one. Down there men catch them just as they catch Lobsters up here. Sometimes they are called Prawns, but Shrimp is the usual name."

Graywing walked along the shore. A short distance away was another tiny pool left by the tide. He stopped beside it and looked into it. "Come over here," he called. Reddy and Jimmy went over at once. "There's another member of the family," said Graywing.

"I see him!" cried Reddy. "He is smaller than that other one."

Graywing nodded. "Yes," said he, "he is quite a bit smaller. This fellow is called the Common Prawn. If you'll notice, his legs

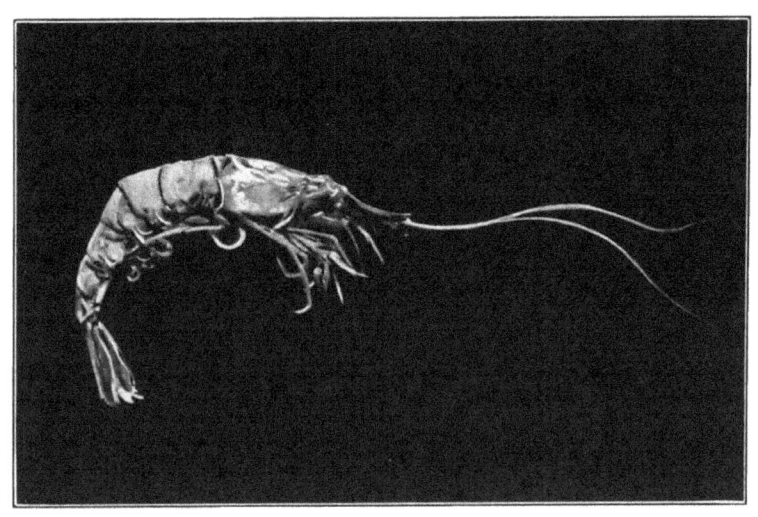

COMMON SAND SHRIMP.
Crangon vulgaris.

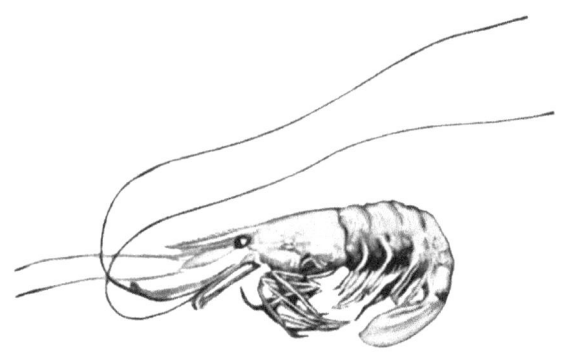

COMMON PRAWN.
Palaemonetes vulgaris.

are more slender than the other's. So are those feelers smaller than the feelers of that fellow back at the other pool. This fellow as a rule likes a muddy bottom. You'll find lots of them where the water is only slightly salt, as where creeks and rivers run into the ocean. By the way, that one that you found first, back there in the other pool, sometimes gets left on the beach when the tide goes out."

"He ought to be easy to catch then," said Jimmy Skunk.

"He might be for you, because you are a good digger," replied Graywing. "He isn't for me, unless I happen to be on hand just when he is left by the water. He promptly digs in and it doesn't take him long. Then he waits for the tide to come in again. Did you notice how both of these you have last seen swim?"

Reddy nodded. "Just like the Lobster," said he.

"That's it," said Graywing. "They swim backward. But you'll notice that when they walk along the bottom they walk forward, and that is like a Lobster too."

"Well," said Reddy, "they may not be Lobsters. Of course, they are not, if you say so. But just the same, I shall always think of them as little Lobsters."

" 'Way, 'way down south lives, to my mind, the prettiest of the Shrimps," said Graywing. "He is a spiny little chap and he has three bands of bright scarlet across the body. Sometimes he is found quite far north, but he is most at home in the south.

"Then there is another little member of the family called the Featherfooted Shrimp," continued Graywing. "He has spines on the sides of his body and feathery hairs on his legs and feelers. He is brown, and I see him most often in winter. Well, I guess it is time for me to be moving along. Talking about these Shrimps has given me an appetite. So long, Reddy. So long, Jimmy." Graywing gave a little hop into the air and away he flew out over the water. A moment or two later they saw him dart down to the water and come up with a little fish in his bill.

XXXIII. Reddy Finds Graywing in Trouble

It was early in the morning. Reddy Fox came up over the sand dunes and looked out across the beach to the sea. It was calm. It was so calm that it was glassy. The tide had just turned to come in. Right in front of Reddy was a long sandbar. Out in the water off the end of this sandbar Reddy's sharp eyes at once saw something white on the water.

"It must be Graywing the Gull," thought Reddy, who often had seen Graywing swimming, or resting on the water. Reddy looked down the beach and up the beach. No one was in sight. His eyes once more returned to that white spot on the water. Then he noticed that it seemed to be moving queerly. Every now and then a pair of wings would lift and flap. It was Graywing, beyond a doubt. But though he flapped and flapped his wings, he did not rise from the water.

Reddy stared long and hard. "I never saw Graywing act like that before," he muttered. "I wonder what he's doing out there. I believe I'll run out and get a little nearer."

So Reddy trotted out to the beginning of the sandbar and then out along the sandbar until he reached the very end. Then he stood and stared. It was Graywing out there beyond any question, but there was something wrong with him. Graywing kept plunging his head under water. He was back to Reddy, so that Reddy could not see his head, excepting from the back. It would be lifted and then plunged back and there would be a little splash. Every time that Graywing lifted his head a little, he would beat his wings.

"Something is wrong with Graywing," thought Reddy. "He

CORAL SHRIMP.
Stenopus hispidus.

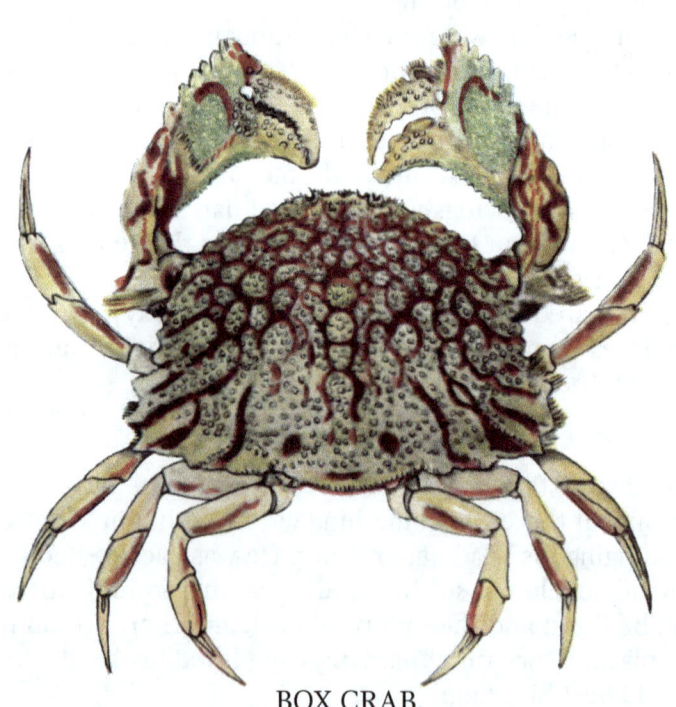

BOX CRAB.
Calappa flammea.

must be hurt! He is trying to fly and cannot. I wonder if some one with a dreadful gun has shot him. Certainly there is something very much out of the way with Graywing. I'll speak to him."

So Reddy barked sharply two or three times. It was so still that morning his bark could be heard a long distance. He knew that it must have carried far beyond Graywing. But Graywing paid no attention. That wasn't like Graywing. It wasn't a bit like him. Reddy began to feel uneasy. There was a mystery about Graywing's actions, and Reddy doesn't like mysteries. So intent was he on watching Graywing that he paid no attention to anything else until he felt the water creeping around his feet. The tide was coming in. Then he realized that Graywing was coming in with it.

"If I wait long enough, perhaps he'll come ashore and then I can find out about it," thought Reddy. He backed up a short distance and sat down. Presently he saw Screamer the Tern flying up along the shore. Reddy always liked to watch Screamer, with his white coat, black cap, and forked tail. Sometimes he is called the Mackerel Gull, but he is a Tern, not a Gull. As usual, Screamer was making his presence known by his somewhat harsh voice. It would be impossible for Screamer to keep his tongue still for very long at a time.

Suddenly Screamer discovered Graywing and began to fly faster as he headed toward him. And how he did scream now! In a few moments a lot of his friends and relatives began to appear, hurrying towards the scene. In almost no time at all there was a whole flock of Terns wheeling and turning above Graywing, all screaming at the top of their lungs. It reminded Reddy very much of the way he had often seen Blacky the Crow call all his relatives when there was something interesting or exciting.

Meanwhile, Graywing was slowly drifting nearer the shore as the tide came in. Once more Reddy had to back up to keep from getting his feet wet. Graywing had turned now, so that once in a while Reddy got a side view of him. It seemed as if Graywing had something big in his bill which he wouldn't let go of. Reddy wondered if he had caught a fish too big for him to lift. Graywing was doing a lot of splashing, so that Reddy was unable to get a good view of that thing Graywing had. With every minute he grew more curious. It was a queer performance. And, my, how excited those Terns were! They would swoop down close to Graywing, but none touched him. Reddy did wish that Graywing would get ashore, so that he might see what it was that was giving him so much trouble.

In all the excitement Reddy had forgotten his usual watchfulness. So it was that he did not see a man coming along the beach until the man was very near the beginning of the sandbar. Then Reddy happened to turn. Instantly he forgot all about Graywing. In his haste he almost turned a back somersault and away he raced back along that sandbar, across the beach and disappeared behind the sand dunes. Once out of sight of the man, Reddy stopped. Then very cautiously he crept back to a place from which he could peep through the grass on the edge of a sand dune. He was much relieved to see that the man had no terrible gun.

By this time the man had started out along the sandbar. Reddy looked over to Graywing, still struggling in the water. The Terns were already moving farther out. Why didn't Graywing let go of that thing and fly to safety? He didn't. He continued to flap his wings and splash and paid no attention to that man.

Then Reddy saw a most amazing thing. That man reached the end of the sandbar and waited a few minutes. Presently he waded out into the water and stooping picked up Graywing the Gull. Then he turned and waded ashore with Graywing in his arms. Reddy could see that Graywing still held fast to something with his bill. The man brought him up on the beach and sat down. He put Graywing down on the sand and got something from his pocket. Graywing continued to flap helplessly. The man opened a big knife he had taken from his pocket. Then he once more picked up Graywing. Reddy couldn't see just what he was doing, but he seemed to be using that big knife.

"He must be killing Graywing," thought Reddy. "Poor Graywing!"

For some little time the man was very busy. But at last he put the knife down, then very gently he set Graywing on his feet. Graywing stood motionless for a moment or two. Then, slowly, he flew away as if it were a great effort and he was very, very

SURF CLAM OR SEA CLAM.
Spisula solidissima.

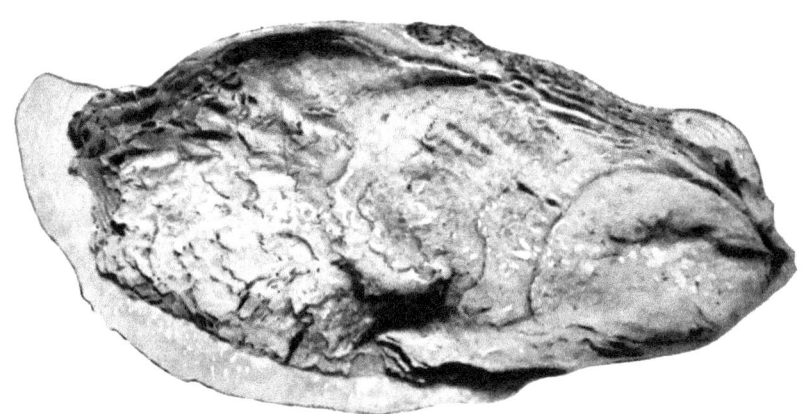

COMMON OYSTER.
Ostrea virginica.

tired. He flew to a rock only a short distance away,—a rock that was out in the water. There he alighted, and the man watched him. For a long time Graywing stood on that rock. At last, apparently rested, he once more spread his big wings and flew away.

The man appeared to be looking at whatever it was Graywing had held in his bill. Finally he tossed it aside, got up and went off down the beach. Reddy watched him until he had disappeared. Then Reddy trotted down to look at the thing the man had tossed aside. When he got there his eyes opened very wide. It wasn't a fish as he had supposed it was. It was a Clam. But such a Clam! Reddy hadn't dreamed that a Clam could grow so big. And such a shell as it had! It was open now, for the man had forced it open. Reddy was tempted to eat the Clam out of the shell, but the fact that that man had been handling it made him suspicious. Finally he trotted off down the beach to look for a fish, for he was beginning to get hungry.

It was some time later when Reddy returned that way. To his surprise there stood Graywing beside that great Clam. Reddy hurried over at once. He noticed immediately that the shell was empty now. He looked at Graywing inquiringly.

"I'm even with him now," said Graywing.

"How so?" asked Reddy, looking puzzled.

"I've eaten him," declared Graywing.

"But how is that getting even with him?" persisted Reddy. "You caught him in the first place, didn't you?"

"No," replied Graywing, "he caught me."

"What?" cried Reddy, and on his face was the most surprised look that ever a Fox wore.

"He caught me," repeated Graywing. "I have heard of such a thing happening to a member of my family before, but I never expected it to happen to me. He was lying partly buried in the sand in shallow water and his shell was partly open. I thought I could pull him out. But he was too quick for me. He closed his shell on my bill and he was so strong that I couldn't get him off. He was so heavy that I couldn't fly up with him. I guess if that man hadn't come along, I would have starved to death, or else would have been drowned. Just look at my bill!"

Reddy looked. He could see where Graywing's bill had been

badly hurt by the pinching of those two halves of the big Clam's shell. Reddy looked down at one half of that big shell. "I didn't suppose," said he, "that a Clam ever grew as big as that."

"This kind does," replied Graywing. "This is a Clam you have never seen before. It is called the Surf Clam. Some folks call it the Sea Clam. It lives out on sandy places where the water covers it most of the time. It doesn't burrow into the sand very deep, but lives right near the surface and is sometimes washed in by storms. I should have known enough to leave it alone. As it is, I guess I'm a lucky bird."

"I guess you are," replied Reddy.

XXXIV. Some Curious Worms

THERE WAS one little ledge of rocks which even at high tide was seldom covered with water. Reddy Fox used to like to go out on that ledge, for from it he could look down into the water and see many curious things which could not be seen unless one were looking directly down. Out there he could see things swimming, and often he wondered what they were. Sometimes he found out and sometimes there was no one to tell him what he wanted to know.

Early one morning Reddy saw Graywing the Gull sitting on the outer end of this ledge of rocks. Reddy carefully made his way out along the ledge until he was almost out to where Graywing stood.

"It's a fine morning," said Graywing.

"It is, indeed," replied Reddy. "Have you seen anything of interest this morning?"

"Nothing of special interest to me," replied Graywing. "I've seen some things which might be of interest to you, but you were not here and now they are not here. What are you looking at?"

Reddy was staring intently into the water and appeared to be paying no attention to Graywing. Nevertheless, he heard what Graywing said. "I don't know what I'm looking at," replied Reddy, "but it is very curious. I have been trying to make up my mind whether or not it is alive. I believe it is. But what it is I haven't the slightest idea. It seems to be swimming, yet it isn't a fish. At least, I don't think it is."

Graywing moved over where he could see too.

"Oh," said he after the first glance, "that is a Worm."

Reddy looked up quickly to see if Graywing really meant that, or if he were joking. The thing moving along down in the water there was perhaps six feet long and about three quarters of an inch wide. It was flat like a strip of ribbon, and in color was yellowish-white. The two ends were somewhat pointed. It was moving along through the water somewhat in the manner of a snake. "Do you mean that that thing is a Worm?" cried Reddy. "It doesn't look like a Worm to me."

"Do you think I would have told you it is a Worm, if it were not?" demanded Graywing somewhat crossly, for he was a little bit put out.

"No, Graywing, no, of course I don't," Reddy hastened to reply. "Somehow, it seems queer to think of that thing as a Worm. It doesn't look like any Worm I've ever seen."

"Just the same, it is one," replied Graywing. "He's probably going ashore to burrow into the sand. If you follow along you may see him dig in. He is called the Ribbon-Worm."

"That's a good name for him," chuckled Reddy, as he moved along towards the beach, keeping that big, flat Worm in sight all the time.

When the Worm reached the place where the water and the land met with the tide out, it began to bore its way into the sand. It was surprising how fast that long body disappeared from view. In a very short time it had entirely disappeared.

"Well, I never!" exclaimed Reddy. "I never did! I wouldn't have believed there could be a Worm so long and flat and wide as that. Ribbon-Worm is certainly a good name."

"There is another Ribbon-Worm that lives along this beach," said Graywing. "It isn't anywhere near as big as this one, and it is of different color. It is dull red and it lives in the sand near the low-water mark. They call it the Pink Ribbon-Worm. What's the matter with your ear, Reddy?"

Reddy was sitting down and scratching his right ear with his right hindfoot. There was a funny expression on his face. "I'm just trying to scratch the ignorance out of my head," said he, and chuckled. "You see, it is a new idea to me that Worms can live in salt water and in the sands of the seashore. This is about the last place in the world I would think of, to come looking for Worms."

"Ho!" exclaimed Graywing. "There are all sorts of Worms

CLAM WORM.
Nereis pelagica.

SEA MOUSE.
Aphrodita aculeata.

around salt water. Haven't you ever seen a Clam Worm? Of course you have. Every one who goes to the seashore sees a Clam Worm, if he uses his eyes."

"I haven't," replied Reddy. "At least, I don't think I have. If I have, I didn't know what it was when I saw it."

"Well, I shall have to show you one sometime," replied Graywing.

"There's no time like the present," said Reddy. "I should like to see one. Why is it called a Clam Worm?"

"I don't know, Reddy. I really don't know," said Graywing. "Perhaps it is because they are likely to be found in muddy places, such places as Clams like. I've often seen men dig them up when they were digging Clams."

"Do they live in the ground, the same as Earth-Worms do on dry land?" inquired Reddy.

"Something the same," replied Graywing, "only you don't find them where it is dry. You follow me; perhaps I'll find one for you."

Graywing took to his wings and slowly flew along down towards a muddy flat where Reddy had often seen men digging Clams. Reddy trotted after him. Graywing alighted on the flat and began to walk about. Suddenly his head darted down. When he lifted it a second later, there was something wriggling in his bill. Reddy hurried over. He saw at once that Graywing held a Worm. But it was unlike any Worm he had ever seen. It was widest near the middle, but not very much wider. It was flat on the under side, but the upper side was rounded. It was about five inches long and at first glance seemed to be reddish-brown.

Then as Graywing dropped it, Reddy noticed that it seemed to have changing colors, such as are seen on some birds. You will see it on a pigeon's breast. As the sun strikes the feathers, the colors seem to change. Things that change color in this way are said to be iridescent. This Worm that Reddy was looking at was iridescent. At the head were ten tiny feelers and there were four black eyes. But the thing that interested Reddy right away was the fact that this Worm seemed to be made up of a series of rings and each ring had a pair of what he called feet. But instead of being on the under part of the body, as a caterpillar's feet are, they were on the sides of the body, which made the Worm look as if it were fringed on both sides. You see, these little feet were not for use in walking or crawling. They were for use in swimming, for at night this Worm comes out and swims about. That is, it comes out on calm nights in the summer.

Reddy looked at Graywing inquiringly.

"There's your Clam Worm," said Graywing. "This is the most common one here, but there are a couple of others. One is more than twice as long as this fellow, but in general they look a good deal alike. Now you have seen a Ribbon-Worm and a Clam Worm. But there are several other Worms you ought to see. If you use your eyes you will be likely to see some of them. They are quite well worth looking for."

"Thank you, Graywing," replied Reddy. "I think I am beginning to use my eyes better than I used to."

"I think you are," said Graywing.

"And I have you to thank for it," continued Reddy. "I don't like to think of how much I should have missed if I had not made your acquaintance."

Graywing looked pleased. You know it always pleases people to be appreciated.

"If you should find any of those other Worms," said Reddy, "and I happen to be anywhere in sight, just give me a call. You know your voice carries a long distance."

"I will do that," said Graywing. "I certainly will do that."

Reddy glanced down where the Worm had been. It was not there. "Where did that fellow go to?" he exclaimed.

"Down into the mud, I suspect," chuckled Graywing.

Reddy sighed. "I wanted another good look at him," said he. "I had never supposed that a Worm could be beautiful, but those changing colors on that fellow were beautiful."

"Oh, that is nothing," said Graywing. "Some of the Sea Worms are very lovely when you see them in the right light. I must be going now. I'll see you some other time, Reddy."

"So long and thank you," replied Reddy.

XXXV. Reddy Finds Some More Worms

"If any one had told me that I would ever be interested in Worms," said Reddy Fox, "I would have laughed at them."

"I wouldn't," said Jimmy Skunk. "Some Worms are very good eating. But you don't find Worms on the seashore. What are you chuckling about, Reddy Fox?"

"I've seen the biggest Worms I've ever seen anywhere right here at the seashore," declared Reddy. "Come with me and perhaps I can show you some."

Reddy led Jimmy over to the nearest mud flat and began to poke around. Presently he found a Clam Worm. Jimmy Skunk looked the surprise he felt. It pleased Reddy greatly to be able to show Jimmy Skunk something.

"That's nothing," said Reddy. "You should see a Ribbon-Worm. I saw one yesterday. I wouldn't have known it was a Worm if Graywing hadn't told me. Listen, there is Graywing calling now!"

They looked up along the beach and, sure enough, there was Graywing standing on a rock and calling to them. "He has found something," said Reddy. "We'll go up there and see what it is."

The Rock on which Graywing was sitting was beside a little tide pool.

"Did you ever see a Mouse?" inquired Graywing.

"Did we ever see a Mouse!" exclaimed Reddy. "Why, before I came down to the seashore I pretty nearly lived on Mice."

Jimmy Skunk was slowly licking his lips. "I wouldn't mind finding a nest of young Mice right now," said he.

"I mean, have you ever seen a Sea Mouse?" said Graywing.

Both Reddy and Jimmy looked interested at once. "No," said Reddy, "but if a Sea Mouse is as good eating as a land Mouse, I should like to see one right away."

"There is one right down in this little pool," said Graywing.

Reddy and Jimmy looked into the pool eagerly and a look of disappointment crossed their faces as they saw what Graywing was looking at.

"That isn't a Mouse!" exclaimed Reddy indignantly.

Graywing chuckled that throaty little chuckle of his. "That's true, Reddy," said he. "It isn't a real Mouse, but it is called a Sea Mouse; though why, I haven't the least idea. It isn't even related to the Mouse family. It is a Worm."

Reddy looked down at the curious little creature in the water and then looked up at Graywing. "What are you talking about, Graywing?" he demanded. "That is no more a Worm than it is a Mouse."

"Oh, yes, it is!" replied Graywing. "When you first saw that Ribbon-Worm you didn't believe it was a Worm. I'll admit that this one doesn't look like a Worm, but it is one, just the same. It is just luck that you have a chance to see him in here. He must have been washed up by the water and left in here when the tide went out. He lives in the mud, but once in a while he gets washed out."

"But," protested Jimmy Skunk, who had been intently watching the curious little creature, "he isn't shaped at all like a Worm, and he looks as if he had a fur coat. Whoever heard of a Worm with a fur coat?"

Graywing was enjoying showing off this new find. It was about three inches long and half as wide, oval in shape, and the sides and back were covered with bristles. As the sun struck these bristles, they were bright green and red and yellow, making the little Sea Mouse very beautiful. On the head was a pair of little feelers. It certainly didn't look like a Mouse and it certainly didn't look like a Worm, but when Reddy and Jimmy discovered that it had about forty pairs of legs, they agreed that it might be a member of the Worm family. And this was a fact. While they were watching it, it burrowed down into the sandy mud at the bottom of a little tide pool and disappeared.

"Are there other kinds of Worms?" inquired Jimmy Skunk.

"Many," replied Graywing, "and some of them are very interesting and curious. Wait a minute, and perhaps I can find another one for you."

RIBBON WORM.
Cerebratulus lacteus.

PINK RIBBON WORM.
Micrura leidyi.

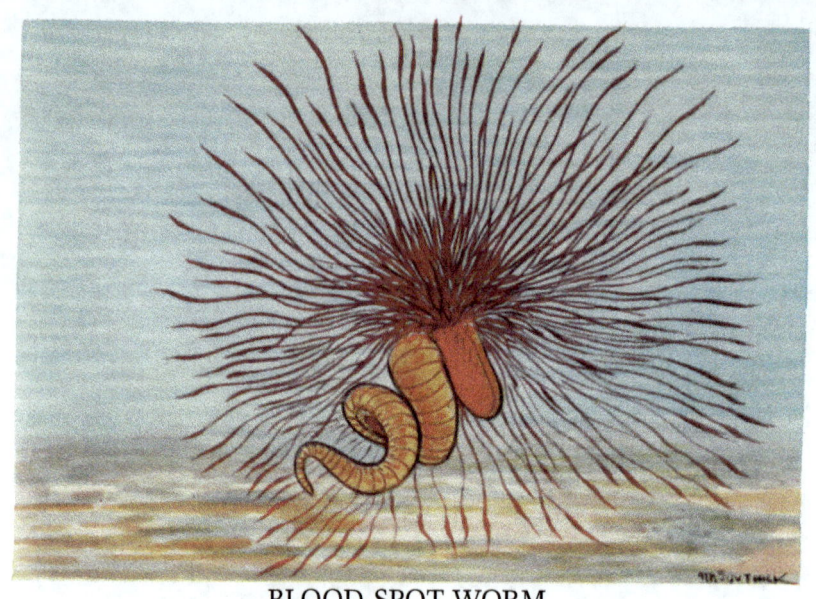

BLOOD-SPOT WORM.
Polycirrus eximius.

FRINGED WORM.
Cirratulus grandis.

Graywing spread his wings and flew slowly along the edge of the water, looking down intently. He had gone but a short distance when he dropped down on the beach and called. Reddy and Jimmy hurried over to join him. In a little pool of water lay half of a Scallop shell. "Do you see that shell down there?" said Graywing.

"Of course we see it," replied Reddy. "What of it?"

"Do you see anything out of the way about it?" asked Graywing.

Reddy and Jimmy looked more closely. "Yes," said Reddy, "it looks as if something had grown on it, the way Barnacles grow on rocks, only these things are sort of worm shape. They look as if they were made of shell. Are they?"

"Well, they are made of something very like shell," replied Graywing. "They are hollow and they were made by Worms. Each one of those little tubes is really sort of a house for a Worm. If you'll sit perfectly still, perhaps you'll have a chance to see one of those Worms come out."

So Reddy and Jimmy sat perfectly still, with their eyes fixed on that shell in the water. It was some time before anything happened, and they were beginning to get a little impatient. Suddenly, what seemed like a little door opened at one end of one of those tubes and out came a lot of little feathery feelers. They were really what are called gills. Reddy held his breath. So did Jimmy Skunk. Graywing didn't move, but his eyes twinkled. Those little feathery gills began to move about in the water. Reddy and Jimmy kept hoping that the owner of that funny little house would come farther out, but he didn't. Finally Reddy moved and instantly those little feathery gills disappeared and the door was closed. Reddy looked up at Graywing. "Well?" said he.

"That was a Shell Worm," explained Graywing. "He built that little house and he'll live in it until he dies."

"Doesn't he ever leave it?" asked Jimmy Skunk.

"Never," replied Graywing.

"Then how does he get his food?" demanded Jimmy.

"You saw those little feathery things waving around in the water, didn't you?" inquired Graywing. Then, without waiting for a reply, he continued: "There are tiny particles of food in the water and Mr. Worm washes them into his mouth with those feathery things."

RED THREAD WORM.
Lumbrineris tenuis.

OPAL WORM.
Arabella opalina.

Just then Graywing took to his wings. He was hungry and his sharp eyes had seen a little flash in the water, which he knew had been made by a small fish near the surface. So, without so much as saying good-by, he started out to go fishing. Reddy and Jimmy continued along the shore. Jimmy stopped now and then to pull over a stone. It was when he pulled over one of these which was surrounded by a little bit of water that he made a discovery. He knew it was a Worm the instant he saw it, because the body was decidedly wormlike. But at one end—he was sure it must be the head end—was a mass of fine threads, which were what are known as tentacles. These were red. They were as red as blood. The forward half of the body was also bright red. Jimmy had found what was known as the Blood-Spot Worm.

Reddy Fox did not see this one, for he had trotted on ahead and had himself made a discovery.

He had found a little hole in the sand right at the edge of the water and out of curiosity had dug it open. In doing this he brought out another Worm, different from any he had yet seen. It was four or five inches long and was yellowish in color. From all along the body extended red and yellow threads like a fringe. These threads were really gills. You will remember the Shell Worm had gills.

Reddy called to Jimmy Skunk and Jimmy hurried over.

"What have you got?" Jimmy demanded as he came up.

"A Worm," replied Reddy. "It must be a Worm, but of course I don't know what kind. If I were asked to name it, I should call it a Fringed Worm. Do you see that fringe on it?"

Reddy's name for it was quite appropriate. As a matter of fact, that is just what this particular Worm is called.

Meanwhile, Jimmy Skunk had begun to dig around a little and almost at once he brought out a Worm almost a foot long. At least, it would have been as long as that had he not broken it in digging it out. It was like a red thread, and Red Thread Worm is what it is called. Later, both Jimmy and Reddy found many of these brightly colored Worms when they were digging in sandy mud.

XXXVI. A Worm That Isn't a Worm

Lying on the beach was part of the wreck of a ship. There was part of the keel and some of the ribs. They had lain there a long time. Graywing the Gull often perched on one of the ribs that stuck up in the air. Reddy Fox was very familiar with that old wreck. At high tide it would be nearly covered with water, but at low tide Reddy could poke around the timbers which were half-buried in the sand.

To the ribs themselves Reddy had never given much attention. To him they were just pieces of water-soaked wood. He wasn't interested in water-soaked wood. So he had hardly looked at these old ship timbers. But there came a day when Reddy did become interested. He had discovered Graywing sitting on his favorite perch on top of the highest rib and had trotted over for a little friendly gossip. Reddy is like every one else, he does love to gossip once in a while. As he sat on the sand looking up at Graywing he happened to notice that there were many little holes in that old rib. He glanced at the remainder of that wreck and he discovered that the wood was full of little holes. They looked for all the world like wormholes that Reddy had often seen in dead wood on land. Graywing noticed that Reddy seemed suddenly interested.

"What are you looking at, Reddy?" said he.

"I've just noticed those little wormholes," said Reddy. "Of course, they must be wormholes, for they are just like wormholes in old wood that I have seen before. I was wondering if any of the Worms that I have seen made those holes."

"What would you say if I should tell you that they are not wormholes?" Graywing asked.

"I would say that you probably know what you are talking about, but that they look like wormholes to me," replied Reddy.

"Well, they are and they are not wormholes," said Graywing.

"Why don't you talk sense?" exclaimed Reddy, as if he were a little out of sorts. "Nothing can be and yet not be. If they are wormholes, they are wormholes. And if they are not wormholes, then they are not wormholes. That's all there is to that."

Graywing chuckled. "Of course you are right, Reddy," said he. "The things that make those holes are called Worms, but they are not Worms. They are commonly called Ship-Worms. Hardly any one calls them anything else. You will be surprised when I tell you to whom they are related."

"All right," said Reddy, "I'm ready to be surprised. To whom are these Worms that are not Worms related?"

"Clams," replied Graywing, his eyes twinkling.

"What?" cried Reddy.

"Clams," repeated Graywing.

"Honest and true?" demanded Reddy.

"Honest and true," replied Graywing.

"But how can anything related to Clams bore holes in wood, I'd like to know," said Reddy.

"I don't know how they do it, but they do it," replied Graywing. "Those fellows do an awful lot of damage. Any wood that stands in the sea very long is pretty sure to be bored full of holes. And those holes go a long way sometimes. Of course it ruins the wood."

"Of course," replied Reddy, as if he knew all about it. "I've seen wood ruined that way by Worms on land. But I still don't see how a Clam can bore into anything but the mud."

"I didn't say it was a Clam," declared Graywing. "I said it was related to the Clam."

"Well, if it is related to the Clam, it ought to have a shell," said Reddy.

"It does have," replied Graywing.

"It can't," Reddy insisted. "No, sir, it can't! Nothing with a shell could bore into a solid piece of wood."

"If you know so much about it, it is of no use for me to try to tell you anything," retorted Graywing.

"I beg your pardon, Graywing. I beg your pardon," cried Reddy hastily. "I didn't mean it that way. I don't know anything about it. I said what I said because it is so hard to believe that anything with a shell could possibly make a hole like one of those, let alone get into the hole after it was made. Does it live in its shell?"

"Not exactly," replied Graywing. "You see, when it starts to bore into a piece of wood it is very tiny,—no bigger than a coarse grain of sand. There are two parts to the shell, just as there are to a Clam shell. When it gets into the wood it begins to grow, so the opening that you see is smaller than the tunnel which it bores. But the shell never does get very big."

"Well, does the Worm, or Clam, or whatever it is, always live in that shell?" inquired Reddy.

"One end of it does," replied Graywing.

Reddy looked puzzled. "Just what do you mean by that?" he asked.

"Well," replied Graywing, "this borer grows in length as the tunnel it bores increases in length. As it bores in, it lines the tunnel with a shell-like substance. But this, you understand, isn't really its shell. It is just a shell lining to the tunnel."

"I understand," said Reddy, who was trying very hard to understand.

"The real shell is at the head end, while the body grows down in the tunnel as it is bored out. It makes the thing look like a Worm. Most folks think it is a Worm. So it is called the Ship-Worm. That is because it bores into ships,—wooden ships, of course. It is also called Teredo."

"I suppose," said Reddy, "that it eats the wood."

"Wrong again," replied Graywing. "It doesn't eat the wood."

"Then why does it bore into it?" asked Reddy.

"For the same reason that some Worms bore down into the ground," explained Graywing. "It bores a tunnel into the wood to make a home for itself."

"And you say it doesn't eat the wood?" repeated Reddy.

"No, it doesn't eat the wood," repeated Graywing.

"Then what does it eat?" demanded Reddy.

"Food that it finds in the water," said Graywing. "The tail end of the body, which is very much smaller than the head end, is always down near the opening of the tunnel, and there it draws in the water and finds food in it."

Reddy thought this over for a moment or two. Then he had another question to ask. "Does it ever leave the tunnel to swim about?" he inquired.

Graywing shook his head. "How can it?" he asked. "Didn't I tell you that it grows bigger after it gets inside? Naturally, it couldn't get out of that opening if it wanted to, which it doesn't."

"I hadn't thought of that," said Reddy. "No, sir, I hadn't thought of that. Of course, it couldn't get out."

"Now do you see why I called it a Worm that isn't a Worm?" demanded Graywing.

Reddy nodded. "I see," said he. "My goodness, what a lot of queer things there are in the sea! I begin to feel as if I know almost nothing about the sea."

"And that is just about what you do know," replied Graywing. "Even I, who was born where the spray from the waves was blown over me, and who have lived all my life along the seashore, know very little about the curious creatures that live in, under and around the ocean. Almost every day I learn something new."

"If I knew one tenth of what you know, Graywing, I should think I knew a lot," said Reddy. Whereat Graywing looked pleased.

XXXVII. Reddy and Jimmy Go Fishing

"What luck?" asked Reddy Fox as he met Jimmy Skunk just above the low-water mark early one morning.

Jimmy knew what he meant. "No luck," he grumbled. "I haven't found a thing to eat this morning. If a fellow could crack shells, he might find plenty, but my teeth are not good enough for that. What luck have you had?"

"Just the same," replied Reddy. "I'm almost hungry enough to try cracking one of those Clams. Hello, what is Screamer the Tern so excited about?"

Reddy and Jimmy looked towards the water. Screamer and a flock of his relatives were flying low over the water close to shore and continually darting down to touch the water. And such a screaming as there was! It was very clear that they were greatly excited by something. Reddy and Jimmy moved along in that direction. There was a sandbar running out into the water and it was along the edge of this sandbar that the Terns were continually darting down. Reddy caught a gleam of something silvery flashing in the water. He saw Screamer the Tern dart down and when he was once more in the air there was a small silvery fish in his bill.

"They are fishing!" exclaimed Reddy excitedly. "That's what they are doing,—fishing! I wish they would catch some for us."

By this time Reddy and Jimmy had reached the sandbar and before them was a most exciting scene. The water was fairly alive with small silvery fishes. They had come in a great school. No wonder the Terns were excited, for they were catching these little fishes as fast as they could dart down for them.

And the Terns were not the only ones who were fishing. Reddy every now and then got a glimpse of a big fish rushing in and snapping right and left in the midst of that school of frightened little fishes. The big fishes were driving them in.

Suddenly there was a rush of the little fishes straight towards the sandbar. So many fishes were crowded together that the water seemed to fairly boil. Dozens of them, like little silvery flashes, leaped out of water in their efforts to escape. And then a strange thing happened. Rushing heedlessly towards that sandbar dozens of these little fishes came flopping right out on the sand. Yes, sir, out they came, right in front of Reddy and Jimmy! There all around them were these little fishes turning and flopping and jumping on the sand. In a flash Reddy and Jimmy each had one. They were little fishes about six inches long, with a fin running nearly the whole length of the back, and with sharp pointed heads, the lower jaw being longer than the upper one. They were very slim—very slim indeed. One fish made no more than a bite. Some of them flopped up where the sand was packed and there Jimmy and Reddy caught several. The Terns meanwhile were swooping down and picking them up.

When there were no more to be found on the sand, Reddy turned back to the water. The great school was still there. And now, as Reddy looked, he noticed a great stirring of the sand and he suddenly discovered that those little fishes were disappearing in the sand at the bottom. He could hardly believe his eyes. "Jimmy," he cried, "they are boring down into the sand. That is as sure as you're alive! If only there wasn't water there, we could dig them out."

Every now and then a little fish would be forced out on to the sandbar and Reddy or Jimmy was almost always on hand to seize it before it could get back to the water. Meanwhile, the tide was still going out. Presently the school moved away, the Terns following it along the shore.

"Well," said Jimmy, "I guess that's the end of our fishing. My, I would have liked a few more of those fellows. Those were good eating, Reddy Fox."

Reddy smacked his lips. "I'll say so!" said he. "I had just enough to give me an appetite. I wish they would come back here."

Just then they were joined by Graywing the Gull. Graywing was in good humor. He had eaten his fill of those little fishes, too. He had caught and eaten all he could hold.

"You fellows look rather excited," said Graywing. "What is it all about?"

Reddy told him what had happened.

"I know," said Graywing. "Those were Sand Eels. They are not true Eels, but the common name for them is Sand Eels. I have just breakfasted on a lot of them myself. Did you get all you wanted?"

Reddy shook his head in a very decided way. "I did not," said he. "I could eat twice as many more. My, I wish they would come back."

"Why don't you dig some out?" inquired Graywing, and you should have seen his eyes twinkle.

"What are you talking about?" demanded Reddy.

"Sand Eels," replied Graywing.

"What was that you said about digging?" inquired Jimmy Skunk.

"I asked why you don't dig some of those Sand Eels out," repeated Graywing.

"Out of what?" interrupted Reddy.

"Out of the sand, of course," returned Graywing.

"But they are not in the sand, they are in the water," protested Reddy. "They all swam away. They are up there where Screamer and his friends are making such a racket."

"That is your mistake," said Graywing. "They are not all up there. I have an idea that there are some right under your feet this very minute."

Reddy stared at Graywing as if he hadn't understood him. "I don't know what you mean," said he.

But Jimmy Skunk had begun to dig as soon as the words were out of Graywing's mouth. He was digging in the wet sand very near the edge of the water. He had dug down only two or three inches when he gave a little grunt of satisfaction and pulled out a little fish.

I wish you could have seen the eyes of Reddy Fox. They looked as if they would pop out of his head. He looked at Jimmy Skunk, then he looked at Graywing, and then back at Jimmy Skunk. The forked tail of that little fish was just disappearing in Jimmy's mouth. Already Jimmy was starting to dig again. Then Reddy began to dig. How he did make those black paws of his fly! Reddy is a very good digger, as you know. Wet sand flew out behind him. Then he gave a little yelp of satisfaction. He had one of those little fishes!

For some time the edge of that sandbar just above the water was a lively place. Reddy and Jimmy were making the sand fly in every direction. They kicked it in each other's face. They filled each other's coat with sand. Each got in the other's way, and for a minute each would lose his temper. But every few minutes one or the other would catch a Sand Eel.

At last Jimmy Skunk admitted he had enough. "I couldn't eat another one if I tried," said he.

Reddy wasn't quite satisfied yet, so he kept on digging. But after a while he admitted that he, too, had eaten enough. Then he looked at Jimmy Skunk and Jimmy looked at him. Both began to grin. Such a looking Fox and such a looking Skunk you never saw. Their coats were wet and covered with sand. Reddy's big tail was a sorry looking sight. But they were happy. They had had the breakfast they had so wanted and it was a good breakfast.

"That is the queerest fishing I ever did in all my life," declared Reddy. "Whoever heard of digging for fish? I don't understand it yet."

"It is simple enough," said Graywing. "When those Sand Eels were driven in, a lot of them just burrowed down in the sand. That was the safest thing for them to do. Then the tide went out and left them there and you dug them out. I don't see anything queer about that."

"But wouldn't they have died buried down there in the sand?" Jimmy Skunk asked.

Graywing shook his head. "No," said he, "they would have remained there until the tide came in again. Then they would have come out."

"Just the same," declared Reddy, "I think it was a queer way of catching fishes. Did you say they are not Eels?"

"That is what I said," replied Graywing. "I have heard them called another name—Launce—and I've heard them called Lant. But most folks call them Sand Eels."

"Thanks," replied Reddy. "Now I think I'll go see if I can clean myself up a little and take a nap. This seashore certainly is a queer place. Yes, sir, it certainly is a queer place."

XXXVIII. Some Feathered Beach Folk

Reddy Fox and Jimmy Skunk had, as you know, become very well acquainted with Graywing the Herring Gull and Screamer the Common Tern. Both of these feathered folk they saw and heard every day. But there were other feathered folk whom they saw almost as often, though these little people were too shy and too busy, and perhaps a little too suspicious, to become really friendly. Almost always there would be some of them running along the beach right at the edge of the water. At low tide there would be whole parties of them out on the sandbars.

When Reddy had first come to the beach he had discovered that it was useless to try to catch any of these feathered people. They were always out in the open where there was no chance to steal up on them. So he had speedily lost all interest in them. But after a while, especially after he had begun to learn really to use his eyes, he had noticed such a difference between some of these busy little feathered folk that he became interested. After that he spent much time, when he had nothing else to do, in watching them. Occasionally he saw Peep the Least Sandpiper running along the edge of the water. But Peep spent most of his time over on the mud flats of the marshes, excepting when they were covered by high water.

It happened one morning that, as Reddy Fox sat gossiping with Graywing the Gull, a flock of Sandpipers alighted on the beach not far from them and immediately began running along the edge of the water. As a tiny wavelet would roll back, two or three of the little fellows would follow it. Then, as it broke on the beach, they would run back just ahead of it.

"It looks to me as if Peep and his friends have grown," remarked Reddy. "I've seen them often over on the mud flats, but somehow they seemed smaller there."

Graywing gave Reddy a quick glance to see if he had really meant what he said. He saw that Reddy was in earnest. He started to chuckle, but then thought better of it. "So you think those are the Sandpipers you saw on the mud flats," he remarked.

Reddy looked up with a little air of surprise. "Aren't they?" said he.

"Didn't you just say that they look bigger than Peep and his friends of the mud flats?" asked Graywing.

"It seems so to me," replied Reddy, "but I might easily be mistaken."

"You are not," said Graywing. "They are just a little bigger. Otherwise, they look very much like Peep, whom you already know. They are Peep's nearest cousins. The Peep over on the marshes is the Mud Peep, or Least Sandpiper. These here are the Semipalmated Sandpipers, but are called Sand Peep and Beach Peep."

Reddy was looking at them with new interest. Several of them were still running about, but a number of them appeared to be resting. Suddenly Reddy opened his eyes a little wider. "Look, Graywing!" he exclaimed. "Those Sandpipers must have been shot at by a hunter with a terrible gun."

"What makes you think so?" inquired Graywing.

"Don't you see for yourself?" cried Reddy. "There are one—two—three—four—five—with only one leg apiece. The other legs must have been shot off."

It was true. Five of those little birds appeared to have but one leg each. All of them were resting. But presently one of the five began to hop along on his one leg. Pretty soon two more did the same thing. Graywing said nothing, but there was a twinkle of fun in his eyes. Reddy continued to watch one of those one-legged Sandpipers. Suddenly, as if by magic, that little bird was running on two feet. Reddy actually rubbed his eyes. He hastily looked at the other one-legged Sandpipers. Another suddenly developed two legs. Such a funny expression as there was on Reddy's face as he looked at Graywing.

"That is a favorite trick of theirs," explained Graywing.

"Those missing feet were simply drawn up into their feathers. They have a way of resting on one foot. Hello, there's Beetlehead over on the sandbar!"

Reddy looked over to the bar. Running back and forth close to the water was a bird about twice the size of Peep, but quite different in appearance. The breast and sides, and throat and sides of head, were black. The forehead and sides of head above the eye and down to the upper breast were white. The rest of the lower parts were white also. The back was a mixture of gray and brown.

"I suppose that is another of the Sandpiper family," remarked Reddy.

"Wrong," replied Graywing. "Beetlehead isn't a Sandpiper at all. He is a member of the Plover family. I believe he is known as the Black-bellied Plover, but he is also called Beetlehead, Bullhead, Blackbreast and Blackheart. If you will notice, his bill isn't as slender as those of the Sandpipers."

"But he lives on the seashore," protested Reddy.

Graywing chuckled. "Why not?" he asked. "All sorts of birds live inland, so why shouldn't there be different kinds of birds along the seashore?"

This was more than Reddy could answer, so he once more turned his attention to Beetlehead. He was just in time to see Beetlehead pull a Worm out of the sand and swallow it. "Well," remarked Reddy, "I know now where some of those Sea Worms go to."

Meanwhile, Beetlehead had been joined by some more of his own kind. A moment later another flock of birds alighted near by. Reddy's eyes brightened.

"Speaking of Plovers," said he, "there is my old friend Killdeer. He and Mrs. Killdeer used to nest every spring up in an old pasture I was familiar with."

"Which one is Killdeer?" inquired Graywing.

"Why, the one with the ring around his neck," said Reddy.

"Which one?" repeated Graywing.

For the first time, Reddy noticed that there were two, each with a black collar and each with a white breast and each with a white throat and a ring of white above the black collar. He had mistaken them for the same kind of bird at first. Now, as they happened to come nearer together, he saw that one wore a dark cap, while the other had a very light-brown cap with a little band of dark color just above the forehead. The back of this one was also very light brown, whereas the back of the other one was very much darker. Before he could note other differences, Graywing spoke. "Neither one of those is Killdeer," said he. "If you will rub up your memory a little, you will recall that Killdeer has two black collars. Neither of these fellows here has but one."

Reddy looked a little crestfallen. "That's so," said he. "Now that you mention it, I do recall it. Anyway, those fellows out there must be cousins of Killdeer. They are members of the Plover family all right. What are their names?" inquired Reddy.

"Well, that one with the darkest back is called Ringneck, and the other one is also called Ringneck," explained Graywing.

"If they are different kinds of birds, how can they both have the same name?" inquired Reddy.

"They shouldn't have," said Graywing. "Of course, they shouldn't have. Fortunately, Ringneck is just a common name. The real name of the dark-backed one is Semipalmated Plover. The other one is sometimes called Pale Ringneck; also Beach Plover, Clam Bird, Butter Bird, and some other names. His proper name, however, is Piping Plover."

"Oh!" said Reddy. "They both remind me of Killdeer, but now I can see the difference. I wonder where they nest."

"On the ground," replied Graywing. "The light-colored one— the Piping Plover—makes its nest right on the beach. It isn't much of a nest. It is simply a little hollow in the sand and the eggs look much like pebbles. The other one sometimes nests on the beach, but she sometimes nests on higher ground too. Both those birds used to be shot by those two-legged creatures with terrible guns. It got so there was danger that there would soon be no more Ringnecks. But now they are not shot as they used to be."

"It's queer," remarked Reddy, "how Men seem to want to kill everything lovely. I can understand why they want to kill me, because my coat is so warm and handsome. But why they should

BLACK-BELLIED PLOVER OR BEETLE-HEAD.
Squatarola squatarola cynosurae.
SEMIPALMATED PLOVER OR LITTLE RING-NECK.
Charadrius semipalmatus.
PIPING PLOVER OR RING-NECK.
Charadrius melodus.

want to kill little feathered folk like those is beyond me. Why, one of them wouldn't make a bite. I never killed anything in my life just for the fun of killing it, but a lot of these hunters with terrible guns seem to do that very thing. I don't understand it."

A lot of other people do not understand it any more than Reddy does. The bird life of our seashore has been sadly depleted by reckless shooting.

XXXIX. The Stake Driver

WHILE REDDY Fox and Jimmy Skunk were spending most of their waking hours on the beach, Danny Meadow Mouse was content to stay on the marsh. He still had his home in the old log at the edge of the marsh and from that he had cut a lot of little paths in various directions through the coarse marsh grass. He felt that the open beach was no place for a Mouse, especially with Reddy Fox and Jimmy Skunk about.

Danny Meadow Mouse is an industrious little fellow. He was forever cutting new paths. In these little runways he felt quite safe. Sometimes he went quite a distance from home. He had one little path that led way over to the big creek that wound through the marsh. It was while he was over there at sun-up one morning that he received one of the worst frights he had had for a long time.

It was low tide, so the water in the creek was low. This made a high bank. Danny's little path, cut through the grass, led right out to the edge of this bank. He liked to sit there and look up and down the creek to see what was going on. He often went there.

This morning he had almost reached the edge of the bank when he heard a noise that made his heart jump right up in his mouth. At least, that is the way it felt to him. He stopped instantly and held his breath. Again he heard that noise. Then he turned and ran back along his little path as fast as his short little legs could take him.

After going a little way Danny stopped to look behind. No one was there. Nowhere could he see an enemy. But he could hear that noise again and every time he heard it his heart jumped. So he ran a little farther before once more stopping. By this time his heart didn't jump quite so much. He was getting used to that noise. He sat down to listen and try to remember when and where he had heard a noise like that. You see, it had a familiar sound. Yes, sir, it had a familiar sound.

"I've heard something like that before," said Danny to himself. "I certainly have. Now where did I hear it? And when did I hear it? And what made it?"

Danny scratched the tip of his nose. That didn't help him any, so he scratched his right ear. That didn't help him any, so he scratched his left ear. Whether or not this had anything to do with it I cannot say, but when he scratched his left ear he remembered something. He remembered that once Farmer Brown's Boy was driving some stakes over in the Green Meadows. Every time he hit one of those stakes there was a noise almost exactly like the noise Danny was listening to now.

"There must be some one down there in the bed of the river, driving stakes," thought Danny. "I'll go back, peep over the edge of the bank and see who the stake driver is."

Danny didn't run straight back to the edge of the bank. His courage wasn't quite equal to that. He ran a few steps and waited. When he had gained a little more courage he ran a few steps more. So, little by little, he got back to the edge of the bank. And all the time the stake driver kept on driving stakes. Anyway, that noise continued.

Now that he had reached the edge of the bank Danny couldn't quite make up his mind to peep over. But at last curiosity got the best of timidity. He parted the grass and poked his head out where he could see the bed of the creek. He expected to see a man there driving a stake. He didn't see any man and he didn't see any stake.

At first Danny saw no one. He rubbed his eyes and looked and looked, but saw no one. It was clear that that stake driver was not just below him, as he had thought. Now the sound seemed to come from a little way up the creek. Whack, whack, whack! came the sound. It must be that stake driver was around the bend, so Danny couldn't see him.

Now that he had made up his mind to see that stake driver and couldn't, Danny wanted to more than ever. What to do? Danny sat down to think it over.

"I suppose," said he to himself, "that I could climb down

this bank and run along the mud at the foot of it. I don't like to, because if danger should suddenly appear I would have to scramble up the bank. Of course I could work my way through the grass on the top of the bank, but that would be long, slow, hard work."

Just then Peep the Least Sandpiper and his friends came skimming along and alighted on a little mud flat just opposite the turn in the creek. They began running about, picking up their breakfast. It was clear that they saw nothing to be afraid of.

"If they are not afraid I shouldn't be," said Danny, and scrambled down the bank. Then, keeping close under the overhanging edge of the bank, he started up the creek. He felt far safer than he had thought he would.

Whack, whack, whack! That stake driver must be driving a lot of stakes. Yes, sir, any one who could keep it up like that must be driving a lot of stakes. Danny scampered just as fast as he could. In a few minutes he would be able to look around that bend. Then he would see what was going on there.

Peep the Least Sandpiper and his friends passed him and disappeared around the bend. Danny was getting out of breath, but he ran faster than ever. He reached a point where he could look around the bend into a little cove. There, running along the edge of the water, were the Sandpipers. Once more Danny rubbed his eyes. The sound of that stake driving seemed to come from around the next bend.

If ever anybody in all the Great World was disappointed, that one was Danny Meadow Mouse. He hadn't for a moment doubted that he would find there a man driving stakes. But he still heard the noise of the stake driving, seeming to come from around the next bend in the creek. Once more Danny started on. He had to stop to rest every few minutes though. This bend in the creek was such a big one that it changed Danny's position completely in regard to the point from which the noise seemed to come. When he reached the very farthest point of the bend, the sound came from a deep cove on the other side. It was then that Danny noticed that the noise wasn't quite the same as it had been. It didn't sound so much like the driving of a stake. Danny turned the bend. The sound sounded less and less like

BLACK CROWNED NIGHT HERON OR QUAWK.
Nycticorax nycticorax naevius.
AMERICAN BITTERN OR STAKE DRIVER.
Botaurus lentiginosus.

that of a stake being driven. It reminded Danny of something else. He sat down to think it over.

"Now what is it I have heard that sounds like that?" said Danny, and listened more intently than before. Then it came to him. "Why," he exclaimed in that funny little squeaky voice of his, "it sounds like that old wooden pump up in Farmer Brown's dooryard. I don't see why there should be a pump down here. That stake driver seems to have stopped driving stakes and now he's pumping. It is queer, very queer."

Pump-er-lunk, pump-er-lunk, pump-er-lunk! It certainly did sound as if there were a pump going down in that cove. Danny was so excited that he forgot all about the stake driver. He forgot that he was tired. His little short legs fairly twinkled he made them go so fast. He was well around the bend, almost into the cove, when he stopped abruptly. There was something queer going on. First somebody had stopped driving stakes and had begun pumping. Now that somebody had stopped pumping and was making other noises. There was something very mysterious about it. Danny was undecided whether to go on or to go back. He began to think that he had gone far enough. Still, he couldn't make up his mind to go back.

Presently he stole forward just a wee bit and stopped. He kept doing this until he was where he could see clearly the shore in that little cove. At first he saw no one. You see, he was looking for one of those two-legged creatures called men. Presently a little motion caught his attention. Already Danny had rubbed his eyes two or three times that morning, but now he rubbed them again. There, close to the grass, stood a brown bird. Had it not been for that motion, Danny would not have seen him. He had a long bill pointed straight up at the sky. When he was motionless he didn't look like a bird at all. He looked like a brown stick.

As Danny watched, this fellow went through a queer performance. He opened his bill and seemed to be swallowing air. Then followed a lot of curious motions with his neck. "My goodness," thought Danny, "that fellow must be sick! Perhaps he tried to swallow a fish and it stuck in his throat. There, I guess he has swallowed it now."

The bird was once more standing with his bill pointing to the sky. Danny had been so interested that he had quite forgotten about those queer noises. Now he began to look about hastily for the maker of them, but there was no one else to be seen. He glanced back at the brown stranger. "Goodness," he exclaimed again, "he must be going to swallow another fish, or something!"

Just as Danny looked the bird began to go through all those queer motions again. And then suddenly it dawned on Danny that all those strange noises were coming from right where that bird stood. Danny opened his eyes very wide and stared in the rudest manner. The bird stopped his queer motions. The noise stopped too. Then Danny Meadow Mouse waked up.

"I do believe," he cried, in that squeaky little voice of his, "that that fellow is the stake driver and the pumper and the maker of those other queer sounds."

"Of course," said a voice close to him. "Didn't you know that? I could have told you that." It was Peep the Sandpiper.

"No, I didn't know it," replied Danny. "Who is he, anyway?"

"He is Pumper the Bittern. That's who he is, Pumper the Bittern," replied Peep. "Did you ever hear such a noise from one of his size?"

"I never did," replied Danny.

XL. Two Long-Legged Cousins

Danny Meadow Mouse was sorry for Pumper the Bittern. You see, Pumper went through such a performance while he was making those noises that sounded like the driving of a stake and the pumping of water in an old-fashioned wooden pump, that it looked as if he must be most uncomfortable. He seemed to work so hard to get those sounds out that when he had finished, he looked sick and tired. So Danny was sorry for him.

"What does he do it for?" asked Danny of Peep the Sandpiper.

"He does it because he is in love," chuckled Peep. "He does it because he is in love and I suspect he thinks he is singing."

"Not really?" cried Danny.

"Yes, really," replied Peep.

"He must know he isn't singing," declared Danny.

"Just what is singing?" asked Peep.

Danny thought over all the different kinds of singing he had heard and then decided he wouldn't answer that question. "I suppose," said he, "that he likes the sound of his own voice."

"Some one else likes it too," replied Peep.

"Who?" demanded Danny. "Who under the sun can like such a noise as that?"

"Mrs. Bittern," replied Peep promptly. "I guess if you should ask her, she would tell you that is the finest singing in the world. You know love is the only real judge of singing."

"I am going over to get acquainted with that fellow," declared Danny.

"Watch out!" warned Peep. "He's got a long bill and a sharp one and he's got a long neck."

"He doesn't look it," declared Danny. "I mean, he doesn't

look as if he had a long neck. I wonder what you call a long neck, anyway."

"If you get too near that fellow, you may find out," replied Peep. "Yes, sir, you may find out. If you do, don't say that I didn't warn you."

Danny moved around to where he could get a good view of Pumper. Pumper got a glimpse of him and suddenly straightened out his neck, which he had had folded back between his shoulders. Danny saw then that he did have a long neck. He had a long neck and fairly long legs. He was of a general brownish color, quite light in places and quite dark in other places. His legs and feet were greenish-yellow. He reminded Danny of one of the children of Quawk the Night Heron, who dress all in brown.

Now that Danny had had a good look at that long sharp bill, he decided that Peep's advice was very good advice. So he was very polite. He remained at a respectful distance and, in his funny, squeaky, little voice, he said, "I hope you're feeling very fine to-day, Mr. Bittern."

Pumper looked at Danny and Danny was a little uncomfortable. He imagined a hungry look in Pumper's eyes. So he took care to keep beyond reach of that long bill.

"Did you speak to me?" croaked Pumper.

"I did," replied Danny in his squeaky little voice. "I said I hope you are feeling very fine to-day."

"Thank you," replied Pumper. "I am. What brought you over here?"

"I came," replied Danny, "to see who was making all that—I mean, to see who it was I heard singing."

Pumper the Bittern looked very hard at Danny and suspicion was in those rather fierce-looking eyes. Danny saw it. "You know," he hastened to say, "I could hear you 'way over across the marsh, and it was such a wonderful song that I just had to come over here to find out who the singer was."

Pumper looked pleased. He was pleased. He was so pleased that he had to hear the sound of his own voice again, and he went through that same funny-looking, distressing performance that Danny had seen before. When he had finished, he asked: "How did you like that?"

"It was splendid!" cried Danny. "I really don't see how you do it. I don't indeed."

Pumper looked flattered. He was flattered. The folks most easily flattered are those who think they can do something that they cannot do at all. So Pumper was flattered. "You have an excellent ear," said he. "I don't believe I've seen you around here before."

"No," replied Danny, "I don't think you have. My home is up on the Green Meadows. May I ask what family you belong to?"

"Look at me," commanded Pumper. "Do you really need to ask what family I belong to?"

"Well," replied Danny, "if I hadn't been told that your name is Bittern, I should have said that it was Heron."

"It is both," replied Pumper. "That is to say, I belong to the Heron family."

"Oh," said Danny, "that's it. You certainly do look like a Heron. Do you nest in trees like your cousins, the Night Herons and the Green Herons and the Great Blue Herons?"

Pumper shook his head. "Mrs. Bittern and I much prefer to nest on the ground," said he. "Yes, indeed, we very much prefer to nest on the ground. My, how plump you are!"

As he said this Pumper took a long step towards Danny. Danny dodged behind a little bunch of marsh grass. He peeped through it. Slowly, but carefully, Pumper the Bittern was coming his way, and in Pumper's eyes was a hungry look.

"I'm going home," said Danny, and turned to go back the way he had come.

Danny had not gone very far when he discovered another long-legged bird, a trifle bigger than Pumper the Bittern. This one was all white underneath, while his back and top of head were a bluish-black. Those long legs were yellow. His wings were pale gray. He was standing on a tussock in the edge of the water and his head was down between his shoulders so that he seemed to have no neck at all. But Danny knew him. He had seen him before. He had seen him up at the Smiling Pool on the Green Meadows. "It is Quawk the Night Heron," thought Danny, "and he must be fishing."

Even as Danny thought this, Quawk's head darted out and

down, and when he lifted it he held his neck at full length while he turned a little fish in his bill, so that it would go down headfirst. It was a long neck, indeed, and a very pretty one, for it was all white. Danny didn't make himself known. Instead, he made himself as small as possible behind a little lump of mud. He didn't dare try to scramble up that high bank. He knew that Quawk the Night Heron had a liking for fat Meadow Mice and he knew that without one of his little paths to run along, he would have little chance to get away from this fisherman.

"There's nothing to do," thought Danny, "but wait until he gets tired of fishing, and goodness knows when that will be. Oh dear, why ever did I get so curious?"

But Danny didn't have to wait as long as he had feared he would. You see, Quawk likes to do his fishing in the dusk, rather than in broad daylight, so as no more fish came his way, he soon grew tired of waiting. He spread his great wings, tucked his head back between his shoulders, so that he looked as if he had no neck at all, trailed his long legs out behind him, and flew away over the marsh.

Danny sighed with relief. Then he started on again. This time he didn't stop until he had reached that comfortable home of his in the hollow log between the marsh and the sand dunes. There he promptly curled up for a long nap.

And there we will leave him. And under a certain bathhouse we will leave Jimmy Skunk curled up. And over in the sand dunes we will leave Reddy Fox taking a sunbath. Over on the beach we will leave the Crabs and the Sandpipers and all the other little shore folk. For just a moment we will listen to the voice of Barker the Seal out on the rocks, and to the cries of Screamer the Tern, as he fishes along the shore. We'll draw a full breath of the salt air and then, regretfully perhaps, but with a promise that some day we will return, we'll turn our backs on the seashore and go home to think over all the wonders of which we have learned.

THE END

Appendix

Of necessity descriptions must be very general in character in the body of this book. Therefore, this appendix is inserted as an aid to identification of the various species described. The arrangement is according to groups, as being the most convenient method for the reader, and here again technical terms are avoided as far as possible.

ALGAE

DULSE *(Rhodymenia palmata)*. The frond is hand-shaped, hence the name. Color dark purplish-red. Stem short, cylindrical, spreading into a fan-shaped membrane six to twelve inches long and two thirds as wide at top. Deeply cleft and each division in turn more or less indented on the outer margin. Fairly common on New England and California coasts, growing below low watermark. It is edible and is dried and sold in markets along the eastern coast.

IRISH MOSS *(Chondrus crispus)*. The front has flattened stem, divided and subdivided in varying degrees, the whole being in general fan-shaped. Some divisions are only slightly indented along the margins, while others are so greatly indented as to be fringed in appearance. Found in shallow tide pools, it is white or whitish, sometimes with a tinge of pink. In deep water under shelter of rocks it becomes dark purplish-red. It is edible and once was much used along the coast in the making of blanc-mange. Common along the shore from New York north.

SEAWEED *(Chorda filum)*. Stringlike; one to forty feet in length, though usually twelve or less. One fourth to one half inch in diameter, tapering at each end. Hollow, divided into sections internally. Young plants covered with fine transparent hairs, but older plant brown and leatherlike. Often grows in masses below low watermark and is common along northern shores.

SEAWEED *(Laminaria saccharina)*. This is commonly called the Sea Tangle. It is ribbon-like in the lamina, or leaf, and has a short, solid stem, which may be three inches to four feet long. The lamina, or leaf proper, may be three to thirty feet long and six to eighteen inches wide. The margin is much waved and the plant is olive green in color and semi-transparent. Its Latin name is taken from a saccharine substance which it contains. This weed is found along the northern shores of the Atlantic and Pacific.

SEAWEED *(Ulva latissima)*. Largest of the genus. Frond a flat membrane of indefinite shape, as a rule roughly oval in outline. It is twelve to twenty-four inches long; sometimes much lobed, often perforated with small holes and is smooth, glossy, and green in color. Very common on muddy shores.

BIRDS

AMERICAN BITTERN *(Botaurus lentiginosus)*. Heron family. Common names, Marsh Hen, Pump Bird, Stake Driver. Adult sexes are alike. General color light brown; top of head and back of neck bluish-slate with buffy markings. On each side of neck is a long velvety black patch. Bill usually pale yellowish or yellowish-green. Legs and feet yellowish-green. Tail short and rounded. Back generally brown. Wings brown, tipped with black. Neck long, as with all members of the Heron family. Flies with head drawn back on shoulders and legs straight out behind. Length 23 to 34 inches; wing spread 32 to 50 inches.

BLACK-CROWNED NIGHT HERON *(Nycticorax nycticorax naevius)*. Heron family. Common name, Quawk. Adult sexes are alike. Forehead, neck and underparts white or whitish; crown, back and scapulars black with a bluish or greenish gloss. In breeding season usually three long, narrow, white tapering feathers depend from back of head. Rump and tail coverts, wings and tail, pale bluish-gray. Legs and feet yellow. Bill stouter than with most Herons. Neck long and carried back on shoulders in flight. Length 23 to 28 inches. Wing spread 43 to 48 inches.

BLACK-BELLIED PLOVER (*Squatarola squatarola cynosuræ*). Plover family. Other common names, Black-breast, Black-heart, Bullhead, Beetle-head, Chuckle-head. Adult sexes practically alike. Strictly speaking, this bird is not black-bellied, but is black-breasted, the lower belly being white. The tail also is white barred with black. The sides of the head and neck and upper breast are white. Top of head, back of neck and back, more or less brownish-black. Bill black. Front toes webbed at the base. Hind toe very small and higher than others. Length 10.50 to 13.65 inches. Spread of wing 22 to 25 inches. Weight 6 to 10.5 ounces.

COMMON TERN (*Sterna hirundo*). Gull family. Other names, Wilson's Tern, Mackerel Gull, Sea Swallow, Summer Gull. Adult sexes alike. Top of head and forehead deep black. Back and wings pearl-gray. Throat white. Breast and underparts pale gray. Tips of outer primaries black. Tail deeply forked. Bill red at base and black at tip. Length 13 to 16 inches. Wing spread 29 to 32 inches.

PIPING PLOVER (*Charadrius melodus*). Plover family. Other names, Ring-neck, Beach Bird, Clam Bird, Pale Ring-neck. Adult sexes alike. Top of head and back very light brown. Cheeks same color. Underparts, throat, forehead and line above eye, white. A line of black between forehead and top of head. A narrow collar of black at base of throat, sometimes extending completely around the neck. Bill orange with black tip. Legs and feet orange. Outer pair of tail feathers blackish near tips. Primaries blackish. Length 6 to 7.80 inches. Wing spread 14 to 16 inches.

SEMIPALMATED PLOVER (*Charadrius semipalmatus*). Plover family. Other common names, Ring-neck and Little Ring-neck. Adult sexes alike. Top of head, back and wings, brown. Forehead, throat and collar extending around the neck, white. Below this is a black collar. Underparts white. Tail blackish near end. Bill yellow with black tip. Legs and feet yellowish to orange. Feet with small webs at base of toes, giving the bird its name. Length 6.50 to 8.05 inches. Wing spread 14 to 16 inches.

LEAST SANDPIPER *(Pisobia minutilla)*. Sandpiper family. Common names, Peep, Mud-peep. Adult sexes alike. This is the smallest of the sandpipers. Top of the head rather buffy, streaked with blackish. Over the eye is a broad light streak; back a general brownish color, marked with black, the feather centers being blackish. Underparts white. Slender black bill. Legs and feet greenish to yellowish-green. This bird is sparrow size, but with long legs. Length 5 to 6.76 inches. Wing spread 11 to 12.17 inches. Frequents mud flats in marshes.

SEMIPALMATED SANDPIPER *(Ereunetes pusillus)*. Sandpiper family. Common names, Peep, Sandpeep, Beach Peep, Oxeye. Adult sexes alike. Closely resembles the Least Sandpiper, but may be distinguished by small web at base of toes, stouter bill and blackish legs and feet. Length 5.50 to 6.86 inches. Wing spread 11.14 to 12.80 inches. Frequents beaches rather than mud flats.

GREATER YELLOWLEGS *(Totanus melanoleucus)*. Tattler family. Other common names, Winter Yellowlegs, Big Yellowlegs, Greater Tattler, Greater Telltale. Adult sexes alike. This bird resembles a giant sandpiper. The upper parts are dark brown to blackish, the head and neck being streaked and the back spotted with white or ashy color. The middle of the belly is white. The breast and sides are heavily spotted with brown to black. The legs are yellow. Between the outer and middle toes is a small web connecting the bases. The bill is black, long and slender. White tail coverts are conspicuous. Length 12.15 to 15 inches. Wing spread 23 to 26 inches. Weight 5 to 10 ounces.

HERRING GULL *(Larus argentatus)*. Gull family. Common names, Harbor Gull, Gray Gull, Winter Gull. Adult sexes alike. Head, neck, breast and underparts white. Wings and back pale bluish-gray. Primaries marked with black and white spots. Bill yellow with spot of red on the lower mandible. Legs and feet pale flesh color. Length 22.50 to 26 inches. Wing spread 54 to 58 inches.

CRUSTACEANS
BEACH FLEA

COMMON *(Orchestia agilis)*. A familiar crustacean of the beach; olive green or brown, not more than half an inch long. It burrows in sand under masses of seaweed. When disturbed it leaps like a giant flea.

CRABS

BLUE *(Callinectes sapidus)*. Carapace about twice as broad as it is long and having long sharp spine projecting outward on each side. Between the long spines and the eyes on each side are eight short spines. Four unequal teeth and a small spine underneath are between the eyes. Chelæ, or pinching claws, large and unequal in size. Back of these are three pairs of simple feet and then a pair flattened for swimming. Carapace and abdomen fringed with fine hairs along margins. Upper surface dark green and lower surface dingy white. Feet blue. Carapace covered with minute granulations. In the South this crab is known as the Sea Crab. It ranges from Cape Cod to Florida.

BOX *(Calappa flammea)*. This crab is unique in that the chelæ, which are large, broad and flattened, when folded fit closely together across the front, so that with the smaller legs drawn in, the crab is in effect boxed in; hence the name Box Crab. This crab is four to five inches wide and two to three inches long, with the body one and one half inches thick. It is found on sandy and muddy bottoms from North Carolina southward.

FIDDLER *(Uca minax)*. The Fiddler Crabs are easily distinguished by the fact that one of the chelæ of the male is small, while the other is proportionately very large. This big claw is carried aloft and held like a fiddler's bow. Both chelæ of the female are small. These are small crabs and live in large colonies, burrowing in the mud or sand and retreating to these holes at the first hint of danger. They are pugnacious little fellows. The eyes are on stalks. This species is the largest of the Fiddler Crabs and may be distinguished by red spots at the joints of the legs. It is found along banks of rivers where the water is brackish. Over the mouth of its burrow it builds a little ovenlike archway of mud. It ranges from southern New England to Florida.

FIDDLER *(Uca pugilator).* Somewhat smaller than *Uca minax,* rectangular in outline and having a highly polished surface to the carapace. Abundant on sandy and muddy flats from Cape Cod to Florida.

GHOST; SAND *(Ocypode albicans).* Carapace almost square, with the anterior corners ending in a spine. Body about an inch thick. Eyes on long stalks. One of the chelæ a little longer than the other and the joints of both toothed. The other four pairs of legs fringed with hairs. Color that of the sand. These crabs are very quick-moving and run and dodge with surprising speed. They are found on sandy beaches above tide mark from Long Island to South America. They are great burrowers.

GREEN *(Carcinides maenas).* Carapace with five sharp-edged teeth on each side of the forward part. Color dark green with yellow to yellowish-green spots. Size, about three inches wide by two inches long. Right chela larger and blunter than left. Range, North Atlantic Coast to Cape Cod; it is also found in northern Europe. It is a rapid runner.

HERMIT *(Pagurus longicarpus).* This is the smallest of the Hermit Crabs and one of the most abundant. Like other members of the family, it is without a shell of its own and the soft abdomen is inserted into an empty shell, usually that of a gastropod mollusk, such as the periwinkle. The curious little crab then has the appearance of carrying the shell about on its back. When alarmed it withdraws into the shell and the claws and feet fold in such a way as to close the entrance. This species can be recognized by its dull yellowish-white legs, more or less marked with gray or blue.

HERMIT *(Pagarus pollicaris).* This species is larger than the other and therefore occupies larger shells. It is pale red and the claws are more or less granulated. It is found from Massachusetts to Florida, preferring rocky and shelly bottoms.

HORSESHOE; KING *(Limulus polyphemus)*. This is not a true crab, but is included herewith because of its common names. It is more nearly related to spiders and scorpions. It is the last survivor of an otherwise extinct group of animals. The shell is domelike and in shape resembles a horseshoe, so far as the forward or larger part is concerned. Joined to this is the abdomen, which is composed of six fused segments. This ends in a long, sharp spine which is movable and which is often called the "tail." There are seven pairs of legs, the first six ending in nip-perlike claws. On the abdomen are five pairs of leaflike appendages, which are used for swimming and as gills. These curious creatures come up on the beaches in the spring to deposit their eggs in holes which they scoop out in the sand. They are common from Maine to Central America.

JONAH *(Cancer borealis)*. This is closely related to the Rock Crab, but its rougher shell and the saw-edged teeth of the front of the carapace distinguish it. It grows to a greater size than the Rock Crab and lives on rocky shores from Long Island to Nova Scotia.

KELP *(Pugettia producta)*. This is the most common Spider Crab of the California and Oregon coasts. It is about two inches long and practically of the same width. There are two spines on each side. It is called Kelp Crab because it is found among the seaweeds on rocks just below the low-tide mark. It is about the same color as the seaweeds among which it lives.

LADY *(Ovalipes ocellatus)*. This is also called Sand Crab and is one of the most attractive of the crabs, if a crab can be said to be attractive. The color is whitish or a delicate greenish-yellow, covered with spots of red and purple arranged in little rings. The chelae are stout and powerful. It is about three inches broad and two and one half inches long and on each side are five spines. The rear pair of legs have been developed into swimming feet or paddles. This crab delights to bury itself in the sand up to the eyes at the low-water mark.

MUD *(Panopeus herbstii)*. As the name implies, these crabs are fond of muddy shores. This species ranges from southern New England to South America and lives in burrows, in muddy banks, or under stones on muddy bottoms. It is one and one-half inches to two inches broad and a dull brownish-green. The claws are tipped with black.

ORCHID *(Gecarcinus lateralis).* This is the well-known land crab of Florida and is found through the West Indies and on the coast of South America. It is about two inches wide and nearly as long. The sides of the shell and the large claws are red, while the middle of the back is dark purple, almost black; and the walking legs and underparts are dull yellow. While this crab visits the ocean for breeding purposes, it spends most of its life on land, living in burrows and under damp logs. It is often found fully twenty feet above high-tide level. It will sometimes be seen scuttling across a road near the Florida Coast. It comes abroad chiefly at night, when it seeks all sorts of carrion and refuse. It is a good runner and a good climber.

OYSTER *(Pinnotheres ostreum).* There is no mistaking the female of this species, for it is found only in the gill cavity of an oyster. This tiny crab has a very thin shell, which is pinkish-white. Having no use for legs and claws, the latter are too weak to be of any service. The male is even smaller and, curiously enough, is an independent little fellow, not living in an oyster. Therefore, he is protected with a shell and has strong claws and legs. A closely related species, *Pinnotheres maculatum,* is found in the cavity of the shells of the Common Mussel and the Scallop.

ROCK *(Cancer irroratus).* This is one of the most common crabs along the New England Coast, especially the northern part. The limits of its range are Labrador and South Carolina. As its name implies, it is usually found in rocky locations, under stones or in crevices. It is sometimes found nearly buried in sand or gravel. The carapace is one third broader than long. It is often three to four inches in width. The eyes are on short stalks set in deep circular holes. This is not a swimming crab, so the walking legs end in a sharp spine instead of in paddlelike swimming feet. It is speckled with small brownish spots.

SAND BUG *(Emerita talpoida)*. This curious little animal does not look much like a crab. It is one of the anomalous forms and as it is related to the Hermit Crabs is included here. It is about two and one half inches long, has an arched back, with smooth, hard, yellowish-white shell, and has antennæ that are plumelike, reminding one of the antennæ of a big moth. The abdomen is long and folds under the body almost to the front. It lives in shallow water along sandy beaches and is a good swimmer. It can also burrow with astonishing rapidity. It ranges from Cape Cod to Florida.

TOAD *(Hyas coarctatus)*. This is a species of Spider Crab and is found from Greenland to New Jersey in shallow water and deep water as well. Its legs are slender and weak for the size of its body, which resembles in form and size that of a toad, which accounts for its common name. Often it is covered with seaweed, which the crab affixes to its body and legs.

BARNACLES

ROCK *(Balanus balanoides)*. These are the crustaceans that whiten rocks and the piling of wharves between tides, being covered with water at high tide and exposed at low tide. Shell small, white, and variable in shape and firmly attached to rock or pile. Shell is composed of a number of plates and a lid, or operculum. The latter has two valves. When covered with water, the valves are open and feathery jointed legs are thrust out to sweep food into the mouth. These valves can be closed at will. The young, on leaving the egg, is free-swimming. After molting several times, during which a number of changes takes place, the little barnacle attaches itself head-on to a rock or some other solid substance and gradually attains the mature form. These barnacles are known as Sea Acorns. They crowd together in unbelievable numbers.

STALKED *(Lepas anatifera)*. Commonly known as the Ship Barnacle and sometimes called Goose Barnacle. The former name comes from the fact that it is frequently found attached to ships, while the latter name was given it because of an old folklore belief that geese hatched from these barnacles. Instead of the shell being attached directly to the ship, there is a long fleshy stalk, which is the head end of the creature. This stalk is from one to six inches long. The shell is only an inch long. It is an animal of warm waters, but is carried to all parts of the world on ships' bottoms.

WHALE *(Coronula diadema)*. This Barnacle attaches to the skin of whales and is an inch and a half wide and an inch high. The skin of the Whale is drawn up into the Barnacle.

LOBSTERS

COMMON *(Homarus americanus)*. This is the common lobster of the Atlantic Coast from North Carolina to southern Labrador. The enormous pincer claws are the characteristic feature of this animal. As with the crab, these great claws are a development of the first pair of walking feet. The next two pairs of feet are furnished with small claws, while the remaining two pairs end in simple hooks. The abdomen is protected by a jointed shell that makes it flexible. The animal has two long antennæ. The color varies, but is usually dark-green with red or blue mottlings. The lobster is one of the creeping forms and uses its legs for creeping forward, but swims backward. It lives in deep water on rocky bottoms, hiding amongst stones. Like the crabs, it is a scavenger, living on dead and decaying animal matter. The male lobster, when fully grown, molts twice a year, while the female molts once a year.

SPINY *(Panulirus argus)*. This is the lobster of the Florida Coast. In general it resembles the northern lobster, save that it wholly lacks the big pincer claws. It has five pairs of walking feet, none armed with claws. It is armed with a number of sharp-pointed spines around the forward part of the body; hence the name. It is richly marked with blue, yellow and brown. On the Pacific Coast is a closely related species, *Panulirus interruptus*.

SHRIMPS

COMMON SAND *(Crangon vulgaris)*. Lobster-like in general form, but small, lacking pincer claws. The abdomen bends sharply down from the carapace, giving a broken-back appearance. The carapace covering the forward part of the body is of thin shell. This shrimp is about two inches long and is camouflaged by being the color of its immediate surroundings. Abundant on sandy shores at low-water mark from Labrador to North Carolina and along the Pacific Coast. When left by the tide, it buries itself in the sand.

COMMON PRAWN (*Palaemonetes vulgaris*). It can be distinguished from the preceding species by its longer antennæ and a sharp spine between the eyes. It is abundant in brackish water over muddy bottoms from Massachusetts to Florida and is one and one half inches long. It is used as bait by fishermen. The body is translucent, almost colorless.

CORAL (*Stenopus hispidus*). This is the most beautiful of the shrimps. It is about three inches long and has three bands of bright scarlet across the body, the background being white. There are short sharp spines on the body and the legs end in claws. It is found from New York to Brazil, but is more peculiarly a southern species, being found among the corals.

EDIBLE (*Penaeus setiferus*). This is the edible shrimp of the South, the shrimp fisheries being of considerable value. The larger ones are called Prawns and the smaller ones Shrimps. It attains a size of six inches and is found from Virginia to Texas. There is a ridge along the middle of the carapace, ending in a sharp toothed spine which projects forward between the eyes.

FEATHER-FOOTED (*Mysis stenolepis*). *This* little shrimp is only about half an inch long. It is called "Feather-Footed" because of the feathery hairs on its legs. There are spines on the sides of the body. It is most abundant in winter and often is found in great numbers in muddy or grassy places.

FISHES

SEA HORSE (*Hippocampus hudsonius*). There is no mistaking one of these curious little creatures as it swims upright in the water or remains stationary with tail anchored to a bit of seaweed. The head is curiously horse-like in shape and the little creature bears a quaint resemblance to a "knight" in an ordinary set of wooden chessmen. Neck, body and tail are covered with rings of bony plates. Each body ring is armed with four blunt spines. The color is light brown or dusty to ashen gray or yellow, variously mottled. Adults may be three to six inches long. The male possesses a brood-pouch in which the eggs are deposited by the female. The young are carried in this pouch for a short time. This curious little fish is found along the Atlantic Coast from South Carolina to Cape Cod and occasionally north of it.

SKATE; COMMON *(Raja erinacea)*. Other names, Little, Bonnet, Summer, Hedgehog, and Old Maid. The outline of a Skate is disklike, thin and with long tail. The various species are much alike in appearance. This particular Skate is found from the Gulf of St. Lawrence to Virginia. It is small in size, being but sixteen to twenty-four inches in length. One of the latter size would be a little over a foot in width. It has a blunt nose and no thorns along the midline of the back. Females are more spiny than males, having their spines scattered all over the upper surface, excepting along the midline. Color grayish to dark brown; white or grayish beneath. It is found in depths of from five to forty fathoms. In the matter of food it is omnivorous.

SAND EEL *(Ammodytes americanus)*. Also called Launce and Lant. Not a true Eel, but a slender little fish with long head, sharply pointed nose and lower jaw projecting far beyond the upper. It has one long, low dorsal fin running almost the whole length of the body. The tail is forked deeply. The ventral fin is a little less than half as long as the dorsal fin. This little fish is about six inches long and its width is about one tenth of its total length. It is olive brownish or bluish-green above, while the sides are silvery and the belly is a duller white. Sometimes there is a stripe of steel-blue iridescence on each side. Sand Eels are found from Labrador to Cape Hatteras and are plentiful along sandy shores. Their most interesting habit is their burrowing in the sand, which they do for a depth of several inches. Often they are thus left by the outgoing tide and come out again when the tide returns.

STICKLEBACK; THREE-SPINED *(Gasterosteus aculeatus)*. Other names, Pinfish, Thornfish and Thornback. This is a small minnow-like fish which is mature at two inches, but sometimes does attain a length of four inches. Like all the members of the Stickleback family, it is distinguished by stout free spines on the back in front of the dorsal fin. In this species there are usually three of these spines, two about the middle of the back and one just in front of the dorsal fin. This latter is much smaller than the other two. Each ventral fin is represented by a large spine. There is also a very small anal spine. There is considerable variation in the size and number of the spines in this species. There is also much variation in color, it being gray, olive, greenish-brown, or sometimes blue, above. The belly is silvery, but in the breeding season the males are reddish from nose to vent. At this time the female may be reddish all over with the exception of the back. This Stickleback is found in coastal and fresh water from Labrador to New Jersey; and a similar form, which may prove to be the same species, is found on the northwestern coast. The Sticklebacks are peculiarly interesting because of the nest-building by the male.

HYDROIDS AND JELLYFISHES
HYDROID

SEA PLUME *(Obelia commissuralis)*. The common name of this little animal, which does not in any way resemble an animal, is derived from the fact that it resembles a delicate sea plant or plume. It has a main stem from which branches run nearly at right angles. On each branch are a number of little flower like parts, which in reality are so many little mouths surrounded by tentacles. These interesting little Hydroids give birth to little Jellyfishes. In turn, these cast out eggs from which spring more Sea Plumes. This little Hydroid is found attached to stones or seaweed, or old wharves.

JELLYFISHES

MILKY DISK *(Aurelia flavidula)*. This Jellyfish gets its name from the color, which is slightly milky. The disk is about a foot in diameter. The mouth is at the center of the concave side. From the central stomach to the edge of the disk sixteen straight and as many more pitchfork-shaped vessels extend. This Jellyfish is found from Cape Cod to the Arctic Ocean.

SPECKLED *(Dactylometra quinquecirro)*. The disk is one to one and one half feet in diameter. Around the mouth are veil-like lips sometimes more than two feet in length. Pendant from the margin are forty tentacles. The margin is notched. On the upper or convex side are sixteen short bars composed of reddish specks. This Jellyfish is very handsome, the color being somewhat pinkish. It appears from time to time in bays all along the Atlantic Coast.

THIMBLE *(Melicertum campanula)*. It is well named, for it is like a large thimble of jellylike substance, which is clear. From the stomach at the center of the concave side, eight yellow canals extend to the edges after the manner of spokes. Tentacles hang from the edge of the disk or bell. It is found north of Cape Cod to the Arctic.

Orchistoma tentaculata. This is one of the hydromedusa, which means that it is the medusa stage of some hydroid. The ball is six millimeters high. The gelatinous part of the upper bell is very thick. This leaves a rather shallow concavity in the lower part of the bell. The margin of the bell turns outward slightly. There are thirty-two tentacles. The velum is well developed. There are no marginal sense organs. The proboscis is flat and shallow, with eight lips.

MOLLUSKS
CLAMS

BLOODY *(Arca campechiensis pexata)*. This clam gets its name from the fact that the gills and circulatory fluid are red. The shell is slightly over an inch wide, covered with a rough brown skin and there are about thirty-two ridges from the beak to the edge. It is found under stones or on gravelly beaches below tide level from Cape Cod to Florida.

HARD-SHELL *(Venus mercenaria)*. Other names, Little-neck, Cherrystone and Quahaug. This is also sometimes called the Round Clam and is distinguished by its shape and hard shell. The small size is known as the Little-neck and the medium size as the Cherry-stone. These are the clams served on the half-shell. When fully grown it is no longer served in this way and becomes the Quahaug, from which a delicious chowder is made. It is found from Nova Scotia to Central America, but is common only from Cape Cod to the Carolinas. It is found chiefly in shallow bays, where it lives below the level of low tide. The siphon is short and blunt and forked at the end. The shell is covered by grayish, or brownish-gray skin. The rings of growth are quite clearly marked on the shell.

RAZOR *(Ensis directus)*. This clam is so named because of its shape, which is very like that of the handle of an old-fashioned razor. It is about six inches long by an inch in width. It is found from Labrador to Florida and is common along the New England and Jersey coasts. This clam has a long powerful foot which projects from one end of the shell and can be pushed out to a length of about five inches or withdrawn completely. This clam is found on sandy beaches and on sandbars. It burrows with amazing rapidity. It does this by pushing the foot down into the sand and then forcing water into the foot so that it expands, pushing away the sand on all sides. The end of the foot is then expanded into a disk with which the animal clings and draws the shell down. This is an edible clam.

SAND-BAR *(Siliqua costata)*. This little clam is a lover of pure ocean water and is found from Nova Scotia to the Carolinas on loose sandy beaches and bars below low-water mark. This clam is about three quarters of an inch wide and an inch and three quarters long. Shell covered with rich brown skin. Foot broad and muscular. Siphon slender. It burrows but a short distance below the surface. It travels along the surface at a smart pace for a clam.

SOFT-SHELL *(Mya arenaria)*. Other names, Long Clam and Nanninose. This is the favorite clam for clambakes along the coast. The shell is comparatively thin and is white. It is found along the North Atlantic Coast of America and the northern coasts of Europe wherever there are sandy or muddy shores. A favorite place is around the mouths of streams flowing into the ocean. It burrows into the mud or sand with the long neck or siphon pointing up. This neck may be several inches long, but can be contracted and drawn into the shell at will. Served steamed, these clams are considered a great delicacy.

SURF *(Spisula solidissima).* Other names, Sea Clam, Hen Clam. As the first two names imply, this is a clam of the open water. It is found on sandy bottoms below the low-water mark to a depth of about sixty feet. Occasionally it is washed up on the beach by the surf. In shape it is more like the Hard-shell Clam than any of the others and its shell is thick and hard, and is covered with a light-brown skin. It is, when fully grown, six inches long by four wide. The neck, or siphon, is short, but the foot is large and stout, so that the clam is able to dig rapidly. However, it does not burrow deeply.

SWIMMING *(Solemya velum).* This is a little clam, being only three quarters of an inch long. It can swim both forward and backward; hence the name. The shell is thin and flexible. The foot can be expanded so that at its apex it is umbrella-shaped. When it is thus expanded and is suddenly driven forward, the clam swims backward. When the foot is suddenly withdrawn it swims forward. It burrows in sandy or muddy beaches just below the tide level from North Carolina to Nova Scotia.

SHIPWORM *(Teredo navalis).* Other common name, Teredo. While not strictly a clam, this creature is not a worm and is so nearly related to the clams that it is included herewith. This curious little creature bores into submerged timbers and sometimes plays havoc with the bottoms of wooden ships. At the upper end is a small bivalve shell. When it first begins to bore into the wood it is not bigger than the head of a pin. As it extends the burrow, the latter is lined with a shelly substance and the body of the Teredo increases in length until in tropical waters it sometimes attains a length of two feet. This body is worm-shaped and tapers at the posterior end, which is equipped with two long extensible siphons. At the base of these siphons are two shelly appendages called pallets which close the opening of the burrow when the siphons are withdrawn. The Shipworm causes enormous damage and great sums of money have been spent in efforts to successfully combat it.

OYSTER

COMMON, American *(Ostrea virginica)*. This favorite shellfish, in which a business running into the millions is done annually, hardly needs description. It cannot be mistaken for anything else. The oyster is stationary and the lower shell, or valve, is usually fastened to a rock or to another shell by means of a shelly secretion. Thus oysters are found growing in a group together. The lower shell is quite deep and convex, while the upper shell is flatter. The inside of the shell is lined with a membrane called the mantle. The mouth is close to the hinge at the apex of the shell. There is a stomach surrounded by a green-colored liver. The heavy rough shells are bound together by a strong adductor muscle. The eggs are cast forth into the water and the baby oysters are free-swimming larvæ.

MUSSELS

BEARDED *(Modiolus modiolus)*. Other name, Horse Mussel. This group contains a number of species of shellfish closely related to the clams. Whereas clams are not attached, but are free-moving, mussels have become stationary and by means of a tough fibrous byssus they attach themselves firmly to various objects, although some of them can move by means of this same byssus. This particular species is of large size, being four to five inches in length. It is covered with a chestnut-brown skin, which flakes off around the edges of the shell, forming a ragged fringe; hence its name of Bearded Mussel. It is a deep-water animal, being attached to the rocks well below the low-water mark. Severe storms often wrench these mussels free and cast them upon the beach. They are familiar along New England beaches. They are found from New Jersey to the Arctic Ocean. In Alaskan waters this mussel is known as the Great Horse Mussel.

COMMON EDIBLE *(Mytilus edulis)*. This species lives in great colonies on mud flats, and especially where there are plenty of pebbles. Masses of these mussels are often found fastened together by the strong yellow byssus threads which they secrete. The skin, or epidermis, which covers the shell is black. The shell itself is violet and about two and one half inches long. This mussel is found from North Carolina to New England and has been introduced on the Pacific Coast. It also occurs in Europe, where it is quite extensively used as food.

WING *(Pinna muricata)*. Other name, Razor Shell. This is a purely southern species, but interesting because of its variation from the typical mussel shape. It is fan-shaped with a very sharp-pointed apex and a wide margin, the edges of which are exceedingly sharp. It attaches itself to a rock below the surface of the sand with just the edge of the shell projecting above. These sharp edges make wading with bare feet a dangerous matter. This mussel is found from North Carolina to Florida and the West Indies.

RIBBED *(Modiolus demissus plicatulus)*. This is one of the most common of all the mussels and is found in great numbers on the mud flats around the mouths of rivers from Nova Scotia to Georgia. It gets its name from the finely ribbed character of the shell. It is far from attractive in appearance, the outer skin being dingy yellowish-green. It is about three inches in length.

SCALLOPS

SCALLOPS, Common *(Pecten irradians)*. This is the familiar shallow-water species which brings such a good price in the market. The shape of the shell accounts for the name. The shell is rounded with radiating ribs. There are two winglike projections at the point where the two valves come together. The adductor muscle is extremely large and it is this and this only which is eaten. Scallops are not stationary, but actually swim by rapidly opening and closing the valves of the shell. The edge of the mantle is ornamented with bright blue eyes. It ranges from Florida to Nova Scotia, but is comparatively rare north of Cape Cod. It is most plentiful around Cape Cod, Long Island Sound and off the Jersey Coast.

SNAILS

MUD-FLAT (*Alectrion obsoleta*). This is one of the small snails and south of Cape Cod is one of the commonest. Where it is found at all it fairly swarms. Its range is as far as Nova Scotia and south to Florida, but is most common from Long Island to Virginia. The shell of this little snail, when clean, is black both outside and in. It is predaceous on other mollusks and in turn is a victim of young Hermit Crabs.

OYSTER-DRILL (*Urosalpinx cinerea*). This little snail gets its common name from its habit of drilling through the shell of young oysters and feeding on them. Next to the Starfish it is perhaps the worst enemy of the oyster. It is found from Florida to Cape Cod. The shell is less than an inch long. The lip is extended to form a sort of snout. The color is dull brownish-gray and there are several whorls to the shell. These are crossed by a number of ridges. Wherever oysters are found, this little pest is almost certain to appear sooner or later.

PERIWINKLE (*Litorina littorea*). This is another small snail belonging to a genus which fairly swarms wherever conditions are favorable. This is a European species which probably came from the northern coasts of Europe. It is an article of food in England. It is found in great colonies along the New England Coast, covering the rocks and seaweed between tide limits. The shell is about five eighths of an inch long with a sharp-pointed but short spire. It is thick and varies from black to a dingy gray in color. This is one of the snails that can live for hours out of water.

ROCK (*Thais lapillus*). This is another probable immigrant from Europe, a lover of cold water, and found in enormous numbers off the New England Coast and north. It is most abundant on rocks covered with barnacles, for it feeds on these. It varies greatly in form and color. One and one half inches is about the limit in America, but in Europe it grows larger. It varies in color from white to dark brown. Sometimes it is banded with yellow and sometimes it is all yellow. The shell may be smooth or very rough. Look for it on the rocks between tides, particularly the barnacle-covered rocks.

SAND COLLAR *(Polinices heros).* This is one of the commonest of the large snails from New England and New Jersey. It is easily recognized by its size, smoothness, bluish-white color, and the very blunt, rounded spire. The opening to the shell is quite large, round, and sharp-edged. It is usually found partly or wholly buried in the sand between tides or in little pools with sandy bottoms. It has a very large foot, which enables it to move about readily. This is the snail that is responsible for the so-called "sand collar," which is a perpetual puzzle to frequenters of the seashore. This so-called sand collar is shaped like a basin with the bottom knocked out and with a break in one side, or like one of the broad collars little boys used to wear in the olden days. It appears to be made wholly of sand. As a matter of fact, it is made of sand and a gelatinous substance in which the eggs of this big snail are deposited in regular order. So the sand collar is in reality an egg case.

SAND-FLAT *(Alectrion trivittata).* This is another of the small snails about the size of the Mud-Flat Snail, it being slightly over half an inch in length. Where the Mud-Flat Snail has a blunt spire, the Sand-Flat Snail has a sharp spire. The surface is granular. It is abundant on the sand flats of Cape Cod and Long Island Sound, but is also found on muddy and stony bottoms extending into the water to a depth of over two hundred feet. It is predatory, feeding on any kind of mollusk it can bore into.

SEAWEED *(Litorina obtusata palliata).* This little snail lives on seaweed. The shell has a low spire and is almost globular. It is found in great numbers on seaweed between tide limits and is apt to be very much the color of the weed on which it is found. It may be yellow, green or red. Often it is mottled. The head of the animal is orange-colored and this is distinctive.

SALT-MARSH *(Melampus lineatus).* This is a little brown snail so small that it is much preyed upon by crabs, seabirds and even by minnows. It is very abundant on the stems of salt-marsh grasses near the high-tide mark. It is found from Cape Cod far south. The opening is narrow and the spire is short and blunt. It is a vegetable eater.

EPITONIUM ANGULATUM. These exc*eedingly* pretty gastropods appear to have no common name. The shells are very apt to be found on the beach from New England to Virginia. They are from one half an inch to an inch in length and conspicuous because of the twisted shape. There are about eight whorls, which are well rounded. These whorls are crossed by elevated, smooth ribs. There are seventeen to nineteen on the body whorl. The aperture, or opening, is almost round. This shell is white with occasionally some revolving brownish lines.

EPITONIUM LINEATUM. This *is* of much the same appearance as the one already described, but there are only nine ribs to each volution and the whorls come together in such a way that these ribs touch. This species is found from Cape Cod to southern Florida.

VERMICULARIA SPIRATA. There is no mistaking this gastropod. The shell starts out like that of a regular snail and then the whorls widen and twist and turn in a worm-like fashion. Indeed, it seems as if nothing but a worm could possibly live in such a shell. It is found in shallow water from New England far south, and the shells are often washed up on the beach.

TEN-RIBBED (*Chrysodomus decemcostatus*). This is a gastropod mollusk of the northern New England Coast, and is fully three inches in length. It is hardly to be mistaken for any other, because of the revolving ribs which encircle it. The normal number is ten. It is yellow-brown in color and is found below the low-tide level. These raised ribs are called "costæ."

SQUIDS

BLUNT-TAILED (*Loligo pealii*). It is difficult to think of the squid as a mollusk, yet that is the classification under which it comes. It is one of the most highly developed mollusks and is related to the clams and snails. Instead of having the shell outside, it is inside. It is embedded in the mantle and what there is of it is called the "pen." It belongs to the class *Cephalopoda*. Cephalopod means "feet around the head." The squid is cylindrical in shape with ten arms, or tentacles, around the mouth. Eight of these are triangular, with two rows of suckers on their inner sides. The other pair is longer, with suckers only on the expanded tips. The body tapers to a point behind, where at the extreme end is a fin resembling in outline an arrowhead. This fin extends well up on the body. There are two great, staring eyes and a parrot-like beak. There are two common species, the Blunt-tailed Squid and the Short-tailed Squid, found along the New England Coast. They are about a foot long. There is also a Giant Squid, which attains a length of fifty feet from the tip of the longest tentacle to the end of the tail, and even larger ones have been reported. The squid projects itself backward through the water by forcing water through a siphon. It possesses an ink bag and clouds the water with an inklike substance as a means of protection. The squid is eaten in some countries. The Short-tailed Squid is extensively used as bait by fishermen.

WHELKS

CHANNELED (*Busycon canaliculatum*). The shells of the whelks are the largest whorled shells north of Cape Hatteras. They are found north to Cape Cod and south to the Gulf of Mexico. They are fully six inches long and the general outline is pear-shaped. There is a long, tapering snout or anterior canal. The Channeled Whelk has no knobs or projections on the whorls and the channel is deep. The shell is covered with a rough skin, which is brown, thick and heavy. The shell is yellowish within and a whitish-gray on the outside. It is this curious mollusk that deposits its eggs in cocoons which are graduated in size and fastened together like a row of yellow checkers on a cord.

KNOBBED (*Busycon carica*). This is similar to the Channeled Whelk, but is slightly smaller and has a row of knobs around the shoulder of the body whorl. Also it lacks the outer skin. The anterior canal is long and open. Like the Channeled Whelk, this whelk is predatory. In both species there is a ribbonlike tongue covered with rasping teeth. The egg cases of the Knobbed Whelk are similar to those of its near relative.

SEA ANEMONES

BROWN *(Metridium dianthus)*. This is the most abundant sea anemone of the northeastern coast and is found from New York northward. It is found in tide pools, crevices of rocks, and on piles of bridges and wharves. The color commonly is yellowish-brown, but some are pure white, pink, orange, or mottled with different colors. Contracted, this curious little animal is a broad, low cone; but when expanded the body is cylindrical, three or four inches high, and the disk is sometimes almost ten inches across. The mouth is surrounded with a fringe of tapering tentacles. This sea anemone is also armed with stinging threads.

CRIMSON *(Tealia crassicornis)*. This medium-sized anemone is found north of Cape Cod and is about two inches high, with short, conical tentacles. The diameter of the disk is about three inches. The color varies from cherry red to bluish-green, mottled with crimson. This little animal constantly changes shape.

WHITE-ARMED *(Cylista leucolena)*. Found from Cape Cod to the Carolinas. It likes dark places, such as the under sides of stones or shaded piles of wharves. This is slender-bodied, being a little more than two inches in length, with tentacles an inch long. The body is a delicate brown, translucent to some extent, and the tentacles are usually white.

SEA CUCUMBERS

BRITTLE *(Synapta inhaerens)*. Sea Cucumbers are closely related to Starfishes and Sea Urchins, but they are wormlike in appearance. This species is long, slender and transparent. It is called brittle because it has the power of breaking itself into pieces. This is done by constriction. The body when extended may be more than a foot long and only about an eighth of an inch in diameter. The mouth is surrounded by twelve branching tentacles. It is viviparous, carrying the young in a body cavity. It is found from Cape Cod to North Carolina.

COMMON *(Cucumaria frondosa)*. This gets its name from its general shape. However, it has the power of changing shape. It may be long and thin, or nearly globular. The surface is almost smooth, whitish on one side and dark purple on the other. Around the mouth are ten tentacles, and these are much branched. It is found on both coasts. Fully grown and expanded it is fifteen to eighteen inches long.

SEA SPIDER

COMMON *(Anoplodactylus lentus)*. These little creatures are not true Spiders, but bear sufficient resemblance to be given this common name. As a matter of fact, their true relationship to other sea creatures has been something of a puzzle to naturalists. The body is so small that the stomach and reproductive organs extend out into the long stout legs. The male carries the eggs fastened to his third pair of legs. When the young hatch they crawl over their father and cling to him in considerable numbers. There are many species, but the one mentioned here is one of the most common. They are found crawling over hydroids and seaweeds. The young live for a time within hydroids.

SEA URCHINS

GREEN *(Strongylocentrotus dröbachiensis)*. In common with other Sea Urchins, this is often called Sea Egg. It resembles a greenish chestnut bur, about two inches in diameter. Sometimes there is a purplish tinge. The spines are moderately slender and about three eighths of an inch long. There are five double rows of long, slender tube feet. It conceals itself by covering itself with bits of seaweed or other matter. It is found on both coasts. It is found from the Arctic Ocean to New Jersey on the east coast and to Washington on the Pacific Coast.

PURPLE *(Arbacia punctulata)*. This is a small Urchin about an inch in diameter, with spines one half to three quarters of an inch long. Color varies from dark brown to deep violet. There are five double rows of feet provided with terminal suckers.

SAND DOLLAR *(Echinarachnius parma)*. This Urchin is sometimes called a Sand Cake. It is flat and about three inches in diameter. When alive it is covered with dense, short, brown, silky spines. The shell of the dead Sand Dollar is usually lacking the spines. The mouth is in the center of the under side. On the upper surface is a slightly raised pattern of a five-rayed star. An indelible ink is prepared from Sand Dollars.

STINGING *(Diadema setosum)*. This Urchin is found along the Florida Coast and in the West Indies. It is velvety black and is covered with extremely brittle spines, which are of unusual length. It is said that in some instances these spines are over three inches long. The Urchin itself is about four inches in diameter. Being brittle, the spines are apt to break off if they penetrate the skin of an enemy and they produce an irritating sting; hence the name.

STARFISHES

BASKET *(Gorgonocephalus agassizii)*. This is one of the Brittle Starfishes. The latter differ from the ordinary starfishes in that the arms are distinct from the body. In the ordinary starfishes the arms are extensions of the body, while in the Brittle Stars the arms are attached to the margin of a central disk. The Basket Starfish, which is sometimes called simply Basket Fish, has a thick, five-sided body. From the body margin extend five arms, which divide and then continue to subdivide until the number of little branches is almost beyond belief. These may be carried curled up or straight out, at will. The animal walks on the tips of these branches and is then one and a half feet in diameter. The name Basketfish has been given to it from its resemblance to a basket when these innumerable little branches are rolled up. It is an animal of the deep water, but is occasionally washed up on shore.

BLOOD *(Henricia sanguinolenta)*. This is smaller than the Common Starfish. It ranges from half an inch to two inches in diameter and varies in color, being red, orange, yellow, purple or flesh color. Ordinarily it is pink or reddish. The ends of the arms often turn up. It moves with two of its arms turned forward. The mother carries the eggs in her mouth until the young are capable of taking care of themselves.

BRITTLE *(Ophiopholis aculeata)*. This is the most common of the Brittle Stars. It is found in deep water from New Jersey to the Arctic Ocean and on the northern coasts of Europe. Either it, or a very similar species, is found on the Pacific Coast. Occasionally it is found in shallow water and is sometimes washed in after a storm. It is a mottled light gray and purplish-brown. There are minute spines on the disk and the arms have rows of thick, compressed spines. Like the other members of this group, they throw off their arms when alarmed, replacing them by growing new ones later.

COMMON *(Asterias forbesii)*. This familiar Starfish is found from Massachusetts to the Gulf of Mexico but is rather rare north of Cape Cod. It closely resembles *Asterias vulgaris,* but the madreporic plate is bright orange, while in the other species it is the same color as the animal. Its arms are blunt tipped and its skin is tough and spiny.

COMMON *(Asterias vulgaris)*. This species is also known as the Common Starfish. It ranges from the northern range of the preceding species up to Labrador. The arms taper to a point. The color varies, being yellow, brown, pink and purple. This species and the preceding one are very destructive to oyster beds.

GIANT *(Pentaceros reticulatus)*. This is a southern species altogether, being found off the Florida Coast and the West Indies. It is the largest of our Starfishes. The disk is sometimes five inches thick and one and one half feet in diameter. In color it is brownish-yellow to brown. Short rounded spines cover the upper surface.

MUD *(Ctenodiscus crispatus)*. This is a deep-water Starfish, occasionally washed up on the shore from Cape Cod to the Arctic Ocean. It lives on muddy bottoms; hence the common name. The sides of the rays are straight and vertical. In color it is a dull yellow or greenish. There are no terminal suckers on the feet.

WORMS

BLOOD-SPOT (*Polycirrus eximius*). This is one of the small worms of our sandy beaches, found under stones below the low-water mark. The forward half of the body is larger than the rear half and is blood-red, while the remaining portion is flesh color. The body is composed of segments and each segment of the forward half bears a pair of branched gills. Surrounding the mouth is a large cluster of tentacles, which are blood red.

CLAM (*Nereis pelagica*). Whoever has dug clams on the coast of New England has made the acquaintance of this big flat worm. The female is four to five inches long, while the male is only two inches long. They may be recognized from the fact that the body is widest in the middle. Worms of this genus are flat on the under side and rounded above. The body is composed of many segments and each segment has a pair of appendages on each side. These are in the nature of flapper-like gill feet. The worm is reddish-brown and beautifully iridescent. They burrow in the sand or mud and on calm nights come out of their burrows and swim about.

FRINGED (*Cirratulus grandis*). This somewhat unusual appearing worm is common in sand or gravel at low-water mark from New Jersey to Cape Cod. It is four to six inches long, a dull brownish yellow and tapering at both ends. Numerous long red or orange-colored threads, some of them as long as the body itself, grow out from the sides and are especially numerous around the head. These act as gills and are called cirri. While the worm itself remains safely hidden in its burrow, the cirri are thrust out into the water.

OPAL (*Arabella opalina*). This worm is twelve to eighteen inches long, cylindrical, tapering at the ends. The color is bronze with opal-like iridescence. Each segment bears a pair of bristled feet. It burrows in sandy mud at low-water mark along the New England Coast.

PINK RIBBON (*Micrura leidyi*). This is a flat, ribbon-like worm, six to eight inches long, one quarter of an inch wide, and red or pink in color. It lives in sand near the low-water mark. This worm secretes a mucus to which the sand adheres.

RED THREAD *(Lumbrineris tenuis).* This is one of the most fragile of the worms. It is twelve inches or more in length, very slender, red in color and somewhat iridescent. It is found in sandy mud from New Jersey northward.

RIBBON *(Cerebratulus lacteus).* This is the common Ribbon Worm of muddy or sandy beaches from Cape Cod to the Carolinas. It has great powers of contraction. When extended, a full grown one may be twelve feet long, an inch in breadth and flat like a ribbon. Contracted, this worm may be only two or three feet long and nearly cylindrical. An average worm is about three feet long. The body is slimy. It is a good swimmer and burrows with ease and rapidity. It has a proboscis, which is a long, threadlike organ and can be thrown out to a great length or completely withdrawn within the body. If thrown out very violently, it may break off and will then wriggle about as if it were a complete worm. A new one will be grown in its place.

SEA MOUSE *(Aphrodita aculeata).* This curious little animal of the sea is not wormlike at all in appearance, being oval, about three inches long, one and one half inches wide, and covered with hairlike bristles on the sides and back. The skin is dull brown, but the bristles are iridescent, in brilliant green, red and yellow. Some of these bristles are quite long. The head bears a pair of tapering feelers. It lives in the mud below the tide mark and is frequently washed ashore.

SHELL *(Serpula dianthus).* This worm can be easily recognized from the fact that it makes crooked shell-like tubes on the surface of other shells. Some of these tubes are three inches long and an eighth of an inch wide. The worm when undisturbed pushes out beautiful feathered gills, variously colored. At the least disturbance these gills are instantly withdrawn and the mouth of the tube is closed, much as a snail closes the opening of its shell. This worm is found from New Jersey to Cape Cod.

www.ingramcontent.com/pod-product-compliance
Lightning Source LLC
LaVergne TN
LVHW021336080526
838202LV00004B/196